ELIZABETH I

Elizabeth I

The Competition for Representation

SUSAN FRYE

ExLibris

MHM

Mitchell M. Harris

New York   Oxford

OXFORD UNIVERSITY PRESS

Oxford University Press

Oxford   New York   Toronto
Delhi   Bombay   Calcutta   Madras   Karachi
Kuala Lumpur   Singapore   Hong Kong   Tokyo
Nairobi   Dar es Salaam   Cape Town
Melbourne   Auckland   Madrid

and associated companies in
Berlin   Ibadan

First published in 1993 by Oxford University Press, Inc.,
198 Madison Avenue, New York, New York 10016-4314

First issued as an Oxford University Press paperback, 1996

Oxford is a registered trademark of Oxford University Press

Library of Congress Cataloging-in-Publication Data
Frye, Susan, 1952–
Elizabeth I : the competition for representation / Susan Frye.
p.   cm.   Includes bibliographical references and index.
ISBN 0-19-508023-8; 0-19-511383-7 (Pbk.)
1. Elizabeth I, Queen of England, 1533–1603.   2. Visits of state—
England—Kenilworth—History—16th century.   3. Pageants—England—
Kenilworth—History—16th century.   4. Coronations—Great Britain—
History—16th century.   5. Patriarchy—Great Britain—History—
16th century   6. Women—England—History—Renaissance, 1450–1600.
7. Spenser, Edmund, 1552?–1599.   Faerie Queene   8.   Great Britain—
History—Elizabeth, 1558–1603.   9. Chastity in literature.
10. Queens in literature.   I. Title.
DA355.F79   1993   942.4′8—dc20   92-37725

3 5 7 9 8 6 4 2

Printed in the United States of America
on acid-free paper

for my parents,
Bruce and Caroline Frye

Preface

This book was born from the conviction that not enough attention has been paid to what Queen Elizabeth I wrote and said about the difficulties of constructing her power within the patriarchal society that she ruled. As the queen who governed England from 1558 to 1603 through four crucial decades of imperial, constitutional, and literary development, Elizabeth has been the focus of innumerable biographies and histories. None has considered how Elizabeth worked to create herself or how her self-creation as an authoritative, unmarried woman competed with her own society's conviction that women should be chaste, silent, and obedient. *Elizabeth I: The Competition for Representation* emphasizes Elizabeth's self-creation and the process of contestation that this construction necessitated. It differs significantly from the wealth of material available on Elizabeth because instead of assuming either that Elizabeth was in full contol of how she was represented or that she was controlled by the special-interest groups surrounding her, my focus is the very issue of her agency. That is, I concentrate on Elizabeth's actions and words (as nearly as they can be determined) in order to ascertain the conscious and unconscious strategies through which she worked to create an identity beyond accepted gender definitions.

I have organized this examination of Elizabeth's agency to center on three essential moments in her representation at fifteen-year intervals: first, the London coronation entry of 1559, during which her relation to her most wealthy subjects was at stake; second, the Kenilworth entertainments of 1575, which staged a representational battle for England's foreign policy toward the Netherlands; and third, the tension, frustration, and even violence with which courtly artists and artful courtiers met the self-constructions of the aging Elizabeth around 1590. The use of historical materials required by this organization made me realize that all but the most revisionist studies of Elizabeth read the reign backward from the perspective of the achievements of the 1580s and 1590s—much as she and her earliest biographers would have preferred. I found myself attempting to read the reign forward, to discover how unforeseen her successes were, to ascertain her self-creation as a response to the continual struggle to define her in accepted gender roles, and to detect the ways in which her vulnerabilities were disguised or incorporated into iconography as well as the mythic biography that remains the primary source for accounts of her life.

This book further differs from other works on Elizabeth in its discussion of the issue of representation itself. Both my feminist argument, that the queen's authority was attained largely through the shifting representational strategies that I term her *agency,* and my historical argument, that Elizabeth's self-representations were more successful in shaping posterity's views of her than her contemporaries' representations were, grew out of a desire to address the complex relation between representation and material practice. In order to relate abstraction and practice, this book proposes a new, particularized definition of the most obvious form of representation, allegory, based on its function in Elizabethan power relations. Moreover, whether discussing allegory or other representational practices, I describe as specifically as possible how representation actually worked and what its impact was on economic, domestic, and foreign policy.

Finally, this book describes Elizabeth I not as a woman who advanced by exercising her feminine wiles, or as a woman who identified only with what her society tended to define as masculine, or as a primarily androgynous figure—although to serve her purposes, she was at times coy, misogynistic, and androgynous. I contend that by using every representational strategy available, she carved out—or *engendered*—a conceptual space from which she could govern. This conceptual space was inevitably a battleground, because in the performance of her power Elizabeth not only acted within but also repeatedly crossed her society's unstable gender distinctions, disrupting them in ways that made her the focus of widespread anxieties. Although she gained considerable material authority by asserting her political self-sufficiency by redefining feminine attributes like her virginity, she remained vulnerable to her countrymen's socially dominant interest in defining the feminine as passive and weak, thereby as requiring defense as the means to control.

To reconceptualize and recontextualize Elizabeth in these ways is part of a historical process that has maintained her as a vital figure in Western culture for four hundred years. Elizabeth was the most visible female in early modern Europe, a woman who exercised power and who also was a prolific writer. As the author of much of her authority, she continues to challenge patriarchal definitions of the feminine. Although Elizabeth resolutely distanced herself from her society's definition of "woman" and left no expression of interest in the status of women as a group, her struggle for self-definition demonstrated the instability of gender categories for future generations as well as her own. Elizabeth remains an icon whose meanings continue to be constructed and contested, whether she is portrayed by Glenda Jackson in all the dignity of a BBC production, by John Cleese cross-dressed as the Fairy Queen with a heavy mustache, or in this book, through which I acknowledge my own critical fascination with the intersection of feminism, history, and representation.

During the years in which this study evolved from a dissertation about allegory into a book about Elizabeth, I have enjoyed many forms of support that it is a pleasure to recall. Stanford University's English department, the Whiting Foundation, the University of Wyoming's English department, and the Institute for Research on Women and Gender at Stanford gave me time, money, and the opportunity to carry on extended conversations with scholars of varied backgrounds and interests. The Spenser Society, in its meetings at both Kalamazoo and the Modern Language Society, provided the occasion to read papers and to engage the responses of its knowledgeable audience. I was also able to read preliminary sections of this book at meetings sponsored by the Renaissance Society of America, the Pacific Northwest Renaissance Society, and the Rocky Mountain Medieval and Renaissace Association.

Many people have generously taken time to read, discuss, and critique this project in draft. In its early stages, John Bender, Morton Bloomfield, Ronald Rebholz, and Louis Montrose offered discriminating guidance. Stephen Orgel has been and continues to be ready with challenging suggestions. Eric Mallin, Elizabeth Robertson, Jeffrey Robinson, Susan Aronstein, Robert Torry, Janice Harris, Duncan Harris, and Jeanne Holland have provided insight in many forms as well as sustaining friendship. In the final stages of this project, Joan Linton, Lowell Gallagher, David Riggs, Mary Crane, and anonymous university press readers made valuable organizational and editorial suggestions. Richard McCoy not only commented on the entire manuscript, but also provided especially formative advice regarding Chapter 2. At a critical moment in revising Chapter 3, Valerie Wayne kindly shared her edition of Edmund Tilney's *Flower of Friendshippe,* together with her introduction, in advance of publication by Cornell University Press. Susan Bell, whose conversation was always influential, was good enough to introduce me to Allison Heisch, who shared not only her knowledge about Elizabeth, but also her meticulously edited texts of Elizabeth's speeches to be published by the University of Wisconsin Press, without which this study would not have been complete.

My final, most personal acknowledgments deserve a public moment as well. Karen Robertson's steadying friendship, erudition, and willingness to read last-minute faxes have had a profound impact on this book. The members of my extended family helped maintain my sense of what is important; the continuing influence of my parents I acknowledge in my dedication. I owe particular thanks to Mark Horowitz, whose support, contentious intelligence, and companionship have proved so enabling during the last two years. My daughter, Lizzie, who was born as I completed my dissertation and is now six, has invested with joy these years of research and writing.

Laramie, Wyo.   S. F.
December 1992

Contents

ELIZABETH I

Introduction:
Who Represents Elizabeth?

Five years ago I began worrying about whether Queen Elizabeth had actually worn armor when she addressed her troops at Tilbury in 1588 when she and her advisers expected a Spanish invasion momentarily. Biographer Alison Plowden confidently asserts that she was "bare-headed and wearing a breastplate"; Elizabeth Jenkins assures us that "a steel corselet was found for her to wear and a helmet with white plumes was given to a page to carry"; and Carolly Erickson concludes—in a description that parallels Garrett Mattingly's—that she was "armed like a queen out of antique mythology in a silver cuirass and silver truncheon. Her gown was white velvet, and there were plumes in her hair like those that waved from the helmets of the mounted soldiers."[1] Not only do the contradictory details of such accounts invite suspicion—Elizabeth bareheaded; Elizabeth wearing plumes or with a plumed helmet carried before her; Elizabeth in a breastplate, a steel corselet, and a silver cuirass—but after a prolonged search of the available textual and visual record, I found no contemporary evidence that she actually wore armor at all.[2] Although this is a small detail, it is not trivial, for her donning armor would have shown that Elizabeth was willing to go beyond the rigid, armorlike stomachers that she is shown wearing in so many portraits to cross-dress openly.

In her cogent analysis of Elizabeth's varying gender roles, Leah Marcus cautiously suggests that Tilbury was "the only recorded occasion on which Elizabeth went to the extreme of adopting male attire."[3] To some extent, Marcus is expanding on Louis Montrose's ground-breaking view of Elizabeth at Tilbury in her "silver cuirass" and "white velvet" as a moment when "Elizabeth incarnated a contradiction at the very center of the Elizabethan sex/gender system."[4] Accepting with Marcus and Montrose that Elizabeth wore armor as she affirmed "I have the body of a feeble woman, but the heart and stomach of a king" and that the dramatically cross-dressed queen provided a moment epitomizing the queen's self-repre-

3

sentation reduces the struggle for her image to a single point that, on closer inspection, tends to vanish.

As dramatic as Elizabeth at Tilbury appears to us today and as well as this picture appears to encapsulate the daring and success of her representational history, as a model it leaves out both process and conflict. The history of Elizabeth's self-representation that my book attempts eschews the image of Elizabeth as a mounted, armored heroine in a single, crystalline moment of time. In focusing on three representational crises spaced at fifteen-year intervals during a forty-five-year reign, I seek instead a sense of the sustained deliberation and drive with which Elizabeth used her culture's assumptions about gender to create herself. I mean to trace the competition for her image that her self-assertion invariably excited. At the same time, I examine the trade-offs in creating power from images. Although these images declared her willingness to make her own decisions about her physical and political bodies, portrayed her hierarchical position in the Christian as well as classical cosmos, and presented her as the logical result of both Roman and English history, they proved so slippery that they also increased her political vulnerability. Although Elizabeth actively participated in the creation of images that have fixed her in our minds as a supremely powerful female figure, many of her contemporaries viewed these same images as points of conflict.

We cannot know whether Elizabeth was consciously a partner in the process of self-representation and competition, but she did believe in an unshakeable relation between the words of the monarch and the monarch herself. That is, she felt that monarchs created themselves through language and the images that language created in its audience. In her writings, this conviction surfaces over thirty years as a restatement of the latter half of a passage of advice to the prince from Isocrates' *To Nicocles:* "Throughout all your life show that you value truth so highly that your word is more to be trusted than the oaths of other men."[5] In 1583 Queen Elizabeth I wrote a tart letter to the young James VI of Scotland reminding him of his promise to follow her counsel by telling him that sovereigns construct themselves. "Among your many studies, my dear Brother and Cousin," she began, "I would Isocrates' noble lesson were not forgotten, that wills the Emperor his sovereign to make his words of more account than other men their oaths, as meetest ensigns to show the truest badge of a Prince's arms." Since an oath is a form of language that promises action—indeed, guarantees that the word and the deed are one and the same—when Elizabeth claims sovereigns' words as oaths, she claims that her every word has authority. As she counseled James, the words of the sovereign go forth into the world as banners or as animated, complex, and visual signs of his authority: A sovereign's words are oaths because they are "meetest ensigns to show the truest badge of a Prince's arms."[6]

Elizabeth's use of this lesson from Isocrates, the rhetorician whose advice to the prince in *To Nicocles* was part of the humanist curriculum, forms a familiar admonition appropriately directed to a young king and ally. It also reveals that Elizabeth took to heart the materials of a humanist education created for men and transformed them to meet her own needs. In this sentence, Elizabeth achieves authority by occupying two male roles at once, that of the schoolmaster reminding James of his lessons and that of a prince who values his every word as producing signs of himself for public consumption. Yet she remains herself as well, a female sovereign who endeavored to see her words as images of fixity in a world whose instabilities of meaning both threatened and helped create her power.

Elizabeth's most important letter before her accession to the throne, written just after having been taken prisoner at the orders of her sister, Queen Mary, also begins with a statement of the connection between sovereign word and sovereign oath. Before pleading that she not be sent to the Tower, where she ran the risk of being executed, the beleaguered Elizabeth wrote: "If any ever did try this olde saynge that a kinges worde was more tha[n] another ma[n]s othe I most humbly beseche your M. to verifie it in me"[7] (Figure 1). On a very different occasion in 1563, Elizabeth's reply to Parliament on the question of her marriage and succession also opened with the following: "There can be no duer debt than princes'

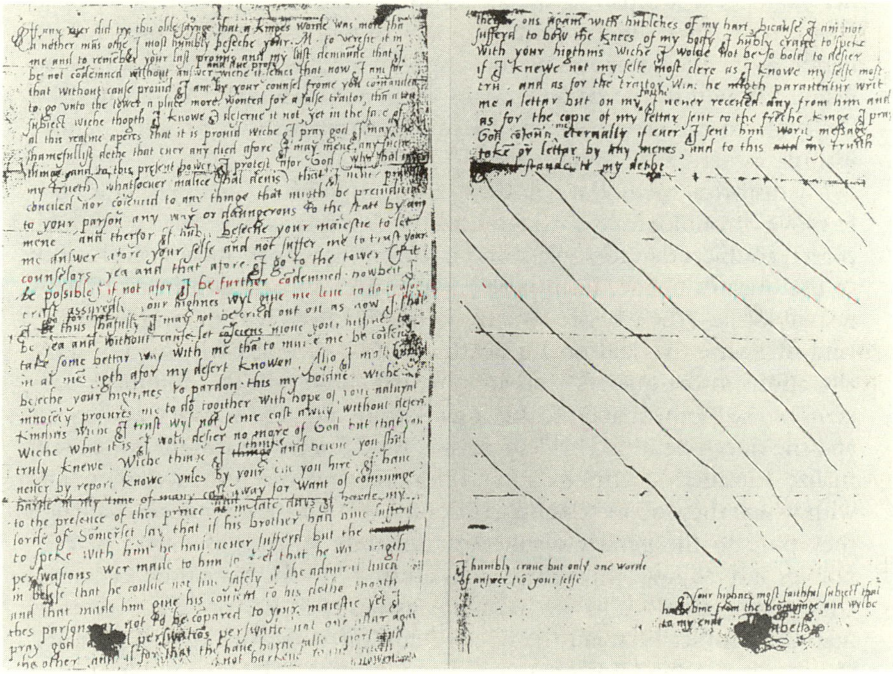

Figure 1. The "Tide Letter," written in 1554, in which the Lady Elizabeth entreats Mary Tudor for an audience before being sent to the Tower. (Crown copyright material in the Public Record Office, reproduced by permission of the Controller of Her Majesty's Stationery)

words, [which I would observe, therefore I answer to the same]."[8]

In each of these three different texts written for James VI, Mary Tudor, and the members of Parliament, Isocrates' equation of words with public image begins her remarks. Clearly, the lesson was so central to Elizabeth's conception of the relation between her words and her images, her promises and her authority, that it came to mind as her starting point when she most needed to persuade her audience and to assert herself.

Elizabeth claimed the words of the sovereign as an active, secured force in the world and expected others to do the same. But she was continually frustrated in her attempt to control the representation of her person for reasons relating to the role that representation plays in producing meaning. I use "representation" here as Michel Foucault uses it in *The Order of Things,* as a "resemblance" and "repetition" of resemblance,[9] a definition that conveys an awareness that no representation can be a precise likeness. Instead, each attempt at reproducing or reimaging Elizabeth's body brings into play culturally derived codes.

This book focuses on the struggle for the meanings embodied in the queen's body by treating Elizabeth I as a discursive agent, as a woman engaged in a continual, fluid struggle for the images she became. By engaging in her own construction through language and action, by declaring herself to be a woman at the same time that she acted outside defined female roles, by politicizing the language of virginity, and by establishing herself as the mediator among those special-interest groups that sought to define her within the parameters of their needs, Elizabeth constitutes a challenge to the essentialist patriarchal sign system that presents gender identity as natural and immutable.

My historical method for studying the competition for representation is to move chronologically through Elizabeth's reign, concentrating on three central conflicts that took place about fifteen years apart during the history of the queen's image. Each moment provides an occasion in a different textual locale—the city of London, Leicester's Kenilworth, and Spenser's land of Faerie overlaid on Elizabeth's court—through which to observe alterations in the queen's iconography, depending on the dominant concerns of the moment and the varying relations among sponsors, audiences, and the queen herself. These successive time frames permit me to contextualize Elizabeth's writings and iconography in the historical moments with which they interacted and to examine them for the semiotic challenge they pose to the gender distinctions inherent in the discourses of economics and religion, chivalry and humanism.[10] At the same time, acknowledging the variations in the meanings assigned to her body allows us to map the conflict between the queen's authority and her contemporaries' views of gender and power as performed in public places or published for an English audience.

Because Elizabeth ruled England during the latter half of the sixteenth century, her image interpenetrates our analyses of nationalism, Protestantism, scientific discourse, imperialism, and the literature that became the means to explore and conceptualize these changes. A number of studies demonstrate the complexities of the relation between Elizabeth's image and the development of English literature. Scholars' opinions are divided regarding the extent to which Elizabeth created her own iconography. The debate is encapsulated in the findings of two recent feminist studies: Whereas Philippa Berry sees Elizabeth occupying a "curious conjunction of roles which [she] had perforce to play," Leah Marcus credits Elizabeth with victory in the field of symbolic meaning during her lifetime, arguing that "gradually, perhaps not consciously, her subjects yielded to the symbolic truths she sought to convey through her precision with vocabulary and modeled their language upon her own."[11] Until now, this split has masked the need to problematize the issue of Elizabeth's agency in its social context, to concentrate on the question of whether Elizabeth is herself responsible for her iconography, as I undertake to do in the following pages.

Part of the problem has been a reluctance to consider the issue of Elizabeth's "agency" because the term appears to assume the existence of the queen as a self-determined subject who was to a large extent in conscious control of the effects she created. Rather than use "agency" in this sense, with Judith Butler I wish to reformulate it "as a question of how signification and resignification work."[12] In my reflections on Elizabeth's self-construction, "agency" describes her conscious and unconscious participation in the practice of signification. Although Elizabeth was fashioned by her culture's complex expressions of gender roles and distinctions, those expressions were unstable enough to be inverted, extended, and contested in the public performance of herself as the ruler of England. To a large degree, the extent of her power was determined by her willingness to engage and restructure the discourses current in her culture that naturalized gender identity. It is this performance or construction of herself that I term her *agency*.

The absence of a theory of agency has perpetuated the split between the passive Elizabeth and the active Elizabeth that lies sedimented within historical accounts of her reign. The nineteenth-century historian James Froude concluded in one of his more charitable phrases that "the great results of her reign were the fruits of policy not her own."[13] Yet some of the most readable and painstaking scholars of the twentieth century, among them John Neale, Garrett Mattingly, and Joel Hurstfield, transmitted a vision of a period blessed, as Neale put it, "while Queen Elizabeth lived to set the hearts of people aflame."[14] Because anyone who studies Elizabeth inherits this split as well as other assumptions of historical scholarship, it is worth considering for a moment some of the other illusions or fallacies harbored in this rich legacy.

The historical subject we call Elizabeth I exists as a composite of texts—speeches, letters, recorded actions, rumors, pictures, spectacles, and literature—in other, interpretive texts termed history or biography. As diverse as these works are, as a group they frequently reproduce three fallacies that tend to distort any attempt at studying Elizabeth. The first fallacy, that she is best explained via the narrative of her greatness—an approach first formulated by John Foxe, Raphael Holinshed's *Chronicles,* and William Camden—is simplistic enough to form the beginning for most revisionist work on the queen. The second fallacy is the assumption that our records of Elizabeth's voice support this Foxe–Holinshed–Camden legacy, an assumption recently contradicted by a few scholars searching for Elizabeth's actual words (insofar as they can be determined). The third fallacy, that Elizabeth and her government formed a monolithic entity that manufactured her image, is my own addition to this list, the starting point for my argument that in studies of the relation among politics, language, and image, Elizabeth and her government should be treated as less absolute than has usually been the case. Despite the amount of recent work on Elizabeth, these three fallacies still prevail, so that I find it useful to clarify my own method by discussing them at greater length.

Queen Elizabeth I was the one woman in early modern Europe whom historians have consistently placed at center stage. Even when she was still living, she became the intellectual property of historians who created a biographical narrative to meet their own divergent needs. John Foxe's widely read account of Elizabeth's life as a Protestant triumph in *Acts and Monuments* (popularly known as *The Book of Martyrs*), which first appeared in 1563, was revised and enlarged in 1570, 1576, and 1583, and went through subsequent editions in 1596, 1610, 1625, and 1632. Large portions of Foxe's text were further reproduced in Holinshed's *Chronicles,* that vast compendium of texts that formed a valuable source for Shakespeare, among others writing about the past. William Camden, whose first English title for his histories of Elizabeth was *Annales: The True and Royall History of the famous Empresse Elizabeth, Queen of England,* had his studies of Elizabeth published in 1615, 1625, 1627, and 1639.[15]

Together, these immensely popular texts helped form a teleological narrative that portrays the queen as moving with resolution and even clairvoyance to solve the religious and political problems of her reign. So pervasive are their views that modern biographies of Elizabeth tend to circle back to them. As Elizabeth Jenkins writes in her biography, *Elizabeth the Great:* "Camden's words enshrined the opinion of his own and succeeding centuries." Her concluding sentence quotes his judgment that "she was a Queen who hath so long and with such great wisdom governed her kingdoms, as . . . the like hath not been read or heard of, either in our own time or since the days of the Roman Emperor Augustus." And Jenkins is only one author in a long apostolic tradition.[16]

How can one avoid reproducing this inherited narrative? One of the problems in writing about Elizabeth is that even updated biographies inadvertently invoke the received story of the late queen of famous memory.[17] Consequently, I have come to think of my own work as a critique of the biographical–historicist tradition. Although speculation about Elizabeth's position and motives forms part of my discussion of the ongoing power struggle for the meanings surrounding the queen's female body, I cannot believe that Elizabeth can be recovered in any absolute sense, even if we finally manage to retrieve more of her voice. That "voice" as it comes to us through her speeches, sayings, letters, prayers, poems, and translations are records of the performance of the only woman allowed to speak and act in public in Renaissance England. They tell us a great deal about her, but as Laurence Olivier remarked concerning his own lack of a fixable identity, "Scratch an actor, and you'll find an actor."[18] Or as Elizabeth observed, "We princes, I tel you, are set on stages, in the sight and viewe of all the world duely observed."[19]

The primary reason that it is easy to imagine Elizabeth within an inherited framework is that no definitive edition of her works exists. Although an abundance of her written work is extant in early copies and manuscripts and she is both a major historical figure and frequently a vigorous prose stylist, in the four intervening centuries since her death her works have not appeared. The volume of letters, though large, is incomplete, and the slim compilations of her poetry, speeches, prayers, and "sayings" are inadequate. Their editors sometimes do not collate texts and even fail to document their sources.[20]

Certainly one reason for the lack of Elizabeth's published works is the logistics of such a project. Allison Heisch took on the extensive editorial work needed to produce scholarly editions of Elizabeth's speeches, and Frances Teague recently edited a short selection of poems and speeches.[21] But the "refusal to edit," as Lee Patterson wrote in regard to the missing and improperly edited texts of the Middle Ages, "is part of the larger refusal to interpret."[22] Without published, modern editions, it is too easy to rely on inherited interpretive structures and to make sense of the inconsistencies and indeterminacies of the records by resuscitating the narrative originating with Foxe, Holinshed's *Chronicles,* and Camden. Even in some new historicist studies, the lack of primary materials continues to limit Elizabeth's voice. Her best-known lines, including "I have the heart and stomach of a king" and "I am Richard II, know ye not that?" are only possibly her own, and they tend to be repeated in a variety of interesting contexts without, however, significantly broadening the scope of our understanding of her or the powerful groups that invested their own needs in her image.

Just as leaving out Elizabeth's lesser-known speeches, letters, and comments reifies the received narrative of her glorious reign, such an omission also makes it easier to assume, with many earlier historians, that Elizabeth's government was fairly monolithic, that her iconography was unquestionably created to serve the Crown. Queen Elizabeth's relative success in representing herself as autonomous and independent makes it easy to take that success for granted. In Roy Strong's classic study, the phrase the "cult of Elizabeth" meant an assemblage of images "skillfully created to buttress public order and, even more, deliberately to replace the pre-Reformation externals of religion."[23] But the now widespread assumption that the queen was able to control her public images or iconography suggests that she approved of her every image and, because she approved, that her image in some sense represents her voice. In her ground-breaking work on these images, Frances Yates saw the queen's virginity, for example, as "a powerful political weapon," without noticing that it was a weapon not always in Elizabeth's hands.[24]

The assumption that the Crown's power was monolithic has made it easier to confuse the proliferation of the royal image with propaganda. Elizabethan attempts at censorship and public relations have been read through the lens of twentieth-century examples of the relation between information dissemination and the state. Roy Strong summarizes this way of thinking when he states that "before the invention of the mechanical mass media of today, the creation of an 'image' of a monarch to draw people's allegiance was the task of humanists, poets, writers and artists." Spenser's *Faerie Queene,* for example, was "written for the glory" of the prince.[25]

Taking representations of the prince at face value eliminates the struggle for meaning that so often motivated the humanist, the writer, and the artist, as well as—to add my own interests to the list—the courtier and the merchant. As this book shows in a variety of historical contexts, those who represented Elizabeth to herself and to one another had interests of their own that they attempted to make hers by dressing them in her image. Elizabeth and her Privy Council, especially William Cecil, were deeply concerned with controlling public opinion and did not hesitate to use proclamations, published speeches and defenses, mandatory sermons, as well as force, to shape and control it. They doubtless saw the queen's carefully staged appearances as helpful in managing that opinion. But to believe that the queen was in complete control of her representations even at court is to fail to recognize the ongoing struggle for control of the queen's image so central to its production.

The "cult of Elizabeth" discussions of royal iconography, useful as they are, are gradually giving way to a recognition of the complex forces creating the image of Elizabeth. This endeavor has been most precisely articulated by Louis Adrian Montrose, for whom Elizabeth's "power to shape her own strategies was itself shaped—at once enabled and constrained—by the existing repertoire of values, institutions, and practices (including the artistic and literary conventions) specific to Elizabethan society and to Elizabeth's position within it." Montrose proposed that Elizabeth "had the capacity to *work* the available terms to serve her culturally conditioned needs and interests. By the same token, however, her subjects might rework those terms to serve their turns."[26]

This book is situated in Montrose's discussion of the working and reworking of "available terms." At the same time, it refigures this process as a competition for authority and self-definition between Elizabeth and those who used her image for their own purposes. Moreover, my analysis extends Montrose's work and that of other new historicists in three areas:

first, by focusing on Elizabeth I herself, her words, and her writings in order to elucidate the issues surrounding her agency or self-construction; second, by spacing my analysis over three distinct moments of her reign in order to separate out particular moments of her vulnerability and authority while tracing the development of the process that I call the competition for representation; and third, by discussing the slippage of meanings that the competition for her image set in motion, why that slippage existed, and what some of its material consequences were.

Elizabeth must have been less grand, less totalized than the heroic image with which so many of us are familiar. Yet if she was not the Augustus that Camden declared her to be (and how does the historical Augustus compare with Camden's image of him?), she was also far more than the sum of grand assessments and a few, variously emplotted, quotations. Upon her accession, she was, like her sister, Mary, perceived as a subject to be created through special interests because she was a woman, as their brother, Edward, had been because he was a child. She was, however, trained in rhetoric (as was any product of a thorough humanist education), well read, and an articulate conversationalist and author aware of the difficulties of constructing power from the elaborate male-oriented codes of English language, law, and religion. Elizabeth's struggle for self-definition within this matrix, for control of a body constructed by the male expectations surrounding her, is visible in her own representations and the importance she attached to them.

Elizabeth's relation to her representations varied, depending on the time and place in which they occurred and on their sponsors and audiences. Sometimes she was in relative control, and at other times she used others' distasteful representations of herself for her own purposes. She exercised the power to censor, interrupt, or critique what did not please her. But there were also times when the proliferation of her image was beyond her control. Representations of Elizabeth were often expected and overt, as when the town of Warwick greeted her in 1572 by creating a staged tableau of herself receiving a "spontaneous" gift of £20 from the town bailiff. She reacted by facing the assembled burgesses to acknowledge graciously that taking the money meant "praying God I may perform, as Mr. Recorder saith, such benefyt as is hopid."[27] At other times, Elizabeth seems to have tolerated representations of herself for her own reasons. *The Four Foster Children of Desire,* which Philip Sidney coauthored, is an allegorical entertainment that staged Elizabeth as an unassailable object of desire for her suitor, the Duke of Anjou. Although Sidney was probably exiled from court for stating similar views in a letter, the spectacle may well have been tolerated as an illustration that, as Elizabeth wrote to Anjou, "the greatest impediments lie in making our people rejoice and applaud" their marriage.[28]

As far as Elizabeth was concerned, even discussions of representation could prove intolerable. The hot debate among Protestants about images of God could easily be extended to questions of the royal image, which helps explain why Elizabeth interrupted Alexander Nowell's sermon at St. Paul's Cross in 1565 before a "great crowd" that the queen contended had gathered "more . . . to see her than to hear the sermon." When Nowell began to "abuse images," Elizabeth immediately ordered him, "Do not talk about that." When he attempted to continue, she "raised her voice and pointedly said to him, 'Leave that, it has nothing to do with your subject, and the matter is now threadbare.'"[29]

But Elizabeth lacked complete control of her images and the subject of representation, as was evident in the many negative representations of her that were performed and published during her lifetime. As is often the case for drama and poetry during this period, her own Master of Revels and the city's censors[30] tolerated images associated with Elizabeth even when they were placed in compromising positions—for example, when the queen of fairies, Titania, sleeps with an ass in *A Midsummer Night's Dream;* when "Celia," the fairy queen of *Tom a Lincolne,* conceives a bastard;[31] or when Elizabeth stands half-naked before the reader's gaze in the figure of Belphoebe in *The Faerie Queene.*

As these examples tell us, whether Elizabeth was allegorized in a celebratory or a more subversive mode, her representation depended to a large extent on the conceptualization of her female but sovereign body. The fact that she was a woman could never be forgotten, even though as head of state she fulfilled many of the functions of a man. Edward Dyer wrote to Christopher Hatton, "First of all you must consider with whom you have to deale, & what wee be towards her, who though she does descend uery much in her Sex as a woman, yet wee may not forgett her Place, & the nature of it as our Sovraigne."[32] The conceptualization of the split between Elizabeth's physical and political bodies as communicated here in a private letter existed as a powerful public conception as well. As Ernst Kantorowitz clarified it in *The King's Two Bodies,* this doctrine, developed from medieval political theory, recognized both the split and the connection between the physical and political bodies of the monarch. When Mary Tudor succeeded to the throne, this doctrine was revised in Parliament to allow her full access, at least in principle, to the power of a king. Parliament

> declared and enacted . . . that the kingly or regal office of the realm, and all dignities, prerogative royal, power, preeminences, privileges, authorities, and jurisdictions thereunto annexed, united, or belonging, being invested either in male or female, are and be and ought to be as fully, wholly, absolutely, and entirely deemed, judged, accepted, invested, and taken in the one as in the other.[33]

Through these words, the legal power of the queen was represented as *interchangeable* with that of a king.

In Elizabeth's hands, the legal conception of the king's two bodies, including its parliamentary accommodation to a woman who inherited the throne, served a purpose for which it had never been intended. As Elizabeth used the conception, her natural body was inevitably female, constructed through cultural norms that placed her below men in the cosmic and social hierarchies. But her political body was constructed within a masculinist legal tradition and thus was often represented as male. This gendering of her two bodies became the queen's justification for what I call *engendering* herself—assuming the assigned gender roles of women, men, or both, or someone in between, as the occasion demanded. Elizabeth recognized that a legal doctrine that could be interpreted with such latitude provided a powerful representational position. On her accession, she asserted herself at the head of the human hierarchy, "ordeyned . . . one bodye naturallye considered though by [God's] permission a Bodye politique to governe," an initial description of her natural female body as inferior, "though" permitted by God to govern.[34] The conceptualization of her two bodies, the one weak and female, the other powerful and male, proved useful to Elizabeth, although as the tone of Dyer's letter reminds us, the discrepancy was always apparent.

What remains undiscussed is that the distinction between Elizabeth's female and male components was not rigidly maintained by either the queen herself or those who developed and used her image to establish their own authority. In a speech of 1569 composed by Elizabeth in conjunction with her Privy Council and ordered read from every pulpit because "the multitude of our good people are unlearned," the queen spoke as "the sovereign prince and queen," a configuration that retains her male body politic and replaces her weaker, natural body with the innovative conception of a female body politic. In effect, she gives herself two political bodies. Throughout her reign, Elizabeth more frequently referred to herself as a single political sex, as male ("prince" or "king") or female ("princess" or "queen"), or as two bodies politic ("prince and queen"), rather than as the accepted conception of the two bodies ("woman" and "king"). In the "Golden Speech" of 1601, for example, she deprecated her "sexelie weaknes" but simultaneously claimed "the glorious name of a King" and the "royall authoritie of a queene."[35] In thus transposing her female body into the political realm inhabited by males, Elizabeth called attention to her society's normative gender roles.

The representations of her body assigned to the queen by her subjects demonstrate their anxiety about the roles and standards appropriate to a female prince. For example, the text of her coronation entry, an assemblage of entertainments staged by the citizens of London, consistently treats Elizabeth as a female who happens to be the sovereign. *The Queen's Majesty's Passage* makes it clear that, like any female's, Elizabeth's position is contingent on her virtue, that is, on her prescribed good, female behavior. This was the point of the device termed the Seate of Worthie Governance, which featured actors as the allegorical figures of Pure Religion, Love of Subjectes, Wisdome, and Justice trampling the vices Rebellion, Insolencie, Follie, Vaine Glorie, Adulacion, and Briberie. These were topped by a figure representing Elizabeth. The text makes it clear that "the Queene's majestie was established in the seate of governement: so she should syt fast in the same so long as she embraced vertue"—but she remains seated only "so long" as she is deemed virtuous. In suggesting that her right to rule depends on the continual assessment of her virtue, the text implicitly challenges the queen's ability to rule according to princely standards.

This device's representation of Elizabeth reminds us how different the feminine and masculine meanings of "virtue" were. Virtue, in the sense expressed in the Italian masculine noun *virtù* (Latin, *virtus,* meaning manliness, strength, vigor, moral perfection), is considered in classical and humanist texts as the principal attribute of nobility and thus of a ruler. In the *Art of Rhetoric,* Aristotle discusses virtue (here derived from the Greek *aretē* rather than the Latin *vir*) in the context of the definition of nobility:

> Virtue . . . is a faculty of providing and preserving good things, a faculty productive of many and great benefits, in fact, of all things in all cases. The components of virtue are justice, courage, self-control, magnificence, magnanimity, liberality, gentleness, practical and speculative wisdom. The greatest virtues are necessarily those which are most useful to others. . . . For this reason justice and courage are the most esteemed. (I.ix)

Humanist scholars set such descriptions at the center of their own admonitory texts for princes and advisers. For Erasmus, virtue in the sense of "good actions" is the first kind of princely nobility.[36] Thus the conception of "virtue" resident in rhetorical and political theory—the "bookes of princes affairs" that Elizabeth was outraged in 1597 that the Polish ambassador had not read[37]—is decidedly active and masculine.

Whereas male virtue was so active that its meaning converges with "service" and "courage," in European culture female virtue was conceptualized as primarily passive. As Vives argued, chastity was the only virtue necessary to a woman, a point of view that illustrates profound anxieties about men's ability to control women. The Seate of Worthie Governance carries the question of virtue outside political theory and into the discursive territory of the queen's female body by collapsing distinctions between political evils like Rebellion, which are to be found in the body politic, and personal evils like Follie and Vaine Glorie, which may reside in the body of any woman.

The figure of Elizabeth, perched atop this tableau of struggling Virtues and Vices, is in jeopardy. Vice's threat is distinctly sexual, for "if vice once gotte up the head, it woulde put the seate of governement in perill of falling." The text's report of Elizabeth's meek acknowledgment of the device's lesson also reminds the audience that the "virtue" under discussion is passive and thus feminine. "The Queenes maiestie when she had heard the childe and understode the pageant at full, gave the citie also thankes there, and most graciouslie promised her good endevour for the maintenance of the sayde vertues, and suppression of vyces."[38] After all, if she did not so promise, as the explication threatens, she would lose her "seate" in its several meanings, including that of the "capital city," London itself, and the "foundation" of her newly acquired "throne" (*Oxford English Dictionary* [OED]). Elizabeth's compliance with the deal that the city elites offered—their support in exchange for her "virtue"—is a bargain that places her where they want her, before the seat of their judgment, even if she never breaks the contract.

How was Elizabeth to represent herself as virtuous—as she would have to do, since *virtù* is central to the conception of leadership in this period— without undermining her own good name and thus her legitimacy? As the Seate of Worthie Governance device demonstrates, Elizabeth could never rely on others to provide her with an iconography that would be palatable, much less powerful. What Elizabeth required was a conceptualization that would mediate between her most powerful subjects and her position as ruler without denying that she was female. As a representational strategy, the queen's two bodies was useful but did not fully meet the need to validate her virtue, even when she used it to give herself two political bodies. She needed a basis for affirming that "I thanke god I am in deed indued with suche qualytes, that yf I were turned owte of the Realme in my pettycote, I were hable to lyue in any place in Chrystendon."[39] She also needed a category that would be familiar to her society but that would place her beyond the restrictions usually imposed on women. As we have seen, she needed a category of virtue that she herself would define, that would assign God, rather than her subjects, to be her judge and thus assert her legitimacy, even if her "virtue" in the sense of "reputation" would always be discussed by others.

In the first speech of her reign, read by Sir John Mason to her Privy Council and the entire first Parliament three weeks after her coronation entry, Elizabeth unveiled the necessary image. She began by declaring her independence of all the other representations that had been associated with her, asserting that "it [is] most true, that at this daie I stand free from anie other meaninge that either I have had in tymes paste, or have at this present." After denying the meanings imposed on her body, she concluded her address by declaring that "in the end this shal be for me sufficient that a marble stone shall declare that a Quene, having raigned such a time lyved and dyed a virgin."[40]

This self-representation accomplished a great deal. It managed to give her subjects what they had requested—the affirmation of her "virtue"—but by redefining the passive, female virtue in terms that located her outside the associated structures of marriage and male control. A virgin queen could permit no male to possess her, since by definition her father and brother were dead and there could be no husband in the picture. A virgin queen could locate herself in a long tradition of anomalous female figures, including Diana, Astraea, the vestal virgins, and the Virgin Mary. At the same time, she could connect her representation directly to material practice. Representing herself as a virgin queen in her case meant a large measure of actual autonomy, with the ownership of her own body as the prelude to commanding her subjects. As the iconography of her virginity developed during the next forty-five years, it frequently took on meanings she did not herself approve. But in 1559, presenting herself as the virgin queen helped Elizabeth elude her subjects' representations of her virtue as female, passive, possessible, and always exposed to scrutiny. Instead, she declared herself to be active and self-possessed, virtuous in terms that only God himself could judge.

My purpose in focusing on Elizabeth's creation of chastity as the "meetest ensign" of her authority is to understand it as the flexible and enduring figure of her political self-sufficiency. Initially created as a response to the immediate pressure to marry and bear her heir while allowing others to define her role as a female queen, as I discuss further in Chapter 1, Elizabeth's chastity became a discursive battleground we can revisit. The terrain in this case is a variety of primary texts, including letters, speeches, city pageantry, court entertainments, committee memoranda, poems, plays, trial transcripts, records of conversations, prayers, and Privy Council records produced over forty years.

Throughout her reign, Elizabeth responded to both material and discursive attempts to limit her authority by asserting the chaste autonomy of her personal and political bodies. As I discuss in Chapter 2, she supplied herself with a personal history in which God had intervened to save her from her sister Mary's imprisonment in order to place her virtuous body on the throne. Chapters 2 and 3 investigate how with the help of those writers and artists seeking to enlist her image in the service of their own ambitions, a special cosmos was also created to enshrine her chastity as magical and divine. The figure of the queen that this history and cosmos helped produce was that of a woman who ruled through the simultaneous invocation and disruption of accustomed gender roles. The response of courtiers and poets to these and related strategies of self-construction, like Elizabeth's increasing physical and figurative isolation in the 1590s, was to address and represent her in increasingly violent terms. In order to examine changes in both the conception of Elizabeth's chastity and the ways in which it was refigured and assailed, I focus on Robert Dudley, Earl of Leicester, and George Gascoigne in Chapter 2 and Edmund Spenser in Chapter 3, with reference to Robert Devereux, Earl of Essex, and Philip Sidney.

Paradoxically, the care Elizabeth took regarding her self-representation helped make her image an attractive locus for the competing interests of merchants, policymakers, courtiers, and other writers. As the queen's own sense of her body as the center of represented power heightened the impact of spectacles featuring her image, she helped create a performative aesthetic in which her representation in general and her allegorization in particular were highly politicized. In fact, because representations of Elizabeth's body were never naturalistic but, rather, sought to convey political abstractions within her visual or verbal image, they were usually allegorical.

The term "allegory" has a long and complex history as a mode of reading and writing. In considering its function in Elizabethan power relations, I have had to develop a highly particularized definition. Allegory as it exists in the competition for represented authority I define as any figure, event, or sequence of events endowed with meaning in order to represent the values it contains as truth.[41] By investing familiar icons with political ideas supporting Elizabeth, the Crown maintained that allegory was its own. But the meanings encoded in allegory were continually altered in the competition for their authority—that is, for control of those meanings. Thus allegory became an important locus of representational conflict between the evolving court discourse of Elizabeth's self-possession and the prevailing masculinist codes.

In analyzing allegory as a discourse through which and for which people sought control, I extend Michel Foucault's analysis of the ways in which we compete for meaning through the development of specialized discourse. "In any society," he writes, "there are manifold relations of power which permeate, characterize and constitute the social body." Because "these relations of power cannot themselves be established, consolidated nor implemented without the production, accumulation, circulation and functioning of a discourse," to study power relations among different social groups is to study specialized discourses—in semiotic terms, sign systems like allegory.[42]

The competition for representation is readily visible in spectacles, literature, and paintings, for the allegorical images of Queen Elizabeth represent not only the self-sufficient chastity of sovereign discourse, but also the woman whose sexuality comes under masculinist control. Examples include published spectacles like Richard Mulcaster's *Queen's Majesty's Passage* and George Gascoigne's *Princely Pleasures at the Courte at Kenelworth*. Literary examples include drama like John Lyly's *Endymion* and Ben Jonson's *Cynthia's Revels,* prose, including Philip Sidney's *Old* and *New Arcadias;* and such poetry as Walter Ralegh's *Book of the Ocean to Cynthia* and Edmund Spenser's *Shepheardes Calender* and *The Faerie Queene*. These texts employ the queen's iconography, the assemblage of allegorical images representing Elizabeth's body. Even the loudest praise encodes messages concerning the needs and claims of its author. This reencoding produced a slippage of meaning through which texts, pictures, tableaux, and dramatic scenes constructed authority both through and in opposition to her image. In spite of, and because of, this search for authority through language and image, allegory became the trope of instability: Every use of the forms representing Elizabeth made them worth appropriating, and every appropriation involved redefinition.

In semiotic terms, the queen could never completely own or stabilize the meanings assigned to her body. The reason is that, as Ferdinand de Saussure elucidated the sign, there exists a disconnection between its two components: the signifier (or referent) and the signified (what the signifier means). Indeed, in defining the "sign," Saussure explains that its first "primordial characteristic" is that "the bond between the signifier and the signified is arbitrary . . . i.e. [the signifier] has no natural connection with the signified."[43]

This disconnection has more recently been termed a "gap" in discussions of sign and that most obvious of signs, allegory. Carolynn Van Dyke points out that "allegory bases itself frankly on the disruption of signifier and signified and therefore renounces the illusions of semantic unity and directness promoted by such modes as symbolism." In "speaking other than what is meant," allegory operates in George Puttenham's Elizabethan terms "as a duplicitie of meaning or dissimulation" or in Paul de Man's deconstructionist terms as a "semantic dissonance."[44] This evident gap between signifier and signified is a linguistic phenomenon with profound social consequences because the resulting instability means that no meaning is ever completely fixed or natural, however it may appear. Thus semiotic instability enables the struggle for meaning to take place, and this struggle for meaning is especially visible in spectacle performances or in texts that create themselves as performances because they stake so much time, money, and effort in making ideas manifest.

Moreover, attention to the gaps between the signifier and the signified, between intention and reception, reveals underlying questions in studies of cultural poetics about the relationship between representations of group needs and ambitions and the degree to which these representations accomplish anything. It has been too often the case that such studies, however excellent, wish to assume a close connection between what is represented and what is. What cultural work did these images of Elizabeth perform? Do they offer evidence for Abner Cohen's assertion that social performances "temporarily resolv[e] contradictions; and always recreate the belief, the conviction of the actors in the validity of their roles in society"?[45] Did they, in fact, allow for the consolidation of Elizabeth's power or the consolidation of anyone's power? One of the reasons that this book contextualizes the dynamics of Elizabeth's iconography is to try to answer these questions. Focusing on specific moments—Elizabeth's coronation entry, the Kenilworth entertainments, and the discussions of chastity in the 1590s—allows us to assess the efficacy of performed representation.

In Elizabethan England, the conflict for social dominance through representation both shaped and was shaped by constructions of gender that have had a continuing impact on material culture. Elizabeth negotiated the signification of her image through her ongoing participation in the public interpretation of her body's meanings. When groups competing with the Crown for authority chose the queen's image to embody their own meanings, they constructed and enforced perceived differences between the sexes, as in the case of the active and passive definitions of virtue. This conflict between the only woman with access to the forums of political debate and the predominantly male interest groups surrounding her helped place questions of gender at the center of performance, whether in city pageantry, court entertainments, poetry, prose, or drama. As language and performance explored the religious, political, and economic questions of the day phrased explicitly or implicitly as questions of gender, they re-created spectacles of authority and dominance stemming in part from the varying social and political relations contested through Elizabeth's image. Thus the struggle for the queen's iconography formed a crucial part of the semiotic system from which much of our literature and even the idea of literature are drawn.

Each of the three chapters of this book offers a different occasion to explore relations among gender, representation, and power. Chapter 1, "Engen-dered Economics: Elizabeth I's Coronation Entry (1559)," discusses the power play for Elizabeth's iconography during her coronation entry, an event published as *The Queen's Majesty's Passage,* a text paid for by the Court of Aldermen, which organized the entry in order to represent its interests. The entry presents the economic interdependence of Crown and city as the queen's feminine dependence—a representation to which the queen acquiesced for precise political and financial reasons. Because (sur-prisingly) Elizabeth's iconography has never been discussed in relation to her finances, I examine the connections between her and the aldermen, addressing the ways that the account of her entry engendered questions of royal authority, religion, and finance.

Although the London aldermen and the queen played out the roles of man and maid, husband and wife-turned-mother, adviser and advisee, the queen was not, finally, the property of London. Given civic support, she headed an executive power with which the wealthier members of the city developed an economic relationship that, with all its stresses and strains, operated productively in the early decades of her reign. I conclude that although the search for the meanings of Elizabeth Tudor's body began when she most needed London's support, in practical, financial terms the entry worked to the advantage of both Crown and city, as Elizabeth, unlike Mary before her, cooperated with city financial interests to their mutual profit. Elizabeth's preliminary attempts to represent herself as self-sufficient and politically capable conflicted with the gendered images of the queen as fertile, malleable, and vulnerable that the entry disseminated. Despite Elizabeth's later success in reworking these images to her advan-tage, they became embedded within her developing iconography.

Chapter 2, "Engendering Policy at Kenilworth (1575)," shifts to Robert Dudley's entertainments for Elizabeth and hers for him at his country estate as described in two very different texts, George Gascoigne's *Princely Pleasures at the Courte at Kenelworth* and *Laneham's Letter.* In breaking with traditional readings of these texts, I find a struggle for control of the entertainments between Dudley and Elizabeth. What was at stake at Kenil-worth was, however, far more than their personal relationship. Rather, the competition for control of these entertainments embodied the debate in the Privy Council between moderates and militant Protestants on the ad-visability of an incursion in the Netherlands and the resulting break with Spain. The unprecedented eighteen days of entertainments gave Elizabeth time to take control of the devices and, with them, the developing imagery of her magical self-sufficiency. I describe how and why the Rescue of the Lady of the Lake—starring Elizabeth as a transcendent goddess—displaced two entertainments she suppressed that featured Dudley's ambitions. Elizabeth's authority was still far from absolute, however: Although she refused to play the roles that the censored entertainments assigned to her, Gascoigne's *Princely Pleasures* prints the suppressed entertainments. Significantly, the queen could prevent such representations from being played but not from being published, and these advanced Dudley's ambition to rule the Netherlands, as he attempted to do within the decade.

The first two chapters focus on central issues in Elizabeth's representation in light of the complex relationships between spectacle and text during two particular historical moments. Chapter 3, "Engendered Violence: Elizabeth, Spenser, and the Definitions of Chastity (1590)," instead considers the material and discursive practices through which Elizabeth's chastity was represented and challenged in the 1590s. By looking at a variety of texts, I examine the transfiguration of Elizabeth's use of Petrarchan and Neoplatonic codes into Edmund Spenser's book 3 of *The Faerie Queene,* in which the poet appropriates, redefines, and even assaults the queen's figure of Chastity.

In the 1590s, Elizabeth worked to create herself as powerful, remote, divinely approved, and magical in her physical location in the privy chamber, as well as in her lyric poetry, speeches, spectacles, and portraiture. Moreover, she made careful political use of the discourses of Petrarchism, Neoplatonism, and medieval political theology. But as an aging unmarried woman, the queen was vulnerable to the redefinition of her represented powers. Of these, the conclusion of *The Faerie Queene*'s book 3 is in many ways the most sophisticated and, until Essex confronted her authority at the end of the decade, the most violent. While examining the complexities of the interrelationships among the queen, the court audience, and the poet, Spenser imposes on Elizabeth's self-possessed virtue of chastity the more socially accepted definition of it as "purity from unlawful intercourse" (OED). In the interests of reclaiming Elizabeth's chastity, book 3 fashions the court's iconography and spectacle, its social and spacial organization, into the violence that could result when a would-be courtier promoted himself through sign systems created to address a remote but dominant queen. Indeed, the House of Busirane cantos mount a rhetorical rape—the enforcement of the dominant meaning of chastity—aimed at Spenser's audience, Elizabeth, in a violent moment exposing the feminized position that the constructions of gender in court spectacle force on the queen and Spenser alike. What is at stake in these conflicting representations is not only how Elizabeth is represented while she lives, but also how she will be remembered and how we will continue to construct her.

The discussions of 1559, 1575, and the 1590s each focus on the particular relation between specific political events and the construction of the queen's image. The many different primary materials that I use indicate that Elizabeth's control of her iconography was weakest at the beginning and the end of her reign. Even when her authority was strongest in the 1570s, representations she did not approve at court were published as presenting alternatives to her policy. The images that Elizabeth preferred threatened male preserves, ambitions, and essentialist definitions of the masculine and feminine while inviting redefinition. Even though Elizabeth herself was no feminist—in the sense that she did not concern herself with the situation of other women—in her own interest she developed and worked for representations of female autonomy and power that both underwrote and jeopardized the apparently natural fabric of signification.

1

Engendered Economics: Elizabeth I's Coronation Entry (1559)

When Elizabeth I participated in her coronation entry, she entered a London as yet unmarked by her reign. As early as 1568, the "Royal Exchange" would be built at the heart of London, the building whose name represents a conflation of royal and mercantile interests.[1] By the 1580s, her image would come to embrace the city, proud of its circumscribed autonomy, with her statue at Ludgate facing west toward the Inns of Court and the royal precincts of Westminster beyond (Figure 2).[2] But in mid-January 1559, when Elizabeth crossed the city to pause for entertainment at six hubs of economic activity, her reign did not yet exist.

Imagining the early years of Elizabeth I's reign without a sense of her developed personality and politics is difficult: Reconstructions have more often resulted in a picture of unity and greatness than of division and detail. Nor is it surprising that we picture this Elizabeth as the incipient commander at Tilbury rather than the unproven great-granddaughter of a London merchant, since the reimaging of Elizabeth's reign began long before her death. We owe much of our feeling for the early Elizabeth to documents produced later in her life and to nostalgic reconstructions from the early seventeenth century. Examples of the refigured Elizabeth are as numerous as her portraits: They include the accounts of John Foxe, Richard Grafton, Raphael Holinshed's *Chronicles,* Fulke Greville, Thomas Heywood, and William Camden, as well as the pictures of a youthful Elizabeth that, like the "coronation" portraits or the "rainbow" portrait,

Figure 2. The statue of Elizabeth erected at Ludgate around 1586 by William Kirwan. In 1760, it was moved to its present location at St. Dunstan's on Fleet Street. (Courtesy of St. Dunstan's-in-the-West)

were painted when she was in her sixties.[3] Although some revisionist scholars have focused on the limits of her power,[4] most people have preferred to see in the twenty-five-year-old queen an incipient invincibility.

Any alteration in this picture must begin with the reminder that in 1559, although her succession was not seriously questioned and her religion had long been understood to be Protestant, the queen's domestic and foreign policies were still largely unformulated. At the moment of the queen's coronation, her most significant plans, from the point of view of many

surrounding her, depended on the deployment of her body. When Elizabeth confidently described herself in 1558 as her "one bodye naturallye
considered though by [God's] permission a Bodye Politique to governe,"[5]
not only was her longevity in question—and fears for her health proved
justified when she nearly died of smallpox in 1562—but the most worri-
some unknown was the degree to which her impending marriage to an
unnamed male would alter present and future policy. As the Count of Feria
wrote in cipher to Philip II, "everything depends upon the husband this
woman may take."[6]

Because questions of marriage and the succession connected her natural
and political bodies in ways that Elizabeth constantly sought to control,
the queen herself became the most politically significant sign of her reign.
As Lucy Gent and Nigel Llewellyn have pointed out, Elizabeth's body
intersects with cultural practice as "a signifier, and therefore, in so far as our
minds are involved . . . [is] constructed by language, by cultural practices encoded in language, and by visual images which mesh with systems
of language."[7] Images of Elizabeth's body, together with scenes or narratives that assign meaning to that body, constitute allegories of Elizabeth, in
the sense that an "allegory" is the most obvious form of representation
whose images embody the ideology of their sponsor.[8] Civic leaders, courtiers, poets, artists, and playwrights representing various political perspectives variously allegorized the queen's body through the overlapping, even
contradictory images that developed and recurred throughout the forty-
five years of her reign. At this, the beginning of her reign, Elizabeth was an
active participant in its construction even when, as in *The Queen's Majesty's
Passage*,[9] her role consisted mainly of a calculated acquiescence from which
she had everything to gain.[10]

The Queen's Majesty's Passage provides a logical starting place for examining the iconography of Elizabeth and its relation to her self-representation.
The description of the eight scenes of the entry itself—the presentation of
the royal genealogy at Fenchurch; the Seate of Worthie Governance device
at Cornhill; the Eight Beatitudes at Sopers Lane; Truth, the Daughter of
Time, presented in Cheapside, with a digression to describe the elaborately
staged presentation of the city's purse to the queen; the oration at St. Paul's
School; Deborah, the married judge dutifully consulting her councillors in
Fleet Street;[11] and the *Brut's* giants presenting the unity of the whole at
Temple Bar—provides the first public, and the first published, allegorical
entertainment of her reign (Figure 3).

In a number of recent anthropological and historicist studies, the entry
has emerged as a particularly evocative text for the study of the spectacle of
power. For Clifford Geertz, Elizabeth's passage reveals the iconographic
center, the locus for charisma, of the Elizabethan regime in the queen
herself; for Steven Mullaney, the entry reveals and defines the city of
London's cultural topography; for Mark Breitenberg, it provides an opportunity to examine neither ruler nor city in particular, but "a single
compound of entertainment" that reveals the workings of the "natural"

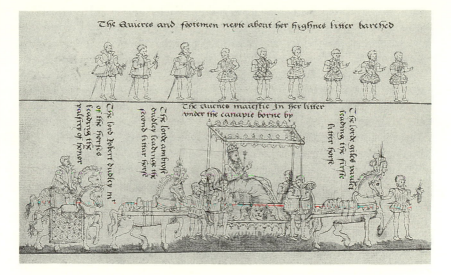

Figure 3. Elizabeth I's coronation procession in 1559, probably drawn by a herald soon after the event. (By permission of the College of Arms)

language of similitude and correspondence in power relations. Most recently, Richard McCoy considered Elizabeth's avoidance of Catholic ceremony during her coronation at Westminster and its "subordination . . . to the civic progress the day before."[12] *The Queen's Majesty's Passage* has accrued an impressive bibliography, but no work has yet discussed the gendered exchanges that produced the text and that an uncritical reading imposes on its audience. This chapter addresses this need, treating the coronation entry as authorizing the views of the London merchants whose anxieties constructed the new queen as compliant, malleable, and grateful—in short, as their metaphoric wife.

The coronation entry tells us at least as much about the aldermen who sponsored the entry as about Elizabeth herself. In the entry, Elizabeth is an economic, political, and social entity without whom the London elites could not function. But to members of a culture that envisioned itself through essentialist distinctions between the sexes, she was fundamentally a woman. Although the debate on the nature of women—on where to draw the line between male and female characteristics—continued throughout the sixteenth century,[13] to be female was to be powerful as procreator, as mother, daughter, and other. These are qualities with which the city's merchants were uneasy, especially when united in a female who had access to the financial and political spheres through which they constructed their own identities. In casting Elizabeth as a mother who receives metaphoric children from the city and as a daughter who receives its advice, the text assigns her the domestic roles that attempt to contain the power and voice of women. Because civic interests authorized themselves through the acts of giving and advising, Elizabeth's role was largely limited to receiving, briefly thanking, and remembering in a show of city wealth and wisdom. Thus the act of reading *The Queen's Majesty's Passage* engages the perspective of civic groups whose primary concern was to establish the values they considered conducive to social stability and financial gain. In producing and paying for the entry, the city elites demonstrated their support of Elizabeth, but expressed that support on their own ground in their own terms.

At the same time that the text records the values of its sponsors and seeks to gloss over conflicts between city and Crown, powerful males and sovereign female, Catholics and Protestants, past and present, its images of Elizabeth reveal the complex nature of political representation during the Elizabethan period. Just as the entry registers a conflict between the city's need for a strong sovereign and its desire to encode her strength as feminine—that is, as contingent on her virtue and public approval—the representations used to impose unity on this paradox are themselves problematic.

Queen Mary as Pre-text

Queen Mary's reign provided a ready model of female governance and its representation in *The Queen's Majesty's Passage*. Because Mary had been entombed only one month to the day chosen for Elizabeth's entry,[14] her reign's associated problems of gender, foreign influence, and civil unrest remained vividly in memory. Queen Mary's gender became the site of general attacks on women rulers like John Knox's *First Blast Against the Monstrous Regiment of Women* and defenses like John Aylmer's *Harborowe for Faithfull and Trewe Subjects*. More particularly, in marital problems made public in Philip's reluctance to remain in England and in gynecological difficulties made public in two false pregnancies, Mary enacted the physical and political risks of a royal marriage in which the sovereign herself attempts to have a child and fails to do so. The only greater danger, as in the later example of Mary Queen of Scots, seems to have been actually to produce one's heir.[15]

Mary Tudor's accession at thirty-seven years of age and her need to replace her immediate heir, the Protestant Elizabeth, with Catholic offspring required her to seek a prompt marriage. Like her immediate predecessor, Lady Jane Grey, whose disastrous marriage began her reign, Mary lacked access to the empowering option that Elizabeth envisioned for herself in her first parliamentary address, that she would reign and die unmarried.[16]

From the first, however, Mary set out just as determinedly as Elizabeth did to wield her female body to best advantage. She could not do so freely because the same circumstances that had kept her unmarried until her accession in July 1553 determined a Spanish match upon her accession. From birth she had been the keystone of Henry VIII's shifting policy between the Spanish imperialists and the French. Princess Mary's life had depended largely on the status of her father's, and then her brother's, negotiations. As foreign policy changed, she was by turns exiled from court and reacknowledged, ignored, and handsomely supported. Once she became the queen, Mary remembered the uncertainties of those years by relying heavily on her mother's family and following the advice of the Spanish ambassador, Simon Renard.[17] Mary's reliance on the Spanish has been overstated, for despite intense pressure she never underwrote England's pro-imperial policy with the funds that Philip desired. Nevertheless, Mary's commitment to the Spanish in order to attain her religious, political, and reproductive goals formed the basis of her relations with the rest of England and with London in particular.

After the iconoclasm of Edward VI's reign, London's citizens celebrated Mary Tudor's accession with "excitement and relief."[18] But this mood dissipated as Mary's political affiliation with Charles V, whom she called "father" in her letters, and her marriage to Philip, negotiated with a speed unusual in the sixteenth century, not only caused considerable anxiety about the effect of foreign influence on everyday life, but also coincided with rapid inflation and economic uncertainty. Mary's political relationship with London was, like Elizabeth's, largely predicated on economics; nevertheless, from the time of her accession, Mary Tudor made decisions that damaged her standing among the convergent London elites of aldermen, Merchant Adventurers, and prominent members of the twelve liveried companies.

One decision especially galled the powerful merchants in the export trade: Mary reversed her brother's, Edward VI's, decision to oversee economic policy in support of the Hanse merchants and in opposition to the Merchant Adventurers. Thomas Gresham, a London financier who served both queens, wrote to Elizabeth upon her accession that Mary's favoring the Germans "hath been the chiefest point of undoing of this your realm, and the merchants of the same."[19] Although by the end of Mary's reign the Adventurers had managed to regain control of the foreign trade in English wool, in the meantime her policy had isolated the Crown from England's most prosperous citizens while reducing Crown revenues. The lack of good faith between Mary and her capital city meant that on occasion she was refused the local loans and guarantees of credit for foreign loans that London merchants usually granted to the monarch.[20] Mary's preference for the Germanic tradesmen in London's Steelyard may have had little to do with the Spanish marriage, but it became part of the general feeling that, as Simon Renard reported to Charles V, Philip and Mary "intended to enrich foreigners by opening the gates of the country to them and impoverish its unfortunate inhabitants."[21]

Nevertheless, the London elites remained loyal to Queen Mary during the rebellion following her announcement of marriage. What happened then helped form the Crown–city dynamics of subordination and legitimation evident in Elizabeth's entry. In order to counter the rebellion's serious threat to her throne, Mary went directly to London for the support of its citizenry. This is the point of *The History of Wyat's Rebellion: With the order and manner of resisting the same* (1555), dedicated to Mary and written by the avowed Catholic clergyman John Proctor, which was as supportive of the Crown as any description of active subversion can be.[22]

Proctor, though a royalist, is most interested in describing a Londoner's view of the uprising. The text, for example, contradicts Mary's contention that Wyatt's rebellion was a religious uprising and agrees with the rebels' own contention that it was a response to her engagement to Philip II.[23] The *History* also records that Mary's strength during the crisis was her ability to come to London, "her Chamber and a city holden of dear price in her princely heart," in order to lay her problem before the aldermen at Guildhall. Proctor implies that this act of obeisance, together with Mary's self-representation as the wife of her realm—a strategy that the *Passage* imposes on Elizabeth by presenting her with metaphoric children and that Elizabeth herself found useful as early as 1559[24]—proved decisive in winning the city's loyalty. Mary asserts that her "first marriage" was to this "realm": "'For,' quod her Grace, 'I am already married to this Common Weal and the faithful members of the same; the spousal ring whereof I have on my finger: which never hitherto was, nor hereafter shall be, left off.'"

According to Holinshed's version of the speech, Mary also found strength in representing herself as her country's mother, another strategy associated more with her successor and imposed on Elizabeth during her coronation entry: "I cannot tell how naturally a mother loueth her children, for I was never the mother of anie; but certeinlie a prince and governor may as naturalie and as earnestly love subjects, as the mother dothe hir child." On the assurance of the political connection expressed through domestic relations, Mary doubted not, "but we together shall be able to giue these rebels a short and speedie overthrow."[25]

In describing the incident, both Proctor and Holinshed wished to display the power of London, but Mary's resolution in coming to Guildhall to request the aid of its powerful merchants may well have saved her throne. As Thomas Wyatt's rebels advanced, aided by at least one band of London troops, still other Londoners closed the city gates to them and later participated in their executions. The language of Mary's submission helped establish a taste for royal deference, imposing a metaphorical reality on Elizabeth's early relationship with her capital.[26] Whether or not Mary actually represented herself as married to her subjects—that is, as the physical property of her audience—is less important than is the memory that she represented her relation with London through the familiar domestic models of female subordination.

Once the rebellion was suppressed and, not incidentally, the queen withdrew her threats to deprive London of revenues by withdrawing the court to York or holding Parliament at Oxford, the Court of Aldermen helped preserve Mary Tudor's right to choose her husband with the approval of her Privy Council. But the aldermen expressed their displeasure with the Spanish marriage by paying Richard Grafton to produce Mary and Philip's entry. Grafton, an ardent Protestant, a chronicler and printer for Henry VIII and Edward VI, and, later, the coauthor of *The Queen's Majesty's Passage,* had lost his position as royal printer for publishing Lady Jane Grey's accession proclamations. His entry planned a gesture of disdain for the royal couple in the device that was to display Henry VIII holding a book entitled *Verbum dei,* despite its Latin title, a representation of the Bible in English, and thus a reminder of her father's break with the church accomplished through the divorce of her mother. This offensive device was apparently censored by Stephen Gardiner, the Bishop of Winchester and Mary's Lord Chancellor, but only after the king had passed,[27] a moment that the account by John Foxe (reproduced in Holinshed's *Chronicles*) also describes as having been performed.

Other devices included a representation of Mary's and Philip's genealogies and an arch paid for by the grateful Hanseatic League. The overt expression of London's doubts about the marriage appeared in a pageant in the commercial center of Cheapside presenting Philip as Orpheus (a clear warning to one whose power might prove deadly to himself) and in a castle erected in Fleet Street where Veritas, like the figure of Henry VIII, held a book titled *Verbum dei.* The route of the entry itself constituted a grim reminder to the entry's sponsors and spectators of the violence occasioned by this marriage: The need to treat both executions and royal entries as staged spectacles meant that some of the stages were erected at the same places where three months earlier Wyatt's rebels had been hanged.[28]

The entertainments presented for Elizabeth were no less pointed than those for her sister and her new husband. On a day of light snow in January with the mud of London's streets newly graveled,[29] Elizabeth's entry, like that of her predecessors, signaled the anxieties and values of the civic elites. Through her cooperation, the new queen acceded to the city's terms in exchange for its support. This public, ceremonious submission formed the basis for subsequent successful Crown–city transactions. Ian Archer, who derived conclusions similar to mine from his very different research in social history, found that "Elizabeth's approach to the metropolis . . . was generally low key and non-interventionist, so that the relationship was more fruitful to the City." Because widespread social unrest does not seem to have been imminent, Archer concluded that Elizabeth's and her councillors' "rather exaggerated perception of [their] own vulnerability" meant that London was "the beneficiary of a monarchy . . . reluctant to press any of its subjects too hard."[30] But Archer's study precludes the message at the heart of *The Queen's Majesty's Passage,* that both the new regime and the London elites regarded the sovereign as vulnerable because of her gender.

Beginning in the following month, the queen transfigured the entry's iconography to present a powerful sovereign that denied her gendered vulnerability at the same time that her government proved itself a business partner capable of pursing its own financial interests. In mid-January 1559, Elizabeth's entry—in its unrecoverable form as it was publicly performed, as well as in the printed version that appeared just eight days after the entry—existed to embody the position of the most powerful London citizens through the allegorized figure of Elizabeth.

Sponsors, Authors, and Meaning in the Entries of Elizabeth and James

The Queen's Majesty's Passage derived its contemporary authority from the Court of Aldermen, the "keystone of the City's constitution" that consisted of an elected member from each of twenty-six city wards. The aldermen— from whom Queen Mary had so wisely sought aid during the rebellion— formed a group that, although factionalized, was equal in power to prominent royal advisers, councillors, and courtiers. Although their privileges were based as much on financial and civic success as on heredity, the aldermen conceived of themselves as gentry because they enjoyed so many of that class's rights and privileges. They acted as magistrates, oversaw civic defense in their wards, and, in short, exercised authority "as great as any county justice's" amid great pomp.[31] The traditional knighting of the annually elected Lord Mayor (if he was not yet a knight) served as an acknowledgment that aldermen formed a powerful group among England's elites, although difficult to categorize at a time when the class designations formulated within the medieval social hierarchy had not yet been revised to include the increasingly self-conscious middle class.

During the sixteenth century, the Lord Mayor's pageants became more elaborate in their expression of the conceptions through which the members of this group saw themselves. Thus it is significant that according to both Holinshed's *Chronicles* and Henry Machyn's diary, Elizabeth's entry into London began by including her in a kind of Lord Mayor's pageant. On the day before her entry, when Elizabeth left Westminster Palace in order to spend the night in the Tower of London, where the procession the next day would begin, she came by water. "The lord maior and aldermen in their barge, and all the citizens with their barges decked and trimmed with targets and banners of mysteries accordinglie attend[ed] on her grace." To the sound of music mingled with artillery fire from the mercers' vessel, Elizabeth's barge passed under London Bridge, and she was followed by the Lord Mayor and other citizens who saw her to "the privie staires at the tower wharfe."[32] Through their pageantry, the city's merchants claimed Elizabeth as a merchant at one remove on the day before her entry and two days before her coronation.

The aldermen and the liveried companies they represented engaged a number of people to write the coronation entry's devices, including the Protestant Richard Grafton; Richard Hilles, who was probably Catholic; Lionel Duckett, a Mercer and later Lord Mayor; and Francis Robinson, a Grocer. City records state that the aldermen paid Richard Mulcaster to produce a final text that is probably the copy text for the printed edition.[33] Mulcaster had a foot in the court, for whose entertainment he wrote verses, including a device at Kenilworth, and directed performances, but he was first and foremost a city man. In the year following the entry, 1560, he assumed the head mastership of the newly founded Merchant Taylor's School, which Edmund Spenser, the last master of Elizabethan allegory, attended from 1561 to 1569. Mulcaster later wrote at least one Lord Mayor's pageant, in 1568, and the court entertainments he directed featured the boys of Merchant Taylor's.[34]

Despite the entry's diverse sponsors and authors in *The Queen's Majesty's Passage,* Mulcaster usually provides a single speaker with a readily identifiable civic ideology. But he does not succeed in producing a seamless text— that is, a text that successfully erases its own anxieties and contradictions. Even this most city-oriented account manages to convey two brief moments when Elizabeth steps outside the roles it assigns her. Nevertheless, the majority of historians and biographers have read this text as straightforward evidence of Elizabeth's triumph and accession to power. The tradition of the uncritical reproduction of the *Passage* begins with Holinshed's *Chronicles,* which prints the text without comment, and continues in Neale's *Queen Elizabeth I: A Biography.*[35] A contemporary example is Arthur Bryant's treatment in *The Elizabethan Deliverance,* an account that introduces its selections from the *Passage* by describing Elizabeth's entry as part of a play she both produced and starred in, "the first act of a drama which was to continue to her dying day."[36] The entry text is, in fact, only one account of the first formal presentation of the new queen staged within the London elites' needs, anxieties, and legitimation practices. To question the apparently sharp focus of *The Queen's Majesty's Passage* and its subsequent treatment by scholars as an objective document, we have only to examine its subtexts of gender, finance, and authority.

One way to de-familiarize the *Passage* is to consider for a moment the more obvious questions of sponsorship and authority raised by the entry of Elizabeth's successor, James I, in 1604. James's entry, delayed for a year after his accession because of plague in the capital, appears in four publications and a variety of accounts whose conflicting details and ideological interests are immediately apparent. Two of the authors—Gilbert Dugdale, who gave a man-in-the-street account that misreads many of the allegories, and Stephen Harrison, who published engravings of the entry's magnificent arches in an attempt to preserve the city's efforts—are clearly city oriented.[37] Two of the authors, Thomas Dekker and his archrival Ben Jonson, provided descriptions and verses for the entry that vied for James's attention. Dekker's account is the longest and attempts what Elizabeth's entry accomplished, to connect the iconography of the current monarch with that of his predecessors. At the same time, Dekker attempts to establish a Jacobean iconography, envisioning a Troynovant, with, however, Elizabeth-like "Pageants built on Faerie land." His difficulty in determining his audience—he walks a tightrope in attempting to recommend himself to the king without offending the city—generates a text that is repetitive and apologetic.[38]

Jonson, on the other hand, seized the occasion to produce a text with an innovative attitude toward allegorical spectacle.[39] Jonson's *Part of the Kings Entertainment in Passing to His Coronation* makes a clear break with the past first by disdaining the repetitive interpretations of Mulcaster and Dekker,[40] second by providing an elaborate scholarly apparatus that represented his learning to both James and a wider audience, and third by creating a new Roman iconography for the king with devices that include Electra welcoming James as Augustus.[41] Although his work was sponsored by the citizens of London and Westminster, Jonson was interested in the way that the text displayed his own abilities, and he was in fact successful in attracting the notice of the king.[42]

The one point on which Dekker's and Jonson's texts agree is the theme of James's entry, that London is the *camera regis,* the chamber of the king. This, as Jonson is at great pains to tell us, is an ancient assignation. But this representation acquired a specifically gendered set of meanings that reverse those of Elizabeth's entry: If James is male, London is female. As Jonson described the situation in the *Panegyre,* his long poem published in addition to his devices,

> When [James] through *London* went,
> The amorous Citie spar'd no ornament,
> That might her beauties heighten; but so drest
> As our ambitious dames, when they make feast,
> And would be courted.[43]

In his entry, James is repeatedly allegorized as entering into London, his "chamber," as a triumphant bridegroom enters his bride. In *The Queen's Majesty's Passage,* the city is no less adamantly gendered as the queen's teacher, father, and husband. London is also a voyeur of Elizabeth, the admiring, dutiful young woman[44] displaying her female anatomy, her "passage," for all to see. Whereas Elizabeth, busily smiling, thanking, and acknowledging the goodness shown her, witnessed condescending allegories of female duty, James's entry into London was proclaimed in the language of mastery. While James felt so confident that he made it clear that his own entry bored him,[45] Dekker's text describes the recorder welcoming him "as a glorious Bridegroome through your Royall Chamber." In short, the new king "rauished" the city "with vnutterable ioyes" by the "vertue . . . begotten in Princes."[46]

In these four accounts, the descriptions of the same scenes differ so much that their reader might well conclude with David Bevington that "the printed text did not always accurately correspond with what took place." The accounts' attitudes toward the king, sponsors, and audience also differ dramatically. In 1559, Mulcaster anonymously placed his competence in the service of the city. In 1604, the authors' names on four different title pages testify to their varied conceptions of representation and audience.

Reading the texts of James's entry thus helps reveal, as I shall discuss in detail later, how gendered and condescending Elizabeth's entertainments were, as well as how anxious the queen herself was to dramatize her commitment to hearing their message. In addition, the sheer variety of the texts, which prevents a satisfying reconstruction of James's entertainment, serves as a reminder that having a single text of Elizabeth's coronation entry does not guarantee that we can know what happened.

Allegory, Instability, and Material Practice

In its attempt to create a new order, an undivided London in an untroubled relationship with its new queen, *The Queen's Majesty's Passage* grapples with the contradictions of constructing a female ruler's power through the unstable media of description and allegorical device. As James's entry illustrates, a single description cannot be more reliable than several descriptions, and yet the more descriptions there are, the less likely it is that a single clear picture will emerge. *The Queen's Majesty's Passage* demonstrates its own descriptive limitations in the gaps and omissions that can be found in its claim of unity. This claim of unity—that London is a homogeneous city, that Crown–city relations are well established and harmonious, and that the text reflects this untroubled picture—inevitably encounters difficulties in the *Passage*. No matter that the text asserts that the "hole matter" will be interpreted. Unity is an impossible achievement for any text, since all writing—especially authoritative writing—summons the very inconsistencies, anxieties, and doubts that it attempts to quash.

For example, the customary genealogical tableau tracing Elizabeth's lineage featured a family tree representing the generational connections affecting the new queen's claim to the throne. Through the crowned figures representing Henry VII and Elizabeth of York, with Henry VIII and Anne Boleyn seated on a stage above them and Elizabeth above *them*, the device represented Elizabeth as their unquestioned heir, "so that unitie was the ende wherat the whole devise shotte . . . that quietnes might be mainteined, and all dissension displaced" (B1, B1v, B2v). Despite this claim, Anne Boleyn's staged presence and her absence from the lengthy explanatory verses call to mind a number of difficulties with this picture. For one thing, Anne had herself once been welcomed by the citizens in a coronation entry representing her as Henry's fertile, chaste queen[47]—and look what happened to her. For another, the physical juxtaposition of Henry VII and Elizabeth with Henry VIII and Anne Boleyn makes Elizabeth's legitimacy (publicly denied in her father's will and the Second Act of Succession[48]) turn on the marital history of her progenitors.

This marital history was not only stormy, but also, as every bystander must have known, implicated in every stir of discontent since the break with Rome twenty years before. Although the text strives to locate all unrest before the Tudors came to power, when the struggle between the Yorks and the Lancasters "had ben the occasion of much debate and civil warre within their realme"(B2v), the citizens of London had to have been concerned with the present possibility of unrest. They were, after all, in transition between the first of Henry VIII's daughters, a Catholic female who married a Spaniard, and the second, an unmarried Protestant female. The device's assertion that now the "two houses were united into one" in the person of Elizabeth, which will end "that jarre . . . and quietnes encrease" (B2), cannot sufficiently whitewash the past or present. Henry's marital history was too complex, his difficulty in producing male heirs too much a part of contemporary events for this tableau not to raise familiar and divisive questions about the relations among gender, religion, sex, procreation, and legitimacy in the minds of its audience.

In an attempt to shut down these disturbing recollections, Mulcaster's text relies heavily on interpretation to delimit the audience's response. The entry consists of five different allegorical devices: the genealogical tree at Fenchurch; the Eight Beatitudes at Sopers Lane; Truth, the Daughter of Time, at the Little Conduit in Cheap; Deborah at the Conduit in Fleet Street; and a general representation of the unity of the various devices at Temple Bar. Each device is packed with explanation. In addition to the figures, their titles and labels "in plaine and perfit writing set upon their breastes easelie to be read of all" (B3v), each pageant featured an official explainer, denoted the "childe" or "poet," who interpreted the device in verse. There were also billboards of Latin and English proverbs. These proverbs, the narrator tells us seven different times, were posted "in every voide space in the pageant," as if to paper over all the other meanings that might occur to an audience that, if literate enough to read them, certainly would know enough to question them.

As a genre, Elizabethan spectacle was too rhetorical, too anxious to represent its argument, to tolerate obscurity or chance its audience's own interpretation of events. Although public allegory during this period depended to a certain extent on the ambiguity and open-endedness of its forms, it could not countenance enigma.[49] Thus in Elizabethan spectacle, representation and explanation attempt to pass as one and the same. All must be exhaustively explained, because the social function of spectacle was to validate a group and suppress dissent by conveying the overwhelming truth of an ideology through the interpretation of allegory.[50] The trouble is that interpretation, especially repetitive, anxious interpretation like the entry's, could not contain the thoughts of its audience. Arguing a supposedly natural and unquestionable position too vehemently tends to expose its ideological origins.

Both description and interpretation prove questionable in *The Queen's Majesty's Passage*. But the entry's reliance on allegory to communicate its civic message reveals even more problems with representing the queen's relation to the city. Allegory, the discourse that Elizabethans believed to be the most authoritative because it provided apprehensible forms for truths located beyond the senses, is also one of the most obviously unstable forms of representation. At the same time that allegory claims to provide an image of truth made visible, it is a form of representation that demonstrates how meaning is constructed. When the text employs allegory, a form of signification calling attention to itself as a form of signification, the fantasy that the truth may be authoritatively represented—that a word or an image corresponds precisely to a given meaning—comes apart. If we consider that a sign—for instance, the Phoenix figuring the Virgin Mary as unique, virginal, and yet fertile—consists of two parts, a signifier (the Phoenix) and a signified (the Virgin Mary, her attributes), then ideological allegory functions by detaching familiar signifiers like the Phoenix from their signifieds and attaching a new signified—for example, Elizabeth. In the coronation entry, the best example of this appropriation of icons from the past is the Truth, the Daughter of Time, device. This device, which I discuss in detail later in this chapter, transforms Mary Tudor's Catholic motto into an occasion to present Elizabeth with the Bible in English.[51]

Through such appropriation—the detachment of traditional signifieds from their signifiers—the sponsors of Elizabethan allegory could connect their messages to the authority of the past.[52] This meant that allegory was constantly being reformed as old signifiers were combined with new signifieds to create new signs. Of course, complications could arise during this process: The signifiers had histories that could not be entirely emptied from the new signs they helped create. Thus they served as reminders of their origin in other, often contradictory, ideologies like Catholicism. Nevertheless, the apparent ease with which an authoritative signifier could be assigned new signifieds in Elizabethan spectacle and the poetry, drama, and visual arts that participated in its sign system meant that allegory proved especially popular as a metalanguage constructed to embody authority. This popularity, however, was not without consequences. The splitting of traditional signifiers and their signifieds reminded people that such connections are in fact arbitrary, that signs are not as natural, as eternal, or as fixed as their creators wish, and that meaning, although created in the contexts of culture and individual experience, is itself a process of shifting acceptances.

Given this instability, can any language or image be of use to us, especially in elaborate systems like allegory? Elizabeth's London entry is evidence that such forms of representation actually accomplish important social business, because it is in the unstable space between signifier and signified that change occurs. It is the instability of language that perpetually undermines its authoritative use. The instability of signs allows not only representation to map conflicting and overlapping discourses, but also the evolution of those discourses as signs—created in part from old sign systems and in part from emergent codes—to alter the distinctions and categories that constitute meaning.

Precisely because signs are unstable and open-ended, they constitute a material practice through which ideas become active.[53] In the case of *The Queen's Majesty's Passage,* city interests sought to categorize the new queen through the metaphoric domestic roles that her predecessor, Mary Tudor, helped develop as the means to connect herself with them. In deploying and developing these categories, the merchants' entertainment of Elizabeth helped construct their authority through representations of the city as her father, husband, and even schoolmaster. Elizabeth, however, gained ground in this situation because the merchants' entertainment situated her within a sign system that assumed, even required, her legitimacy. Thus the entry assigned roles that placed Elizabeth at a disadvantage in the hierarchy of gender, but the mutually constructed fiction of the queen's dependent body served both Crown and city alike.

Elizabeth's Early Self-representation

Before continuing this discussion of ways in which the *Passage* engenders the sexual, financial, and religious questions of the day, I want to consider the extent of Elizabeth's participation in her emergent iconography. The *Passage* grants her only two brief moments of self-representation: her prayer and her response to the city's gift of a purse of gold. The prayer, the single scene that she does not share with the merchants, takes place outside the city gates in front of the Tower and is carefully wrapped in the text's explanation that it forms one of two "principall sygnes" (the other is her acceptance of the city's Bible) that "she in all doinges doth shew herself most mindful of [God's] goodnes and mercie shewed unto her" (E4). Elizabeth's prayer deserves this cautious packaging because it forms a moment of careful self-representation as the new queen thanks God for his mercy in language that associates her with a powerful male image: "I acknowledge that thou hast dealt as wonderfully and as mercifully with me, as thou didst with thy true and faithfull servant Daniel thy prophete whom thou deliveredst out of the denne from the crueltie of the gredy and rageing Lyons: even so was I overwhelmed, and only by thee delivered" (E4–E4v).

In this, the only moment in which she is allowed to represent herself in the entry text, Elizabeth compares herself with Daniel—well educated, male, wise in the ways of politics and the supernatural, beloved of God—and compares the lions of Nebuchadnezzar with the lions of the Tower, in which Mary Tudor had imprisoned her in 1554. Regardless of the narrator's attempt to cloak this powerful moment in piety, Elizabeth's construction of the Daniel analogy suggests an attempt to preempt the accepted female roles that the entry assigns her. In this way, she momentarily occupies what was for her the strongest possible representational position, that of a body neither distinctly male nor distinctly female, as in the portrait of herself that she sent to Eric of Sweden in response to his suit in marriage (Figure 4).

At the same time that she claims male attributes by comparing herself with Daniel, Elizabeth took advantage of her moment in front of the crowd to rewrite the history of her imprisonment in the Tower during her

Figure 4. An early, androgynous portrait of Elizabeth, painted around 1560, that she sent to her suitor, Eric of Sweden. (National Swedish Art Museums)

sister's reign. Her prayer reminds her audience of her moment of greatest vulnerability. But in suggesting that God had sponsored her release from prison, she implies that God preserved her for her coronation. During her reign, as I discuss further in Chapters 2 and 3, this claim would become a highly developed and contested component of her representation.

This prayer constituted Elizabeth's first public speech to a citizenry that collectively equated female silence with female virtue. She selected for her speaking debut the relatively modest genre of the womanly prayer, which her stepmother, Katherine Parr, first popularized in print[54] and to which Elizabeth contributed throughout her life. As seemingly unexceptionable as a public prayer may seem, it signals the new queen's willingness to address her subjects as their sovereign, an activity that crosses over into the male realm of public speech even as it represents her as a Daniel and provides her with a history of divine favor.

Elizabeth's seizure of this moment was one of several instances early in her reign in which she actively participated in her own representation. To know how overwhelmingly the entry's representations of Elizabeth express the attitudes of the city's elites, we have only to look at places and times when she was more in control. For example, at court Elizabeth seems to have commanded from the outset. The London merchant Henry Machyn recorded in his diary that on 31 December 1558 "at nyght at the quen['s] court ther was a play a-for her grace, the wyche the plaers plad suche matter that they wher commondyd to leyff off."[55] Even though we do not know for certain what the "matter" was or even if Machyn's report is simply rumor, it is worthy of note that the queen's displeasure and her willingness to act on it were known in the city.

Machyn's account is also consistent with the queen's behavior at other times. In general, the history of Elizabeth's cancellations, interruptions, and expressed disapproval of material provided for her "entertainment" reminds us of her willingness to make her response clear whenever it was politic to do so. This history also reminds us of the delicacy of her position in relation to her own entertainment. Although her Master of Revels, who in 1558 was Thomas Cawarden, had necessarily to approve what was presented to Elizabeth, he and his successor, Edmund Tilney, were some-times not so sensitive as the queen was to potential slights. Inevitably, she must have greeted many new entertainments with suspicion.

Not only did Elizabeth dislike seeing representations she could not ap-prove, but as she came to realize, simply by viewing an entertainment she also created a scene of validation that could become part of court iconogra-phy. In 1565, for example, she watched a staged debate about marriage featuring Juno and Diana. On this occasion, she informed the Spanish ambassador that this is "all against me" but did not interrupt, possibly because the "entertainment" occurred at a wedding. Her irresolution on that occasion helped set the stage for a similar entertainment in 1575, when she was forced to censor a debate with the same theme and figures at Kenilworth.[56] As in these cases and in the instance of the anti-Spanish play she broke off in 1588,[57] whatever the "matter" was in the December 1558 entertainment, she deemed it unsuitable representation.

This first hint of her active participation in the images she created was borne out when Elizabeth publicly attempted to take control of her own representation less than a month after her coronation. On 6 February 1559 she replied to Parliament's first expression of concern that she marry. In speaking to the Privy Council and members of Parliament in a letter read as a speech by Sir John Mason,[58] Elizabeth remained conciliatory but firm while developing her virginity as a metaphor for choice and the autonomy to claim that choice. She begins by employing the circumlocutions she had customarily used when as a powerless dependent but an attractive matrimonial prospect during the reigns of Edward and Mary, preserving her virginity meant retaining control of her body and her prospects.

While Mary Tudor still lived, Sir Thomas Pope wrote her a letter describing his interview with the Lady Elizabeth on the subject of marriage with Prince Eric of Sweden. He reports that Elizabeth remembered that when her brother, Edward, had offered her in marriage, she asked that Edward give her "leave" "to remayne in *that estate* I was, which of all others best lyked, and pleased me," and that she found herself at "present of the sayme mynde, and soe entende to contynnewe" (my emphasis). As for Prince Eric, she preferred not to marry him because "I so well like *this estate,* as I persuade myself there is not *any kind of life* comparable unto it" (my emphasis).[59]

Just two years later, responding to her council and members of Parliament, Elizabeth begins by similarly avoiding any open statement concerning the relation among her physical body, the choice of marriage, and her autonomy: "I happelie chose *this kynde of life* in which I yet lyve," she tells them. She has not sought marriage from either "ambition" or a desire to avoid "perile." If she had found sufficient reasons to marry before, "if any of these, I sai, could have drawne or dessuaded me from *this kynd of life,* I had not remayned in *this estate* wherein yowe see me" (my emphasis). Throughout this speech, she continues to use other phrases for virginity and marriage conveying that what is at issue is the delicate legal and social question of how completely she may "chose" to possess her own body. Virginity is a decision, "this determination," and a place, "to live out of the state of marriage," whereas marriage is "another kind of life."

By the speech's well-known conclusion, the indirect language deriving from and helping to perpetuate her vulnerability disappears completely.[60] When Elizabeth declares, "And in the end this shalbe for me sufficient that a marble stone shall declare that a Quene having raigned such a time lyved and dyed a virgin," she finally names her physical state. In so doing, she asserts herself through a powerful image, imagining her reign as a lifetime in which she would be "sufficient" unto herself.[61]

At the moment when Elizabeth expresses her realization that she is engaged in a struggle for the meanings attached to her body, the circumlocutions of powerlessness give way to the self-sufficient image of the virgin queen that would become the center of her iconography. The shift occurs about midway through the speech, at the end of still another indirect statement and a timid assertion that she has "continued" so "constant in this determynation although my youthe and woordes may seme to some hardlie to agree together." Then she suddenly asserts, "yet is it most true, that at this daie I stand free from anie other meaninge that either I have had in tymes paste, or have at this present." In these words, Elizabeth not only concedes that her body is the center of political meaning, but also attempts to remove that body from the male definitions of the past, of Parliament, her courtiers and advisers, and her coronation entry.

The need to assert her independence of the meanings so long imposed on her coincides with her need to find an image that embodies her desires, a tradition in which to place herself. Because her female body is the topic of discussion, Elizabeth chooses the strongest female role available to her, that of a woman without a father, brother, or husband: the virgin queen. Assuming this role disrupts the connection between her procreative capability and her sovereign female body.

As the new queen continues her speech, without closing the door on the possibility of marriage, she pronounces herself pleased that the parliamentary expression of concern to which she is replying "cont[aineth] no lymitacion of place or person." It would be a mistake to "draw my love to your liking or frame my will to your fantasies," she tells her audience—perhaps because that had been her role for so long, including during her London entry.[62] That she could submit so willingly and consciously to the city in mid-January and write these words during the first week in February suggests how strategic the entry's representations were in establishing a general recognition of her power. Without those submissive gestures through which she allowed London to construct her "meaning," she could not have claimed to Parliament to be "free from anie other meaninge." But, of course, she was not.

The Sexual Economy of the Passage

In exchange for Elizabeth's submission, *The Queen's Majesty's Passage* stages civic authority as wealthy but generous, powerful but supportive. The "Crown"—by which I mean Elizabeth herself, her Privy Council and executive bureaucracy, and those members of the aristocracy who identified their interests with hers—was not monolithic in purpose, action, or iconography. Torn from the start by the kind of factionalism recently elucidated in Eric Mallin's discussion of the end of Elizabeth's reign,[63] the court and executive bureaucracy were nevertheless united in seeking the fulfillment of their desires through the monarchy, and its court, civil service, and judiciary. The term "city" usually refers in this period to the entire London citizenry, inseparable from its geographical milieu. But when *The Queen's Majesty's Passage* writes "city," it is conflating the citizens' interests with those of their rulers, the Court of Aldermen, by presenting the elites' opinions as being held by the entire city.

The Queen's Majesty's Passage casts the queen as triumphant by stressing the citizens' physical solidarity as an aspect of the city topography: "On eyther syde ther was nothing but gladnes, nothing but prayer, nothing but comfort" (A2–A2v). London is "a stage wherin was shewed the wonderfull spectacle, of a noble hearted princesse toward her most louing people, & the people's exceding comfort in beholding so worthy a soveraign" (A2v). Through this image of her in relation to the unquestioning, indivisible crowds, it is the London elites—the liveried companies, the aldermen, and the Merchant Adventurers—that triumph in this text.

Elizabeth's responses lie within the bounds of feminine propriety, appropriate to an England in which, as A. F. Pollard once observed, "Tudor despotism consisted in fact largely in London's dominance over the rest of England."[64] The text cannot allow the queen to forget the trouble to which the city has gone. The most magnificent description is of the "hyghe ende of Chepe," the economic center where the aldermen awaited her amid the members of their companies standing along the street from Fenchurch to the Little Conduit. Quoting this description in full is useful because nearly all discussions of the entry include some of the following text. Short quotations fail to provide the full material context, the sense that this extravagant moment verbally surrounds and sets off the companies long before the queen appears on the scene. The opulence concentrated in Cheapside, near the hall of the wealthiest company, the Mercers,[65] exists as a demonstration of the power of the London merchants, who, Thomas Gresham advised Elizabeth, would "stand by you at all events in your necessity" as long as she could "keep up [her] credit and specially with [her] own merchants."[66] The "aldermen in the hyghe ende of Chepe" and the "companies" (C2v)

> stoode alonge the streates one by another enclosed with rayles, hanged with clothes, and themselves well apparelled with many ryche furres and theyr livery whodes upon theyr shoulders in comely and semely maner, having before them sondry persones well apparelled in silkes and chaines of golde, as wyflers and garders of the said companies, beside a numbre of riche hangynges, aswell of Tapistrie, Arras, clothes of golde, silver, velvet, damaske, Sattyn, and other silkes plentifully hanged all the way as the Quene's highnes passed from the Towre through the citie. Out at the windowes and penhouses of everie house, did hang a number of ryche and costly banners and streamers tyll her grace came to the upper ende of Cheape. (C2v–C3)

The queen arrives only toward the end of this long descriptive sentence to act as the scene's necessary audience. Enshrined in this display of civic opulence is the moment when "the right whorshipfull maister Ranulph Cholmley, Recorder of the citie, presented to the Quenes majestie a purse of crimosin sattin richly wrought with gold, wherin the citie gaue unto the Quenes majestie a thousand markes in gold" (C3). The recorder's appearance is significant, as he was the official liaison between city and Crown whose duties included "raising troops or loans for the Queen, offering civic offices to the friends of a crown officer, securing patents for city merchants . . . and especially maintaining the traditional liberties and privileges of the City."[67] His speech, which Mulcaster paraphrases, asks her directly "not to esteme the value of the gift, but the mynd of the gyvers." Taking the gift "with bothe her handes" (C3) commits her to acknowledge the merchants' "mynd" (purpose) in this staging of the city's socio-economic power. At the same time, the recorder's paraphrased remarks define this moment as one of exchange.

When Elizabeth accepts the purse from the recorder, she stands within the entry's most overt allegory of its sexual economy. It is an allegory at once financial—a gift of gold to a sovereign who will always need money—and sexual—a kind of inseminated vessel. As an object, the purse is so closely connected to financial power that it cannot be as female as its looks suggest. Yet the medieval moral association of the sexual act with money is too prevalent in the Renaissance for the purse not to have the resident connotation on which Iago would play in forty-five years.[68] To accept the gift (as she must) is to accept the implications it transmits.

Once the transaction is complete, the text reassures its city audience that this is a good investment: "When the citie's charge withoute parcialitie, and onely the citie was mencioned unto her grace, she sayd it shoulde not be forgotten" (E3). Elizabeth's speech, replete with the language of gratitude and compensatory self-sacrifice, follows, although it does provide a hint of her own perspective:

> I thanke my lord maior, his brethren, & you all. And wheras your request is that I should continue your good ladie & quene, be ye ensured, that I wil be as good unto you, as ever quene was to her people. No wille in me can lacke, neither doe I trust shall ther lacke any power. And perswade yourselves, that for the safetie and quietnes of you all, I will not spare, if nede be to spend my blood, God thanke youall. (C3v)

"No wille in me can lacke," she starts agreeably, but she finishes the sentence more pointedly: "Neither doe I trust shall ther lacke any power." For just a moment, Elizabeth's response breaks out of the mold of gracious obedience to make sure of the bargain: I will perform my part, but you must support my sovereignty.

This economic bargain held for the most part until the end of Elizabeth's reign. But as we have seen, the queen moved quickly to confuse, if not remove, the gendered assumption of her passivity and vulnerability underlying the exchange. By the 1590s, her ongoing attempt to represent herself in an array of powerful icons had encouraged her address through the hyperbole of mythological, political–theological, Petrarchan, and Neoplatonic discourses. When the recorder Edward Drew welcomed her in 1592, he spoke in terms that form an effective contrast with the representation of Elizabeth in *The Queen's Majesty's Passage*. In particular, his language marks a clear reversal of many of the gendered assumptions made in the entry: The Mayor elected by us is

> a dimme and senceless body untill he receaves light and sence, which is only to be obtayned from your sacred Majesty, being the consecrated lamp from whome all magistrates doe drawe their light, and the only suprem head from whence all motion and senses are dispersed into every member of the body of this Commonweale, from whence all sense and life doth flowe and proceede, unto every member of the incorporate body whereof your Majestie is the sole and supream head.[69]

In 1592, the representational hierarchy of 1559 is reversed: Instead of a daughter–wife to London's father–husband, Elizabeth is twice called the "suprem head" of the commonwealth. The scale of distance between herself and the city is, moreover, cosmic: Elizabeth is the sun in London's heliocentric universe, so that the mayor, her subject, is fittingly her planet. Instead of a grateful recipient of the value bestowed on her by the London elites, in this speech it is she who is the giver of a magical "sense and life" flowing outward from her. The recorder's need to express city–Crown relations by appropriating language that Elizabeth herself was expected to approve, rather than through the coronation entry's gendered metaphors of exchange, shows how completely Elizabeth's more developed iconography could displace the images popularized by the *Passage*. By the 1590s, the Crown still needed the city, and the city, the Crown; but in London and on this occasion at least, the queen's control of her representations predominates.

Truth, the Daughter of the Signifier

The entry's most intriguing juxtaposition of gender and economics occurs in a device concerning religion: Truth, the Daughter of Time, which is the fourth pageant. The city's attitude toward Elizabeth as a female at once powerful and subordinate is particularly evident in this device when we consider that it featured an enlargement of the female anatomy of Brobdinagian proportions. On the stage were "two hylles or mountaynes of conuenient heyghte. The one of them beyng on the North syde of thesame pageaunt, was made cragged, barreyn, and stonye, in the whiche was erected one tree . . . all withered and deadde, with braunches accordinglye" (C3v). This first "hill" was titled "Ruinosa Respublica, A decayed common weale." The other hill "was made fayre, freshe, grene, and beawtifull, the grounde therof full of flowres and beawtie, and on thesame was erected also one tree very freshe and fayre." This second hill was titled "Respublica bene instituta. A florishyng commonweale" (C4). The hills are simultaneously mons and breast: her sister Mary's, barren; Elizabeth's, green. The device suggests multiple readings of Elizabeth's fertility, of the relation between her body and the potential for the commonwealth's prosperity, of the expectation that she, unlike Mary, will produce both offspring and good government. Elizabeth's procreative and political functions are viewed as versions of each other, as the explanatory verses demonstrate:

> Now si[n]ce that Time agai[n] his daughter truth hath brought,
> We trust O worthy quene, thou wilt this truth embrace.
> We trust welth thou wilt plant, and barrennes displace. (C4v)

The contrast between Elizabeth and Mary is also implicit in the pageant's invention, in that Truth, the Daughter of Time, is a device associated with Mary (Figure 5).[70] In appropriating Mary's iconography, the writer (probably Richard Grafton, author of the device featuring the "word of God" at Mary and Philip's entry) constructed an allegory that overtly

Figure 5. Portrait of Mary Tudor (ca. 1554), by Frans Huys. Her motto, "Veritas Temporis Filia" (Truth, the Daughter of Time), is prominent under the portrait. (British Library)

overlays its Catholic associations with Protestant meanings that assert the city's power. Time signifies the teleology that has brought this moment. Time's signified is his daughter, Truth, who herself promotes a new signified: Protestantism. When Truth is "born" from her cave to present Elizabeth with the English Bible, the picture of Elizabeth's body as nourishing and fertile is complete. Indeed, Elizabeth accepts the Bible like a baby. "How reverently did she with both her handes take it, kisse it, & lay it upon her brest to the great comfort of the lookers on" (E4v) comments the text's final paragraph. Elizabeth's acceptance of the Bible is equivalent to a mother's acceptance of her child. That is, the queen's embrace of the Bible forms a contract as permanent and natural as motherhood in her marriage to city interests.

Elizabeth's allegorization as wife to the city's wishes and mother to its truth seems clear. The relation between the allegorized marriage of Crown and city through Protestantism is, however, less so. Other twentieth-century readers of the device Truth, the Daughter of Time, have assumed that this was simply a Protestant device, but like all governmental policy, Elizabethan Protestantism had yet to emerge from parliamentary debate and the subsequent proclamations of June, July, and August 1559. The mass, for example, was abolished and the prayer book instituted in June. At the time of the *Passage,* the city was in transition between two religions and did not yet know what form Protestantism would assume under this second queen.

From November 1558 through May 1559, Elizabeth acted in accordance with the advice contained in a memorandum of 1558/1559 (probably Cecil's) from the committee on the settlement of the Protestant religion. Under the heading "what may be done of her highnes for her own conscience openly, before the whole alteration [of religion]?" stands the suggestion that Elizabeth make few open moves and that the option of Catholic worship be left available. The committee found it advisable "to alter [observed religion] noe further then her majesty hath, except it be to receive the communion as her highnes pleaseth on the feasts. And that there be more chaplines at masse, that they doe alwayes communicat with the executor in both kindes."[71]

For the moment, at least, Catholic and Protestant forms of worship coexisted, which was necessary, in part because the Catholic clergy remained in place. As late as "the end of 1560 no less than thirty-six London livings remained in the hands of their Marian incumbents."[72] The London of January 1559 was still more Catholic than this. The fact that Protestantism was far from institutionalized helps explain why—although Clifford Geertz, Stephen Mullaney, and Mark Breitenberg discuss the entire text as heavily Protestant in tone[73]—it uses religious forms of expression while repressing religious questions.

Indeed, the entry uses Protestant religious discourse for purposes of civic self-definition rather than to institutionalize any particular form of Protestantism. A great deal of evidence points to this conclusion. The text, although pious in its invocation of God, betrays no religious ardor. Except for the *Verbum dei* device, the text is not overtly Protestant. No mention of common Protestant grievances appears, like the execution of heretics during Mary's reign. The text is equally silent on the Protestants' rejoicing at Mary's death, the ongoing Catholic departures for the Continent, and the gradual return of exiles like John Foxe.[74] The text is neither Catholic nor right-wing Protestant; rather, displays of iconoclasm like "the masquerade of friars in the streets of London" and "the statue of St. Thomas stoned and beheaded, which is now thrown down entirely, and the stucco statue of a little girl placed in its stead," as the Venetian ambassador says happened on the eve of Elizabeth's entry, go unremarked.[75] In fact, the account ignores the divisions of faith and loyalty in a London whose citizens simultaneously welcomed the return of Protestantism and attended churches where mass continued to be said. The text occupies this ground of religious centrism not only because it addresses an audience of mixed religion, but also because the Court of Aldermen paying for it was itself of mixed religious conviction. Indeed, three of the ten aldermen for whom biographical information is available (out of a total of eighteen known members of the court) were avowed Catholics.[76]

If the London elites were concerned with defining their political present through what Patrick Collinson called a "consensual Protestantism closely connected to a sense of national identity and to principles of civil obedience and deference,"[77] Elizabeth's own political position was far different. London's leading citizens could afford to conceptualize their break with Mary and Spain through Protestant discourse. But while England remained at war with France, the government was too vulnerable for the queen to offend Catholic Spain. We cannot know how much the historical Elizabeth wanted to display her Protestantism, but as a monarch who often favored ambiguity above frankness, it seems unlikely that she wanted to make a point of her religion at the cost of losing her most powerful foreign ally. At her coronation, at which she and her council exercised more control, she was circumspect about declaring herself a Protestant.[78] She seems to have succeeded in maintaining some doubt about her leanings, since as late as 23 April, Paulo Tiepolo, the Venetian ambassador, along with King Philip, wrote to the doge and the senate that "the Queen would still wish to some extent to feign to profess the Catholic religion, but she can conceal herself no longer."[79]

Within the six months following the entry, Parliament legislated the beginnings of a specifically Elizabethan Protestantism. In time, the Crown fashioned a Protestant iconography that employed maternal, sexual, and fertile images of Elizabeth to assert her independence, popularity, wisdom, and virtue. Even in January 1559, few had any doubts about Elizabeth's religious preference. In the interests of self-definition, however, the London elites forced on Elizabeth the gift of the Bible—a gift, like that of the purse, that she had to accept, acknowledge, and remember. Richard Grafton's Protestant convictions and the device's Protestant implications remain unmistakable. But in the context of *The Queen's Majesty's Passage*, the Truth device enacts England's growing religious movement in a larger context of civic self-definition. Civic order, capitalism, and Protestantism become indistinguishable in this device, funded by the aldermen, Catholic and Protestant alike.

Thus the entry invites us to associate, even conflate, the gifts of gold and the Bible, to read religious concerns as financial in its insistence that Elizabeth's acceptance of the Bible means "welth thou wilt plant, and barrennes displace." The structure of the text itself enforces this relationship by describing the gift of the purse in a digression within the Truth device.

In order to do so, the text even gives us a moment of insight into how uncomfortable Elizabeth was at the idea of receiving the Bible in English. The text's straightforward chronology of events suddenly fractures when Elizabeth, moving from the fourth device to the fifth, inquires what the next entertainment will be. Informed that it is Time, which will give her the Bible in English, Elizabeth tries to avoid receiving it herself: "She thanked the citie for that gift, and sayd that she would oftentimes reade over that booke, comaunding sir John Parrat, one of the knyghtes which helde up her canapy, to goe before and to receive the booke." When the city representative insisted, stating that the Bible "should be delivered unto her grace downe by a silken lace," she caused "him to staye, and so passed forward till she came agaynste thaldermen in the hyghe ende of Chepe" (C2v). Only after receiving the gift of money there does she proceed to the gift of the Bible, as if the 1,000 marks was her price for an overt statement of her Protestantism.

If we want to find a more absolutely religious device, the presentation of the Bible to Mary Queen of Scots during her Edinburgh entry provides an example of a similar pageant without London's economic subtext. In 1561, Scotland's returning queen entered Edinburgh through a portal from whose clouds a boy descended to present her with "the keyis of the toun, togidder with ane bybill and ane psalme buik, coverit with fyne purpourit veluot." John Knox describes her as acknowledging the gifts with a frown and giving the book to Arthoure Erskyn, the captain of her guard, "the most pestilent Papist within the Realme." Mary Stuart's remaining devices, as Randolphe described them to Cecil, "were terrible significations of the vengeance of God upon idolaters." According to the *Diurnal of Remarkable Occurents,* they included the burning of the usual allegory of Catholicism, a dragon, and speeches "concernyng the putting away of the mess."[80] The entry was inspired by John Knox, perhaps even written by him. It fully expressed the more united—and openly hostile—left-wing Protestantism of an Edinburgh business community so closely connected with Knox that its council made several payments to him in 1561 and even helped him repair his house.[81]

The difference between the two entries does not reside in the two queens' religions so much as in their relationships with their merchants. Although Catholic and Protestant, their initial reactions to the forced "gift" were actually similar: Mary Stuart handed the Bible to Arthoure Erskyn, and Elizabeth, when first hearing of the device, attempted to sidestep the Bible's presentation by asking John Parrat to receive it.

Nor was there much difference in their attitudes toward radical Protestantism. Both queens found Knox an irritant and a threat. The crucial difference between these presentations of the Bible lies in the financial relations between queen and community. The London government had, after all, supported the Catholic Mary Tudor once she had acknowledged her proper relation to Guildhall. But Edinburgh, a smaller and more homogeneous city, was composed of radical Protestants who had based their economy on an absentee queen to whom religion was more important than economic cooperation. When Mary Stuart returned to rule Scotland, although highly placed Edinburgh citizens were not averse to dining with her at Holyrood, the Edinburgh Town Council continued zealously to evict Catholics: On 16 June 1561, the council ordered "Sir George Strauchane, prieist, to depesche of this toun and boundis thairof within xii houris nixt heirefter"; and a proclamation of October 1561 aroused Mary's displeasure by ordering "preistis, monkis, freris, and vtheris of the wikit rable of the antechrist the paip," including "nonnys, adulteraris, fornicatouris, and all sic filthy personis," to leave in twenty-four hours.[82]

To describe London as generally tolerant of religious differences would be going too far, but at this historical juncture, religious conformity was not crucial to the pursuit of its socioeconomic goals. Instead, *The Queen's Majesty's Passage* contributes to an overtly Protestant discourse that powerful Catholics also saw as working for them because it contained their hopes for order and trade as established between themselves and the Crown with a minimum of foreign influence.

The cooperation that I believe occurred between powerful Catholic and Protestant merchants through Protestant discourse flies in the face of the Whig interpretation of history, the assumption that "Protestants will be seen to have been fighting for the future."[83] Christopher Hill warns in "Protestantism and the Rise of Capitalism" that "there is nothing in protestantism which leads automatically to capitalism"; "men did not become capitalists because they were protestants, nor protestants because they were capitalists." The evidence of Catholic–Protestant cooperation in city families and government[84] and in Crown–city relations supports Hill's observation that the "main significance" of Protestant theology "is that in any given society it enabled religion to be moulded by those who dominated in that society."[85] In the light of this analysis, it seems reasonable that London Catholic merchants would prefer a Protestant discourse that could create a city in the image of its leaders. The aldermen-supported pageant of emergent Truth is about cooperation and hence about the values and self-perceptions of prosperous men. In embracing Protestant discourse, Londoners, like the Lyonais whom Natalie Zemon Davis has described, "thought in terms of a new measure, redefining how the holy should be present in the world."[86] When Elizabeth embraced as her "child" the Bible, the most Protestant symbol in the interests of articulating her liaison with the city, she was embracing their economic and political interests in religious form.

Profits and Representations

As it turned out, Elizabeth did not "lacke any power" in the ongoing negotiations with London elites throughout her reign. Although the *Passage* strove to place Elizabeth within the exchange of submission for support developed during Mary Tudor's reign, everyday financial relations required the realization that the queen was not city property, a wife or daughter, but an entity apart from paternalistic categories. In the early years of Elizabeth's reign, the economic reality was that Crown and city actively cooperated for their mutual gain. In financial interactions in the twelve months after the coronation, neither Crown nor city seems to have proved itself dominant, although each helped the other. In 1560, for example, as the financial community continued to experience inflation, debased coinage, and the unavailability of hard currency prevalent in Mary's reign, the Crown moved quickly to reform the coinage along the lines developed by Mary's Privy Council. On its side, the Crown, as usual, depended on London for financing and securing the debts incurred in pursuing its foreign policy. At least one early loan around 1560 "was largely subscribed to by members of the Merchant Adventurers Company."[87] The most significant loan of her early reign was the £10,000 borrowed from the city to help finance the unfortunate Normandy expedition of 1562/1563.

Aside from cash transactions, Crown and city also affirmed and checked each other's privileges. In its confirmation of a guild's charter, the Crown helped bring that group's powers and privileges into being by ratifying its place in the socioeconomic order. At the same time, negotiating the charter allowed the Crown to exchange confirmation for concessions. For example, the Stationers Company achieved the goal of having books printed solely under its authority when its charter was confirmed by Elizabeth in 1559, but it also had to comply with a new system for licensing books. This role of royal confirmation explains why, as Erna Auerbach found, the charters of guilds incorporated during Elizabeth's reign frequently bear some of the most unusual, noncourt portraits of Elizabeth, testimony to the interdependence of city–Crown relations as well as to the citizens' preference for their own images of the queen (Figure 6).[88]

Frank Foster points out that "the essence of the greatly interdependent relationship between crown and City was that at many points opportunities arose to do each other favours; these were often followed up in the mutual recognition that continued relations would be smoother as a result."[89] One of the ways in which Crown and city cooperated was that the Crown helped in a sense to underwrite the coronation entry itself, as David Bergeron discovered when he found Elizabeth's holograph order to Sir Thomas Cawarden, Master of Revels.

In this document, the queen ordered Cawarden to "cause to be deliuered vnto John Gresham and John Elyot citizens of our Citie of London suche and so muche of the said apparrell as they shall require for the setting forthe of those pageentes which be appoynted to stande for the shew of our Cytie at the tyme we are to passe thorough thesame towardes our Coronation."[90] This kind of cooperation between Crown and city in staging an entry was apparently commonplace: Edward VI supplied a number of items to the city of London for his coronation entry (Figure 7), including

Figure 6. Portrait of Elizabeth within the initial *E*. From the Charter of the Worshipful Company of Blacksmiths (1571). (By permission of the Worshipful Company of Blacksmiths)

"garmentes for women," two coats with "Tynsyll and Crymsyn velvett," and the intriguing notation, "one spyre for Astronomye."[91] As evidence of the ongoing relation between Crown and city, Elizabeth's order suggests the kind of preparation necessary for a coronation entry. It also suggests that since Elizabeth herself helped in the planning, she may have known in advance the roles she would have to play. Indeed, it is likely that she knew at least the general outlines of the representations she encountered. If she did know the content of her entry beforehand, then perhaps she actively cooperated in the appearance of her own relative passivity.

In addition to its recognition of domestic economic interests and relations, Elizabeth's London entry expressed close cooperation between the Crown and the Merchant Adventurers, the organization that in 1559 administered the vast majority of England's trade overseas. The entry's correlation of the Crown's interests with the Adventurers expressed a crucial relationship, for as it turned out, the Merchant Adventurers determined many of Elizabeth's connections with Europe. "Wherever there are towns," Ferdinand Braudel observes,

> there will also be a form of power, protective and coercive, whatever the shape taken by that power or the social group identified with it. And while power may exist independently of towns, it acquires through them

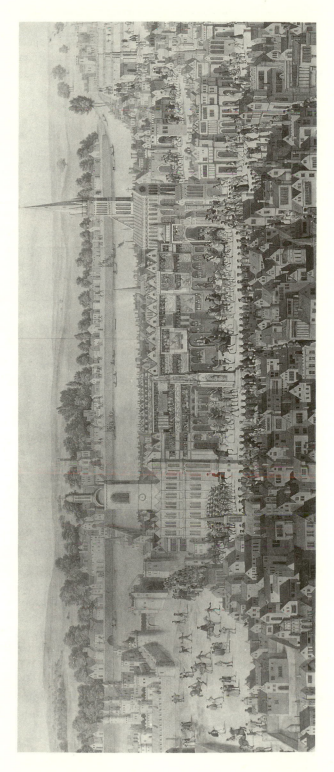

Figure 7. Edward VI's coronation entry into London in 1547, depicted in a watercolor copy of the original, which is now lost. (The Society of Antiquaries of London)

> an extra dimension, a different field of application. Last of all, there can be
> no door to the rest of the world, no international trade without towns.[92]

Whereas Mary had seen Europe through her Hapsburg interests, Elizabeth
and her Privy Council most often saw Europe through issues of trade and
thus through the eyes of London's wealthiest merchants, whose elected
representatives on the Continent frequently doubled as Elizabeth's liaisons
with foreign governments.

To a large extent, the Merchant Adventurers sponsored *The Queen's
Majesty's Passage,* so that its devices represent Elizabeth's relationship with
not only the entire business community, but also its wealthiest members in
particular. Although individual members of the twelve principal companies organizing the entry were dunned for its expenses, all larger aspects
of London city government were determined by the Court of Aldermen,
which paid Richard Mulcaster for producing the entry text. Most of these
aldermen were Merchant Adventurers, as a number of historians, including
D. M. Loades, Robert Ashton, and G. D. Ramsay, have made clear. The
aldermen's families usually invested heavily in foreign trade, especially in
the Continental cloth trade, which comprised the majority of sales abroad.

Although the English economy was increasingly diversified, throughout
Elizabeth's reign, exporting cloth offered a fairly steady income during
periods of internal decay and recession.[93] It should be remembered that
many London merchants had mixed foreign and domestic interests. Nevertheless, Robert Ashton's distinction "between the mass of privileged
merchants in general and merchant princes who had directive interests in
the great chartered companies: and between those whose interests were
confined to orthodox commodity trade"[94] is useful. Those merchants and
merchant princes in the first, privileged group for the most part invested in
foreign trade, identified their interests with the Crown's, and found in the
sixteenth century that Parliament usually stood against them, favoring
domestic over foreign trade. The foreign investors' interests were particularly hegemonic in the sixteenth century: The ease of crossover between
companies in this period meant that Merchant Adventurers joined and
eventually dominated a number of the twelve liveried companies.[95] The
implications of their influence for Elizabeth's *Passage* can be most easily
assessed if we look at what the Adventurers and the Crown had to gain
through cooperation.

The economic relation joining Elizabeth's interests with the Adventurers' is simply stated: Elizabeth's solvency and the aldermen's expectation
of profits abroad rested on their mutual need to bypass Parliament to
secure profits from the foreign sale of cloth. In the middle of the sixteenth
century, Sybil Jack informs us, "London was the dominant centre of international trade," with "four-fifths of all overseas trade normally passing
through the port."[96] London's centrality in turn created an ongoing competition for the control of English wool between London cloth finishers
and dyers and exporters of unfinished cloth to Antwerp.

Early in the century, parliamentary legislation had sought to keep at least the most expensive cloth in England for finishing in order to benefit local craftsmen, and through its Act of 1542, Parliament had set the "permissible price limit for the export of unfinished cloths to £4 for white and £3 for coloured."[97] By the 1550s, the inflationary increase in prices meant that less cloth was available for export. The Merchant Adventurers had two choices if they wanted to continue exporting cloth abroad at similar or increased levels: They had to turn either to Parliament, which at this point favored the domestic trade's desire to lower the price of exportable cloth, or to Elizabeth for royal license to export above the parliamentary limits. The path of less resistance proved to be working with Elizabeth, whose licenses for foreign export were lucrative for the merchants and a primary source of income for the Crown, which received payment for licensing and collected additional levies from the exporters. This income also allowed Elizabeth a crucial degree of autonomy from Parliament.

The partnership between the queen and the Adventurers proved particularly effective in the early years of the reign, as G. D. Ramsay's figures show: "In the financial year 1559–1560, the total customs revenue of England came to £83,024-odd, of which £50,809 was raised in London—61 percent—and the proportion was even greater the following year when . . . London supplied . . . over two-thirds." The "official valuation of exports" rose from "£286,315 odd in the first year of Elizabeth, to over £363,000 in 1562–3, and grew to a little less than £500,000 by 1565–66," Ramsay estimates. Thanks to the activity of the aging William Paulet, once Mary's and now Elizabeth's Lord Treasurer, the Crown had acquired greater control of customs under Francis Englefield, who oversaw a more accurate assessment of the amount of cloth exported. The control of exportations by the Adventurers and the importation of goods made possible by foreign trade ensured that, as Ramsay concludes, "court and City were brought into tighter interdependence than ever before, and the crown was aligned with the most dynamic social force of the age."[98]

The foreign economic picture became bleaker in the 1580s and 1590s. England shared in the rapid inflation present on the Continent; Elizabeth came under attack for her overissuance of monopolies; and as hostilities with Spain made trade with the Netherlands uncertain, the sway of the Merchant Adventurers eventually ended as their competitors, the Company of Clothworkers, gained control over new markets in the Baltic and the Mediterranean.[99] At Elizabeth's accession, however, the Crown and the aldermen-Adventurers stood to gain considerably by forms of cooperation not figured in *The Queen's Majesty's Passage*.[100]

What, then, did civic and monarchical interests gain—or lose—through Elizabeth's coronation entry? In what ways were Crown–city relations maintained or altered, objectified or camouflaged, in its symbolic action? When the city elites seized the opportunity at the outset of the queen's reign to express their paternal support, they succeeded in authorizing their fantasies through Elizabeth's person. Because city groups paid for, produced, and finally published the record of their achievement as *The Queen's Majesty's Passage,* they momentarily created, in the words of Pierre Bourdieu, an "authorized language" invested with the authority of a group."[101] Thus the city's merchants succeeded in staging the queen they preferred to see at that historical moment. Then, in a book entitled *The Queen's Majesty's Passage,* these wealthy males re-created their fantasy as a commodity to be exchanged among themselves.

Because there was a gap between representation and the material world as well as fundamental (if unspoken) divisions among the different groups participating in the spectacle, the cultural work of the entry was significant both in practical terms and in terms of its interaction with the gendered sign system representing the queen. The merchants, especially the most powerful aldermen and Merchant Adventurers, depended on the Crown's help in granting trade licenses, thereby creating a stable political climate in which trade could flourish after the depressed years of Mary's reign. The queen needed the merchants' help in validating her succession to the throne, in borrowing money and establishing her credit rating abroad, in creating revenues that could be taxed with some accuracy, and in generally supporting the Crown's institutions. Thus in practice, the exchange of civic support for Elizabeth's momentary feminine submission enabled the development of a lucrative relationship between the London elites and the Crown. The money and influence resulting from the relations between Crown and powerful merchants in turn allowed the queen to consolidate her power while she took greater control of her representation.

At the same time that the entry's interactions presaged a genuine need to cooperate, the anxieties of its sponsors and authors regarding the queen's sex, relative youth, and religion created images of her that called for her response. In representing herself at the beginning of her entry (although described at the end of the published text) as a Daniel just liberated by God from the lions' den and stating her desire before members of Parliament to "stand free from any other meaning" chosen for her, Elizabeth entered an ongoing struggle for the elusive connections between representation and power. As she discovered, precisely because representations are unstable, they could affirm her right to the throne as well as undermine it, declare her importance as that institutional entity, the Crown, as well as subordinate her because she was a woman.

The history of the queen's representation as a competition begins with *The Queen's Majesty's Passage* because as the first public allegorization of her, it provided a wealth of images that she would later restructure in an attempt to authorize her power. For example, the entry's presentation of Elizabeth as a dutiful daughter became subsumed in more potent images. Her metaphoric motherhood was eventually turned more to her advantage by recasting her subjects as her dependents. As she replied to a Commons petition that she marry, "You [shall] never have . . . a more naturall mother, than I meane to be vnto yow all." The entry's implication that she was the wife of the city she turned into a political metaphor of her marriage with her kingdom in the manner of the doge of Venice and Mary Tudor before her. The new queen's success in the 1560s in altering the entry's iconography may be seen in such texts as Thomas Norton's address "To the queenes maiesties poore deceived subiectes of the northe contreye." Written during the rebellion of 1569, it describes Elizabeth in her preferred terms and even adds a twist: She is "the most louing Mother and nourse of all her good subiects . . . the Husband of the comon weale, maried to the realme."[102] In giving the queen the role of husband, Norton has also astutely reproduced the representations, fully current by 1569, of Elizabeth as male or androgynous.

By the time of the Kenilworth entertainments of 1575, the queen was adept at selecting an iconography of independence and censoring devices that conflicted with that view. Her dual importance as the focal point of representation and its audience always left her somewhat vulnerable, however, to images of herself that required male support, as we shall see in Chapter 2, which considers the competition between Robert Dudley and Elizabeth for control of the Kenilworth entertainments.

2

Engendering Policy at Kenilworth (1575)

Among the Spanish diplomatic dispatches of 1575, news of the entertainments at Kenilworth first appears in Antonio de Guaras's letter of 18 July from London. Writing secretly, de Guaras communicates several news items that betray a certain relish for the historical moment's instability. In the process he reminds us, as I wish to do, that the entertainments took place in relation to external events that also helped construct them in the first place. De Guaras begins with a report on the English involvement in the Palatine, including rumors of troops raised in support of the Dutch revolt and the departures of Englishmen to meet at Heidelberg with members of the Protestant alliance. It describes still more events: Two ships are being fitted at Plymouth to transport soldiers to the Continent. The Prince of Orange is "intimidated" by his loss at Buren. The writer is busy negotiating with Burghley the release of English prisoners of the Spanish Inquisition. The news that arrived a week ago that the Scots treacherously attacked a group of Englishmen "has thrown the Court into great dismay." Only then does an account of the court entertainment intrude: "The Queen, who is now at a castle belonging to Lord Leicester, called Kenilworth, has been entertained with much rejoicing there." This happy picture is disrupted, however, with a rumor of attempted assassination: "It is said that whilst she was going hunting on one of the days, a traitor shot a crossbow at her. He was immediately taken, although other people assert that the man was only shooting at the deer and meant no harm." Although de Guaras, "a Spanish merchant and leading member of the Spanish community in London,"[1] is all too willing to report this event for which no corroborative evidence exists, the rumor itself suggests both the widespread fear of Elizabeth's death and a contemporary skepticism about the glories of Kenilworth.[2]

These details of foreign policy that conclude with the dubious entertainment of Elizabeth are reminders that the two accounts from which scholars reconstruct Kenilworth were themselves constructed at a time when many English were contemplating full-scale military involvement on the Continent for the first time in twenty years. These two texts, *A Letter: Whearin, part of the Entertainment, untoo the Queenz Maiesty, at KILLINGWORTH CASTL,* known as *Laneham's Letter,* and George Gascoigne's *Princely Pleasures at the Courte at Kenelwoorth. That is to saye, The Copies of all such Verses, Proses, or poetical inventions, and other Devices of Pleasure, as were there deuised, and presented by sundry Gentlemen, before the Quene's Majestie,*[3] inform their readers that the entertainments were the most spectacular of Elizabeth's reign, but each writer cautiously avoids mentioning what he thinks of the external events that bore directly not only on the national welfare, but also on the personal welfare of the queen and her courtiers. De Guaras's dispatch has not been considered in discussions of Kenilworth, perhaps because its vision of events there dispels a glorious myth, founded on readings of *Laneham's Letter* and *The Princely Pleasures* that were popularized through the works of Ben Jonson and, two centuries later, Walter Scott, and that have been widely accepted in the twentieth century by many who study Elizabeth's court. But the first three descriptions of Kenilworth were generated through the contemporary connections among gender, court politics, and commerce, as well as domestic and foreign policy.

Both *Laneham's Letter* and *The Princely Pleasures* were published soon after Elizabeth's visit—the *Letter* almost immediately, and the *Pleasures* within six months. Although both have become canonical texts of court spectacle, both exist to some extent at the margins of contemporary accounts of spectacle: *Laneham's Letter,* as I will show, is an elaborate and revealing jest, and *The Princely Pleasures* publishes two entertainments censored by the queen. The best guide to Dudley's interests, at least as interpreted by George Gascoigne, is *The Princely Pleasures.* Although Gascoigne does not include a dedication to Dudley, the work forms a clear bid for the patronage of an earl known for his militant Protestantism, by an author newly returned from his private participation in the Netherlands revolt.

Ambition and Policy

A close look at the sponsors and writers of these entertainments as planned, performed, and printed allows us to approach the representations of spectacle in relation to questions of domestic and foreign policy. By the summer of 1575, the most pressing political debate concerning Robert Dudley and his queen was whether the English should actively support the Dutch revolt against the Spanish. Thus Dudley welcomed the queen to Kenil-worth (Figure 8) in entertainments whose extravagance submerged his dependence on her while elevating his eagerness for more responsibility, specifically for military command of an English intervention in the Nether-lands. At this point in his career, Dudley sought some kind of activity outside the country. As powerful as he found himself in England, Dudley was hampered in his attempts to increase his sphere of influence either in the country or abroad. As long as his prestige derived entirely from his personal relations with Elizabeth, he could never act independently, for fear that she would reduce him to his origins, as she repeatedly threatened to do.

Was Dudley completely at Elizabeth's mercy? In 1566, the Venetian ambassador in France, Giacomo Surian, reported a vicious game that says a great deal about the earl's situation. During the English court's celebra-tions marking Epiphany, a king customarily "was chosen who had lately found favour with Queen Elizabeth." This revels king, most probably Christopher Hatton—of whom Dudley was known to be jealous—"commanded Lord Robert to ask the Queen . . . which was the most difficult to erase from the mind, an evil opinion created by a wicked in-former, or jealousy?" According to the rules of the game, Dudley had no choice but to ask Elizabeth the question that would allow her to rebuke him for his jealousy of Hatton. The queen "replied courteously that both things were difficult to get rid of, but that, in her opinion, it was much more difficult to remove jealousy." Dudley, angered at having been placed in this situation, later threatened that he would beat her new favorite "with a stick." When Elizabeth heard of this, she once again admonished Dudley, saying "that if by her favour he had become insolent he should soon reform, and that she would lower him just as she had at first raised him." Only after Dudley had remained for four days in his rooms, "showing by his despair that he could no longer live," did the queen restore him to favor.[4]

Dudley's elaborate "show" of fury and despair and Elizabeth's equally elaborate show of authority, condescension, and forgiveness in these and similar anecdotes capture the performative quality of the relationship be-tween the two. Each viewed the other's acting with a combination of distaste and admiration that stands at the base of their life-long association.

In 1575, these two princes, whom Frederigo Zuccaro sketched while on a visit from Italy that year (Figure 9), also embodied the two powerful political factions that each represented. Dudley and Walsingham led the militant Protestants, who were united in a desire to seek realms of influence farther from the queen's court, and Elizabeth and Burghley remained united in their willingness to use diplomacy to avoid as long as possible an overt show of aid to the Low Countries. The members of the Protestant faction dreamed that if Dudley were their leader in an incursion in the Netherlands, he and his supporters would enjoy wider fields of action in fighting and governing abroad, perhaps gaining the wealth and social

Figure 8. Kenilworth Castle, the property that Elizabeth granted Robert Dudley, Earl of Leicester, in 1563 and the site of the Kenilworth entertainments of 1575. (Engraving by Wenceslaus Holys. British Library)

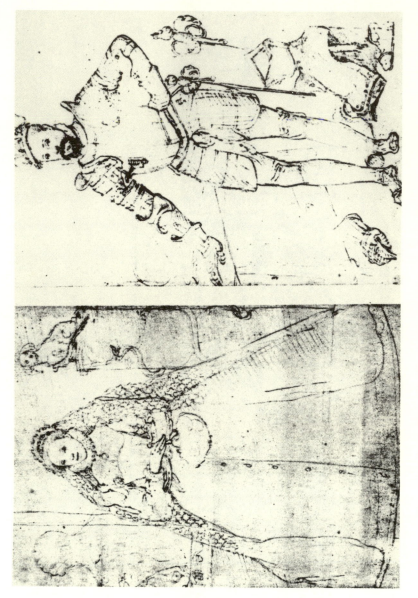

Figure 9. Elizabeth and Dudley in May 1575, as sketched by Frederigo Zuccaro. (British Library)

mobility denied them by Elizabeth. The more cautious thinkers were hesitant to commit the national treasury to a war with Spain, and as it turned out after the English intervention of 1585 to 1587, justifiably so. Despite pressure from Dudley, Walsingham, and William of Orange, in the summer of 1575 the queen remained unwilling to support an open intervention in the Netherlands. But the militant Protestants continued to hope. One of the results of their collective aspirations was the Kenilworth entertainments as they were originally planned, during which Dudley sought to advertise his personal gifts, status, and noble origins in spectacles celebrating the queen as a guest, an observer, and, above all, an unmarried woman who should welcome his masculine attentions.

Elizabeth did not care to see herself displayed as a guest on property that she owned, as an observer of her subordinate's gallant actions, or as a woman in need of a husband or protector. Such terms were anathema to a queen who perpetually had to construct herself as the principal decision maker of the government she headed. Nonetheless, she watched at least the preliminary entertainments, as she sometimes did. Perhaps she watched because at least they mixed the epideictic and the unflattering. Perhaps, in full view of both court and countryside, she chose to appear gracious. Perhaps she watched because she saw such entertainments as inevitable in the dynamic she had helped create, in which courtiers used court ceremony and spectacle to display themselves through their definitions of her.

That Elizabeth recognized Dudley as being dangerous and that she had the power to check him were equally clear. The Elizabeth who had worked hard to maintain her distance from Dudley was by the 1570s a fully empowered viewer of and participant in the spectacles that displayed her and her relations with others. She was skillful at guarding "the natural representation of her majesty's person" from "the errors and deformities already committed by sundry persons," as she and her council worded their concern in a draft of the Proclamation Prohibiting Portraits of the Queen (1563).[5] When Robert Dudley and Elizabeth Tudor met at Kenilworth to perform their relationship for themselves and the varying interests they represented, for the court, and, indeed, for all of Europe, the earl's ambition and the queen's insistence on her authority resulted in the performance of conflicting representations of their personal and political relations, to which de Guaras alludes in his own dismissive way.

Kenilworth's Two Texts

The texts of Gascoigne and "Laneham" offer a view of a world different from that of the Spanish informer. To the English eye, the Kenilworth entertainments were unprecedented. They were, moreover, of a length and expense never again attempted. Unlike the calculated opulence of Queen Elizabeth I's London entry, the entertainments performed for Elizabeth while she was on progress made a more extravagant use of time, space, and money. At Kenilworth, they occurred during eighteen days, in a variety of settings that defined the natural world with the romance architecture of tiltyard, pavilion, open banqueting hall, arbor, and bower. They incorporated nearly every allegorical, narrative, and festive form conceivable: The court hunted, banqueted in open halls attended by poets and wood nymphs, watched bearbaiting, attended a Latin oration, and enjoyed masques, slapstick performances by rustics, plays, and fireworks that had been in preparation for months.

At Kenilworth, these entertainments fell into two groups: those displaying Dudley's interests and those showing Elizabeth's. The Dudley entertainments, which continued for about ten days, included the queen's welcome, a dialogue between a wild man and Echo, and a bride dael—the mock-marriage of an aging, "ill smelling" bride that forms an unflattering paraphrase of Elizabeth as an unmarried middle-aged woman.[6] After that time, however, a change took place. Two of the most intense Dudley-centered devices, the masque of Diana and Iris that argued for marriage, and the military skirmish between a "captain" and the forces of the rapist Sir Bruse sans Pitie, were canceled. In their place were substituted entertainments that centered on Elizabeth, including an elaborate allegorical device featuring Elizabeth's rescue of the Lady of the Lake that rewrote the chivalric narrative of the imprisoned female, the unusual spectacle of her knighting several supporters of her noninterventionist policy, and the application of the royal touch as a potent reminder of Elizabeth's place between God and her subjects in the hierarchy.

In his purported "true copie" of events at Kenilworth, George Gascoigne included these two canceled events featuring Dudley, only to end with the self-deprecating picture of himself trotting after Elizabeth and attempting to entertain her one last time as she finally left. In fact, in his text Gascoigne is playing a double game, working to keep the potential goodwill of Elizabeth while publicizing Dudley's attempt to star in the entertainments for which he was paying. It was not possible to do both, but Gascoigne's pretense that he might simultaneously support Dudley and Elizabeth is at least consistent with his search for patronage during this period.

In 1575 and 1576, Gascoigne threw a wide net for patrons by publishing seven works devoted to various interests: *The Glasse of Government,* dedicated to Sir Owen Hopton; *The Steele Glas* and *The Complaynt of Phylomene* to Lord Gray of Wilton; *The Droome of Doomes day* to the Earl of Bedford; *A Delicate Diet, for Daintiemouthde Droonkardes* to Lewes Dyve of Broomeham; and *The Tale of Hemetes the Heremyte* and *The Grief of Joy* to Elizabeth. Not only did Gascoigne attempt to establish himself as creative retainer to the great; in 1576 he both supported the scheme of his old comrade Humphrey Gilbert to discover a northwest passage and returned to the Netherlands to give Francis Walsingham information while continuing to serve the Protestant cause.

During the varied career that Gascoigne describes in his evocative poem *Woodmanship,* he also constructed himself as a professional author. Certainly he was one of the first Elizabethans to create literature from court codes. It was not an easy road for him to choose, however, given the censorship of both *A Hundred Sundrie Flowers* (1573) and the later version, *Posies* (1576). For all his efforts at forming social ties through his texts, his work demonstrated the innate instabilities of human relations at court, so that Gascoigne was never as diplomatic as he imagined. If *The Princely Pleasures* sets out to please Elizabeth and Dudley alike, its inclusion of materials hostile to the Crown's iconography helps explain why Gascoigne remained downwardly mobile even as he mastered the double voice of court and courtly spectacle.[7]

The title *The Princely Pleasures at the Courte at Kenelwoorth* captures the immediate tension in Gascoigne's life between his desire to praise the remote, parsimonious queen and his desire to publicize his ideological affiliation with the militant, more liberal-handed earl. It contains a central ambiguity: "Princely" can refer to Elizabeth, to the Earl of Leicester, or to the two of them. According to the *Oxford English Dictionary,* in the sixteenth century its meanings shaded from the genuine to the imitative. "Princely" could mean "of, pertaining to a prince, held or exercised by a prince"; "princelike, dignified, stately, noble"; and "like that of a prince, sumptuous, magnificent, munificent." The title thus suggests that the entertainments were worthy of a prince, enjoyed by a prince, and princely in their magnificence, originating in a Leicester who, if not an actual prince, was certainly princely.[8]

This title, like the entertainments Gascoigne selected to publicize, both captures and enlarges the confusion between the personal and political roles that underlay the relationship between female monarch and sometime suitor, the policymaking sovereign and her privy councillor. Their "Princely Pleasures" link the queen and the earl through the pressured give-and-take of their relationship, for upon entering Kenilworth, Elizabeth entered a world that she had given Leicester but that he controlled, albeit at her pleasure and his expense. Thus Gascoigne's account forms a masked advertisement of himself and the Protestant faction while apparently praising his queen.

The story behind the second account of Kenilworth's entertainments is even less straightforward. *Laneham's Letter* is supposedly written by a man named Laneham, also spelled Langham, a loquacious narrator who supplies an almost daily account of the entertainments in a letter to Master Humfrey Martin, a Mercer of London. In his article "William Patten and the Authorship of 'Robert Laneham's *Letter,*'" David Scott persuasively argues that William Patten, a Teller of the Exchequer and retainer of William Cecil, Lord Burghley, wrote the *Letter,* apparently as an elaborate joke on a court officeholder, Robert Langham, whose voluble officiousness the *Letter* imitates and exaggerates. The evidence that David Scott presents includes a real letter from Patten to Cecil dated 10 September 1575. Patten explains in the distinctive spelling evident in the *Letter* itself that he had "this day receyved . . . aunswer fro my good freend the mr of Requests

[Thomas Wilson] hoow the book waz too be supprest for that Langham had complaynd vpon it, and ootherwize for that the honorable enterteinment be not turned intoo a iest."9 So many elements in this message point to the Kenilworth entertainments—the occurrence of the name Langham and the recognition of his complaints, the worry that the "honorable enterteinment" might be turned into a "iest"—that Patten is almost certainly describing Wilson's order that *Laneham's Letter* be suppressed.

Going past David Scott's argument, the last sentence of the preceding quotation also states that Langham's complaints are not the only reason for suppression. The text is "too be supprest for that Langham had complaynd vpon it, and *ootherwize* for that the honorable enterteinment be not turned intoo a *iest*" (my emphasis). Not only is Langham unhappy, but there is "ootherwize" in the text—other material beyond Langham's complaint—that threatens to turn Kenilworth into a "iest." In fact, the *Letter* prints a carefully detailed account of what occurred as part of the jest on Langham, but finally, the target of the jest is not one man so much as the entire courtly assemblage. At one point, while providing a hyperbolic description of one of Leicester's extravagant banquets, as brilliantly lighted "az it wear the Egiptian Pharos relucent untoo all the Alexandrian coast," the *Letter*'s narrator offhandedly explains that the purpose of his text is "too talke merily with my mery freend" (472). That is, the *Letter*'s purpose is to send an insider's description of courtly behavior to an outsider of the nonleisure class, the fictitious Master Humfrey Martin, Mercer, to whom it is supposedly addressed. The assumed existence of this merchant-class audience simultaneously recalls Leicester's source of wealth in his London financial activities and alerts the reader that the text is a critique of court practice.

The narrator provides a number of details that dampen the glory at Kenilworth. For example, on the second day, after hunting had continued by torchlight to around nine o'clock, a savage man appeared in a favorite Gascoigne stratagem to initiate a dialogue with "Echo" that formed a reprise of the previous welcoming entertainments. The narrator, however, is impatient with the self-importance of the courtly group and signals a transition to a humorous anecdote by summoning his noncourt audience: "But I shall tell yoo, Master Martin, by the mass, of a mad adventure." It appears that in the act of making a bow, the savage clumsily broke his staff, which hit "her Highness hors head; whereat he startled." The groom grabbed the horse; the horse "of generositee" calmed itself; and Elizabeth called "no hurt, no hurt!" to calm her subjects' apprehensions. "Which words," observes the *Letter*'s narrator, "I promis yoo wee wear all glad to heer; and took them too be the best part of the Play" (437–38).

The narrator further enlists Elizabeth's reactions to de-glamorize Kenilworth when he describes a banquet that took place a week later. There were three hundred dishes, he guesses, "whearof, whither I myght more muze at the deintynesse, shapez, and the cost." In the midst of the display, "her majesty eat smally or nothing; which understood, the coorsez wear not so orderly served and sizely set doon, but wear by and by az disorderly wasted and coorsly consumed; more courtly methought than curteously" (456). At such moments, the self-congratulatory voice of "Laneham" gives way to satiric comment on the "bouge" of court in the satiric tradition of Skelton's poem "The Bowge of Court," in which the "bouche of court" is simultaneously the rations supplied to courtly retainers and the name of the nightmare ship that the speaker boards in search of favor.[10]

Because the *Letter* exists as a "iest" annoying enough—even dangerous enough—to be suppressed, it provides a view of court unique to texts of this period. It pokes fun at the display of egos in this entertainment for the queen, yet because its humor resides in the address of a courtly participant to a hard-working merchant, it avoids the overtly scandalous tone of *Leicester's Commonwealth*. Unlike such pageant texts as *The Queen's Majesty's Passage* and Gascoigne's *Princely Pleasures*—works recounting spectacles largely for the sake of their sponsors—and authors *Laneham's Letter* declines to smooth over the ideological divisions between the queen and the underwriter of her entertainments. Instead, it delights in describing some of Kenilworth's less glorious moments.[11] Did the *Letter* manufacture the stories that suggest a more negative view of the glories of Kenilworth? Possibly. But the Elizabethan court seethed with disagreements; it seems more likely that the *Letter* underrepresents the moments of exasperation and the general extent of ill temper and ill feeling.

The most important aspect of the *Letter*'s airing of conflict is its use of Elizabeth's opinions to send up the Dudley agenda. The more ceremonious accounts of Mulcaster and Gascoigne have a stake in controlling the queen's voice, in limiting her responses to her gracious approval. In both hushing Elizabeth and casting her as unfailingly grateful, these sponsored texts attempt to represent her as complicitous in less-than-flattering representations of herself. In the *Letter,* although the queen is inevitably included in the courtly group made to look ridiculous, the text attempts to place her beyond both criticism and the suspiciously lavish praise heaped on Dudley. The result is that *Laneham's Letter* grants Elizabeth a dissenting voice—and thus an authority—that Gascoigne's text denies her.

The Terms of the Visit

The Princely Pleasures establishes the terms of Elizabeth's stay before she sets foot inside Kenilworth's gates. Her "welcome" consists of three demonstrations of Dudley's power and Elizabeth's passivity through the allegories suggested by the Arthurian legends of *Layamon's Brut* and *La Morte Darthur*. The Arthurian figures, through which Elizabeth's father and grandfather had encoded a number of dynastic–imperialist claims, at Kenilworth negotiate the social distance between Dudley and his queen. As Elizabeth draws close to Kenilworth—and she must view three lengthy devices before even entering the gates—Arthurian figures present the arriving queen with scenes and language that define her role as part of her welcome.

The first device is of a sibyl, invented and composed by William Hunnis of the Queen's Chapel. "Sybilla" meets Her Majesty on the "way, somewhat neere the Castle," and forms an allegory of the magical virgin whose gift of prophecy the *Brut* associates with Merlin's powers. This sibyl prophesies fortune for Elizabeth's reign in terms that conflate Isaiah's prophecies of Emmanuel with the queen's arrival: "You shall be called the Prince of Peace, and peace shal be your shield, / So that your eyes shall never see the broyls of bloody field" (486–87). Thus far, the device employs the queen's own assertive images of a ruler who transcends the definitions of male and female, human and divine, and who, moreover, oversaw a foreign policy with as little overt violence as possible. But the assertion that the queen's virtue carries religious and magical properties that defend her kingdom from war is quickly undermined in the following two lines as "peace" ceases to mean public accomplishment and becomes a domestic virtue: "*If* perfect peace then glad your minde, he joyes above the rest / Which doth receive into *his* house so *good* and *sweet* a guest" (my emphasis). The speed with which these lines reduce Elizabeth from armed divinity to house guest is dizzying. She is supposed to be "good," which is to say compliant. Assuming that she acquiesces to this representation of her relationship with Dudley will not make it so, however.

Dudley's audacity in sponsoring this welcome is in character, although he stood on shaky ground at Kenilworth, which the queen had bestowed on him in 1563, about the time she raised him to the peerage.[12] From that November day in 1558 when Dudley appeared at Hatfield to offer his services to the new queen with whom he had once shared the Tower, his personal importance depended on his physical proximity to her.[13] At the beginning of their relationship, he had represented himself as her dependent in his tournament impresa of November 1559, "a vine clinging to an obelisk and the motto *te stante virebo,* 'you standing I will flourish,'" at a time when foreign ambassadors gossiped that the queen was about to marry him. As early as 1561/1562, he had consented to his representation at the Inner Temple as Prince Pallaphilos, the second Perseus, in a masque presenting Dudley as Elizabeth's suitor.[14] This representation of Dudley's growing social ambition also occurred within the climate of her regard. In 1562, when Elizabeth believed herself to be dying, she revealed the depth of her trust when she insisted that her council appoint Dudley to be Lord Protector of the Realm, ignoring the blood claims of Lord Huntingdon, the imprisoned Lady Catherine Grey, and Mary Queen of Scots. The following year, she made him Earl of Leicester and gave him Kenilworth. Then, because even such an estate did not immediately supply revenues, Elizabeth granted him £1,000 a year, to come from the customs of London.

In the English financial world, writes G. D. Ramsay, "Dudley was the major beneficiary of the licensing system, especially for the export of undressed cloths," because the Merchant Adventurers were able to secure an export license for only about one-third of their "annual shipment of 30,000 unfinished cloths." For the rest, the Adventurers were forced "to apply to holders of special licenses," especially to Dudley, their principal holder.[15] By 1575 Dudley's city connections were well established. Although he invested in a number of ventures, including the Barbary trade and Martin Frobisher's attempt to implement Humphrey Gilbert's plan to search for a northwest passage, his principal source of income remained the cloth trade. It is this trade that helps explain the anxiety with which Dudley observed events in the Netherlands, where the Merchant Adventurers preferred to market their goods, and his singular lack of interest in such ambitious schemes as promoting plantations in Ireland.[16]

Despite raising him to wealth and high office, by the mid-1560s Elizabeth was careful to keep Robert Dudley in his place, as we have seen in Giacomo Surian's anecdote. Dudley's proximity to her power did not result in his contentment or satisfaction. Instead, proximity inspired ambition, what Richard Terdiman calls "the socialized form of desire."[17] Because ambition functions as the questioning of constraints that prohibit or delay advancement in a given society, it actively seeks social fissures and weaknesses in that society. In practical terms, Dudley's ambitions meant a ceaseless probing of governmental policies to ascertain in what political situation he might assert himself and how he might do so—that is, through what forms of representation of himself and his queen.

Elizabeth was aware that this was the case. "In the latitudes which some modern princes allow to their favourites," wrote Fulke Greville in a dig at King James, "it seems this queen reservedly kept entrenched within her native strengths and sceptre."[18] Elizabeth knew about Dudley's attempts to engage in foreign policy, which would allow him to increase his power abroad. Thus when Dudley renewed his suit for Elizabeth's hand in 1565, she caught him angling for Catherine de Medici and Charles IX's invitation to visit France in order to receive their personal expressions of support. Elizabeth's reported reaction to his proposed trip to France was, first, apparent concern—"I cannot live without seeing you every day"—followed by a rough reminder of his position in the hierarchy—"You are like my lapdog, as soon as he is seen anywhere, the people say that I am coming; and when you are seen, they may say, in like manner, that I am not far off."[19]

In the face of the queen's alternating favor and disfavor, as well as her desire to preserve her place at the summit of the court hierarchy, the 1575 entertainments develop Dudley's princely qualities in the search for a fanciful social equality with his sovereign. In his welcome, he needed simultaneously to acknowledge Elizabeth as the source of his greatness and to turn his hospitality to his advantage by presenting himself as worthy of her gifts, as coming from an ancient house, and as knowing how to entertain a queen. In this world where, as Simon Adams writes, "a clear distinction between the courtier and the bureaucrat is almost impossible to draw,"[20] it is also apparent that the line between amusement and self-legitimation, between court entertainment and policymaking, between self-display and counsel, is equally invisible.

The second welcoming device at the gates of Kenilworth projects a royal welcome through the assertion of Leicester's mythic pedigree, which bears a strong resemblance to the Tudors' claims of descent from Arthur. At the gate appeared "six trumpetters hugelie advaunced, much exceeding the common stature of men in this age." They were outfitted with "likewise huge and monstrous trumpettes counterfetted, wherein they seemed to sound: and behind them were placed certaine trumpetters, who sounded indeede at her Majestie's entrie" (488–90). Gascoigne's description of the scene supplies its ideological content: The show signals the restoration of Kenilworth's glory under Dudley. "And by this dum shew it was ment, that in the daies and reigne of King Arthure, men were of that stature, so that the Castle of Kenelworth should seeme still to be kept by Arthur's heires and their seruants" (490).

As Lawrence Stone explains, "A lengthy pedigree was a useful weapon in the Tudor battle for status."[21] In claiming descent from the ancient Suttons, who had inhabited Kenilworth in ancient times, the upstart Dudleys linked themselves with the idealized past in general and Kenilworth in particular. But as the derisive *Leicester's Commonwealth* reminds us, Robert Dudley was "noble only in two descents and both of them stained with the block," in that both his father and his grandfather had been executed for treason.[22] Since Dudley himself had narrowly avoided a similar fate, he had everything to gain by suppressing his paternity in favor of a pedigree originating in Arthur. In making his presumptuous claims to the person of the queen before her court, Leicester uses spectacle as an opportunity to bring the past into the same conceptual structures that shape the present.[23] An Arthurian view of Dudley's past conveniently predicted his present successes and erased the queen's ability to take them away.

After these two welcoming devices, when the queen arrived at the actual gates of Kenilworth, she still had to wait to be admitted. The figure of a dim-witted giant appeared before her, awed but in the end made bold enough by her presence to present her with the keys to the gate.[24] This slow-moving figure is described as a jest. But viewed at the end of a long day's travel and in the midst of her host's self-aggrandizing welcome, the giant also suggests that Kenilworth is so secure that its porter can be made drolly loutish, and his tardy welcome asserts that Kenilworth's possessor can afford a moment of faint insolence before allowing his sovereign through the splendid gates (490–91).

Once through those gates, Elizabeth meets more insolence in the form of the Lady of the Lake, who welcomes her to Leicester's territory. At this moment, what Gascoigne selects and the *Letter* includes form an interesting contrast. Gascoigne prints the Lady of the Lake's welcome, which makes Dudley's territorial claim to Kenilworth:

l wil attend while you lodge here,
(Most peereless Queene) to Court to make resort;
And as my love to Arthure dyd appeere,
So shl't to you in earnest and in sport.
Passe on, Madame, you need no longer stand;
The Lake, the Lodge, the Lord, are yours for to command.
   (491–92)

Whereas Gascoigne faithfully reports these gorgeous indignities, the *Letter* is impatient with Leicester's Arthurian fantasies of legitimation. Recounting how Kenilworth had only "*most* alleyz" been "in the hands of the Earls of Leycester" (my emphasis), the text gives the queen's response to the verses that claim Kenilworth for Dudley: "It pleazed her Highness too thank this Lady, and too add withall, we had thought indeed the Lake had been oours, and doo you call it yourz noow? Well, we will herein common more with yoo hereafter" (431).

In point of law, Dudley only held Kenilworth for the Crown. Feudal tradition, moreover, allowed the king to occupy any dwelling during a progress. The Lady of the Lake's words ignore the fact that Elizabeth's comment recalls, that Elizabeth was notoriously insistent on her titular sovereignty. It was, for instance, typical of her that in 1570 at Chenies, the long-held property of the Russell family, she dated herself from "our manor of Cheneys."[25] The response "doo you call it yoorz noow?" records the queen's refutation of the claim to the unconditional ownership of Kenilworth that underlies Dudley's welcome. As such, it disturbs the triumphant picture of Leicester's success in welcoming her as an equal.

The *Letter* chooses to include incidents that bring to the outside world an irreverent insider's perspective on these events. Gascoigne's text, although no less insidious in its way, reveals very different principles of selection. Gascoigne concentrated on full texts of the most literary devices, accompanied by the names of their inventors and authors, prose glosses, and descriptions of action. The decorous nature of the text, however, serves as a screen for its emphasis on Dudley and specifically for the two censored entertainments that would have centered on his person. The first is the better-known masque of Diana and Iris, which covertly urged the queen to marry Dudley. The second is the sketch of an unperformed device that has not been critically discussed before, featuring a captain defeating that rapacious attacker of maidens, Sir Bruse sans Pitie.

The publication of this suppressed material means that Gascoigne's claim to publish a "true Copie" of what occurred at Kenilworth is false. Its interest in representing Leicester's close relationship with the queen and his preference for military solutions means that the text fulfills in a particular way the "demaund" of its potential audience, which the introduction describes as "studious and well-disposed yong Gentlemen and others . . .

desyrous to be partakers of those pleasures by a profitable publication"
(486). In printing the suppressed material under the title of "deuised, and
presented," *The Princely Pleasures* publicizes Leicester's ambitions and abilities, thereby offering those gentlemen and others an alternative to the
queen's cherished principles of hesitation and delay. Gascoigne imagines
an audience that shares Leicester's impatience with Elizabeth's unwillingness to commit either her physical body to marriage or her political body of
England to an interventionist policy that would more closely involve the
island kingdom in events on the Continent.

A Proposal of Marriage

Critics of the entertainments at Kenilworth generally agree that Elizabeth
censored Gascoigne's masque of Diana and Iris because it resurrected the
subject of her marriage to Dudley. What has not been discussed is how
much the masque—whether performed or unperformed—worked to raise
Leicester's status. Although by 1575 there was no reason to think that
Elizabeth still considered marriage to Dudley a possibility,[26] the masque of
Diana and Iris assumes a personal relationship between its sponsor and his
queen that was always, at heart, political. Viewed as a political move, the
device forms a particularly male plan for advancing Dudley's hopes: a
masque that makes explicit that he is a man and she is a woman and that he
is powerful enough to express his desire for her. Such a show of ambition
phrased as a proposal of marriage is inevitable in a government headed by a
woman that also conceptualizes itself as the body of its sovereign.

Elizabeth's move to censor this masque was equally inevitable. She declared her dislike for the masque of Juno and Diana presented to her in
March 1565, in which "Jupiter gave a verdit in favour of matrimony."[27] In
1566 she responded to parliamentary concerns about her marriage and
succession with outright irritation that her subjects wanted her to marry
but that no husband would please. "They (I thynke) that mouythe the
same [her marriage] wylbe as redy to myslyke hym with whom I shall
marrie, as theye are nowe to move yt, and then yt will apere they nothynge
mente it." She continued her complaint by pointing out how close such
suggestions were to treason: "Well there was neuer so great a Treason, but
myght be coueryde vndere as fayre a pretence."[28] Inappropriate discussion
of her marriage and succession later resulted in Philip Sidney's banishment
from court, John Stubbs's amputated right hand, and Peter Wentworth's
imprisonment in the Tower until his death.

But declaring talk of the queen's marriage to be treason and punishing
those who gave their opinion of it could not silence the debate. As long as
Elizabeth remained childless and even after James VI of Scotland became
an adult, the succession remained the central political issue in England.
The queen's marriage also remained a potent, if complex, metaphor. At
Kenilworth, Gascoigne's purpose in displaying the Earl of Leicester's
princely qualities was well served by having actors dressed as goddesses

urge the queen to marry when the only apparent candidate was the lord who paid for the entertainment.

It is interesting that neither *Laneham's Letter* nor *The Princely Pleasures* states openly that Elizabeth censored the masque. In failing to acknowledge the real source of the queen's displeasure, both texts subtly undercut her and protect the participants by pretending that her actions are unfounded. Gascoigne introduces his text with the explanation that "there was prepared a shew to have bene presented before her Majestie in the Forest" (502). At its conclusion he adds, "This shewe was devised and penned by M. Gascoigne; and being prepared and redy (every Actor in his garment) two or three days together, yet never came to execution. The cause whereof I cannot attribute to any other thing than to lack of opportunity and seasonable weather" (515). The *Letter* observes in apparent innocence "that had her Highnes hapned this daye too have cummen abrode, there was made reddy a devise of goddessez and nymphes, which az well for the ingenious argument, az for the well handling of it in rime and endighting, would undoubtedly have gained great liking" (459), even though in order to address the highly sensitive issue of marriage, the text casts the queen as a nymph, Zabeta, who is distinctly subservient to the advice givers, Diana and Juno, on the proper disposition of her virginity. To this insult is added a direct challenge to Elizabeth's most cherished chapter in her mythic biography, the story that her release from prison during her sister Mary's reign and her subsequent accession to the throne resulted from God's recognition of her virtue.

In effect, the masque argues for Elizabeth's marriage by using her iconography and biography of virginal autonomy against her. Featuring first Diana and then Iris, Juno's messenger, the masque as printed creates a debate between their respective cases for virginity and marriage staged before the figure of a queen passively playing her role as the nymph Zabeta. At the beginning of the masque, Diana must find Zabeta with the assistance of her nymphs as well as the moss-clad man (Gascoigne again in his favorite disguise) and Echo, both of whom made their first appearance in the device that startled Elizabeth's horse. Diana—a slightly wild, fierce Diana drawn from the legends of Brut and not a particularly congenial model of virgin chastity—has most of the lines, but it is her nymph Castibula who flatly states that Juno's purpose is to lift Zabeta "on Hymen's bed" (507). Elizabeth's reaction to this debate about the uses of her sexuality was predictable, given her open dislike for marriage discussions in general; nevertheless, publishing this material makes her reaction beside the point.

In the second half of the device, Juno's messenger Iris has far fewer lines than Diana does. Iris's argument, however, rests on the issue of how Elizabeth was released from prison during Mary Tudor's reign. At first glance, her argument seems flimsy, but Iris's logic depends on the appropriation and redefinition of a key principle of Elizabeth's self-representation: that her virtue—often figured as her virginity—was responsible for her release. As a result, Iris's lines confront the Crown's own interpretation of its most bitter hour:

> Remember all your life, before you were a Queen:
> And then compare it with the daies which you since then have
>   seene.
> Were you not captive caught? were you not kept in walles?
> Were you not forst to leade a life like other wretched thralles?
> Where was Diana then, why did she you not ayde?
> Why did she not defend your state, which were and are her
>   maide?
> Who brought you out of bryers? who gave you rule of realmes?
> Who crowned first your comely head with princely dyademes?
> Even Juno she, which meant, and yet doth meane likewise
> To geve you more than will can wish, or wit can wel devise.
>   (514)

Had this final scene been allowed at Kenilworth, Iris's address would have forced Elizabeth to acknowledge publicly that while imprisoned in the Tower and at Woodstock her greatest value lay in her marriageability rather than in God's rewarding her virtue with sovereignty. Whether performed or printed, Gascoigne's advancement of Leicester's claim to greatness proceeds through the masque's evocation of a time when Elizabeth, as an uncrowned, legally illegitimate young woman, was physically and politically vulnerable.

Elizabeth's Imprisonment

The masque's willingness to pit Iris's version of the queen's imprisonment against her own version acknowledges how important this episode in Elizabeth's biography had become to her self-representation by 1575. In order to dispel the figure of the mature and independent queen in Dudley's way, the masque attacks Elizabeth's history of her active virginity by reminding the audience that it was as a marriageable body rather than as the virtuous heir to the throne that Elizabeth was imprisoned and finally released. A basic account of Elizabeth's imprisonment in fact supports the assertion of Gascoigne's lines that her marriageability was a key element in the events of 1554/1555.[29] In the early days of Wyatt's rebellion in January 1554, Mary Tudor requested that her sister join her at court because she and her Spanish adviser, Renard, wanted to keep a close watch on her actions. They suspected a conspiracy among Elizabeth, the French, and the rebels to marry her to Edward Courtenay, the great-grandson of Edward IV whom Mary had made Earl of Devon. This would have been a marriage that might well have solidified anti-Marian support and placed Elizabeth on the throne. In order to keep an eye on her youthful sister, Mary invited her to attend her. When Elizabeth replied by excusing herself on the grounds of illness, she invited further suspicion.

A few days later, the uprising against the Spanish marriage led by Thomas Wyatt the Younger began attracting followers in Kent. The Crown felt that under the circumstances it could seize the French ambassador's diplomatic pouch, in which a copy of Lady Elizabeth's excuse to Mary was found among other letters linking Elizabeth's and Courtenay's names to the uprising. Mary responded by *commanding* her heir to come to court. Elizabeth, who claimed herself too ill to travel more than two or three leagues a day, managed to turn her journey into a slow progress, during which she took the opportunity to exhibit her pale face to the London citizens. When Elizabeth finally arrived at court in the third week of February, she was denied Mary's presence and kept under house arrest.

Meanwhile, in early February, Wyatt's failure to rouse London to join his protest against Mary's marriage resulted in his capture and guaranteed not only his own death, but also the executions of Lady Jane Grey, her husband, and her father. A few days after these executions, Mary ordered Elizabeth and Courtenay to the Tower. Elizabeth remained confined for a month to rooms in the Bell Tower on the floor above those that Thomas More had occupied.[30] In late April, she was allowed to walk in the garden, although the Tower was so crowded with prisoners that great care had to be taken in closing windows and forbidding the other prisoners to watch her as she passed.

During the spring of 1554, both Renard and Charles V pushed Mary hard to have Elizabeth and Courtenay tried and executed as traitors before Philip arrived that summer for his wedding to Mary. But sworn evidence against Elizabeth was lacking: If Wyatt had implicated Elizabeth under torture, as seems likely, he publicly repudiated his confession on the scaffold. In the end, no written evidence against Elizabeth could be produced. Although Lord Russel testified that Wyatt had sent her letters informing her of his plans, she had been careful not to respond. Moreover, the French letters implicating Elizabeth were in cipher, which meant that various interpretations were possible. Then the originals of the letters disappeared from Lord Chancellor Gardiner's possession, quite probably because, as Renard claimed, they implicated Courtenay as well as Elizabeth, and Gardiner wished, above all, to shield Courtenay.

The result was that Mary found herself in the awkward position of having to explain to her Spanish supporters why her enemies were not subject to capital punishment. As she told Renard, "Courtenay was certainly accused by several other prisoners of having had a share in the plot." He had communicated with Peter Carew, who had "arranged a marriage between him and Elizabeth" by means of a "cipher, carved on a guitar." Even given these circumstances, Mary explained, "the law as laid down by the English parliament did not inflict the capital penalty on those who had consented to treason if they had committed no overt act."[31]

When even less evidence was found against Elizabeth, she was released to Woodstock under close house arrest. Although convinced that the kingdom would know no peace as long as she lived, Renard tolerated her removal from the Tower because he agreed with Paget's assessment that "if sufficient evidence to put her to death were not discovered he saw no better means of keeping her quiet than to marry her to a foreigner."[32] As both the heir to the throne of a sister who might well die in childbirth and a marriageable commodity in her own right, Lady Elizabeth was too valuable to be married off quickly, however. Instead, she remained in the custody of Thomas Bedingfield, a privy councillor who proved himself an honorable and cautious guardian. Elizabeth was released to court in April 1555 when Mary neared confinement for the child who was never born, in part because with an heir on the way, Mary and the Spanish feared Elizabeth less, but also because if Mary or the child were to die, Philip apparently wanted her near—although whether as a hostage or a potential wife (or both) is unclear.

The claim that the Kenilworth Iris makes that Elizabeth's prospects of marriage, not self-possessed virginity, "brought you out of bryers" and "gave you rule of realmes" is thus supported by the foreign and domestic correspondence available for 1554/1555. But in reminding the queen of the facts, to which Robert Dudley, imprisoned in the Tower at the same time as Elizabeth, was a witness, Gascoigne as author and Leicester as sponsor must have known they were treading on sacred ground. Insofar as Elizabeth was concerned, her imprisonment had formed a supreme test of her character that explained God's endorsement of her claim to the throne, and her most immediate biographers seized her theme (Figure 10). With the memories of Courtenay and other potential husbands carefully eradicated, the story of her imprisonment became the story of a personal struggle. According to the revised biography, she became queen "not . . . without syght of manyfold daungers of lyfe, and crown as one that had the mightiest and greatest to wrestle with," as she put it to Parliament in 1584/1585.[33]

True, Elizabeth's imprisonment represented the nadir of her life, falling between the favor shown her by her brother, Edward VI, after Somerset's fall and her accession. It was unquestionably a time when she lived in fear for her life, as when she first was ordered to the Tower and afterward was unexpectedly transferred to Woodstock. As she summarized her position in 1566, "I stode in dangere of my lyffe, my systere was so ensenst [incensed] ageynst me."[34] In retrospect, Elizabeth never forgot the fear and anger of imposed passivity.

After her accession, her vulnerability became more acceptable when refashioned as her sister's political–religious assault on her body. In retellings of the story, Elizabeth was imprisoned not because of her suspected conspiracy with Courtenay, but because of her sister's fear of her power. "I did dyffere from here in relygeon," she maintained later, "and I was sowght for dyuerse wayes." According to Elizabeth, she was released not because of a lack of evidence against her or because the right marriage was expected to remove her from the political scene as conveniently as death, but because God preserved her to fulfill the destiny that Mary hoped to avert. This

Figure 10. "Many daughters have done well." Frontispiece to the 1631 edition of Thomas Heywood's *Englands Elizabeth, Her Life and Troubles,* showing the implied relationship that developed among Elizabeth's imprisonment (represented by Woodstock in the background), accession, and success as a monarch. (British Library)

version of events allowed Elizabeth to focus on her earlier self as an individual political entity rather than as the young woman who, contemporary letters reveal, was threatening to Mary, Paget, Renard, Philip, and Charles V only when viewed in combination with a husband. Suppressing her connection with Courtenay also had the advantage of suppressing all questions of her passive complicity in the rebellion.

Pictured alone, Elizabeth was not only a frightened yet courageous figure, but also innocent of any passive role in the conspiracy. And when she was viewed as alone and innocent, her imprisonment could be represented as a threat focused on her body in ways that increased the importance of that body. Purged of the marriage question, the memory of this highly personal threat retroactively empowered her, thereby allowing her to turn to good effect the personal humiliation of an imprisonment that was inevitably public and political. During the 1559 entry, Elizabeth, standing before the Tower, reminded the crowd that she was a Daniel who, once imprisoned there, had met with God's favor. The myth of Elizabeth's rewarded virtue continued to develop when in 1563 the first detailed account of her experience appeared in John Foxe's *Actes and Monuments,* in which she figured as a religious martyr.

Foxe's narrative, which Carole Levin notes was ordered "to be installed in every cathedral church" in 1571,[35] was also included in the 1587 edition of Holinshed's *Chronicles* in conjunction with *The Chronicle of Queen Jane* and fleshes out Elizabeth's own view of her imprisonment. It may in part have been constructed with her help, since it provides quotations besides those given in *The Chronicle of Queen Jane* and a wealth of details that only Elizabeth herself could have known. But even if Foxe's account is based on information deriving from the queen, only those representations that Elizabeth herself voiced or directly supervised represent her perspective on events. As Foucault observes of Velázquez's *Las Meninas,* when the scene before us has been arranged by an invisible hand (i.e., Velázquez or, in this case, Foxe), "it is not possible for the . . . image ever to present in a full light both the master who is representing and the sovereign who is being represented."[36]

Foxe uses Elizabeth's image of herself in order to express his own religious conviction, appropriating her experience to serve his ardent Protestantism. As he explains, "I see no cause why the communion of Her Grace's afflictions also, among the other saints of CHRIST, ought to be suppressed in silence: especially since the great and marvellous workings of GOD's glory, chiefly in this Story, appeareth above all the rest."[37] A prisoner of the Catholic threat, Elizabeth was "clapped in the Tower" only to be "tossed from thence, from prison to prison, from post to pillar"[38]— rather like a rag doll. Foxe's elaboration of Elizabeth's imprisonment in subsequent editions places a growing emphasis on her sufferings and offers a titillating fantasy of her momentary powerlessness that has no basis in fact: "[She was] at length, also prisoner in her own house; and guarded with a sort of cutthroats, which ever gaped for the spoil of the same, that they might have been fingering of somewhat" (605).

However much Foxe's descriptions served a prurient desire to imagine the queen as helplessly threatened by the men surrounding her, they did provide the Crown with a powerful allegorical narrative of her imprisoned self and her relation to a God who had, in releasing her, certified her legitimacy.[39] Foxe's embellishments of this account in later editions include a summary of her feelings. Cut off from friends, "desolate, and utterly destitute," she was "fraught full of terror and thraldom" (619). The queen herself later referred to this period as that of her "trouble and thrall." Throughout it all, Elizabeth's virtue and faith remained strong until, at length, God "hath exalted and erected [her], out of thrall, to liberty; out of danger, to peace and rule; from dread, to dignity; from misery, to majesty; from mourning, ruling; briefly of a prisoner, hath made her a Prince."[40]

In this summary of events leading to Elizabeth's accession, as in many other accounts of the queen's life from the 1570s on, the final two years between Elizabeth's release and Mary's death simply disappear because they interrupt the flow of divine interventions. Elizabeth herself thanked God in similar terms in one of her devotions: "How exceeding is thy goodness . . . and in times of most danger, most gracious deliverance: pulling me from the prison to the palace."[41] Although Foxe and Elizabeth leave open whether the virtue that delivered her was approved female behavior or lifelong virginity, both see her virtue as active rather than passive. As her reign progressed, memories of Elizabeth's imprisonment were increasingly associated with the active virtue of her chastity, which, whether defined as virtuous female behavior or lifelong virginity, enabled her accession because God's hand could be read in her release and elevation to sovereignty.[42]

By the 1570s and 1580s, as the queen and those who competed with her for representation produced a complex iconographic system, Elizabeth I's perfections and limitations were increasingly defined through the motif of imprisonment and delivery. The result was a dynamic expressing her court-iers' fantasies of defining and controlling her, as Chapter 3 considers in more detail. Like all of Elizabeth's preferred representations, however, the allegory of her imprisonment cut two ways: It recalled her own courage and sanctity at the same time that it participated in one of the most preva-lent paradigms for the containment and subordination of women. Her patient suffering in prison and the popular support she received when she was moved from Tower to house arrest and finally to freedom foretell subsequent greatness. But embedded in her triumph lies the romance tradition of imprisoning women in castles that metaphorically represent their bodies as well as domestic space, a tradition on which Foxe draws heavily, even when describing Elizabeth's imprisonment as religious per-secution.

If Foxe's "approved" account of the queen's imprisonment revels mo-mentarily in a fantasy of control, Gascoigne's masque attempts to rewrite this crucial episode in her life by asserting that the queen's marriageable virginity, not her self-possessed virginity, was responsible for her delivery. His Iris asks of the queen / Zabeta: "Were you not captive caught? were you not kept in walles? / Were you not forst to leade a life like other wretched thralles?" because in the marriage masque, the emphasis is not on thralldom overcome by virtue, but on Elizabeth's helplessness, a thralldom alleviated only by her identity as a potential marriage partner.

In directly challenging the myth that Elizabeth's virtue was the source of her release from prison, the masque portrays her as helpless, then and now. Asked to compare her life before she was queen with "the daies which you since then have seene," Iris suggests that she has an unpaid debt to Juno. If she will surrender her virginity—"your wealth," which "would have you wed, and, for your farther hire"—she will receive "a world of wealth at wil . . . / In weded state." For "never wight felt perfect blis, but such as wedded bene" (514–15). Like the drawn-out welcoming pageants at Kenilworth, the masque undermines Elizabeth's autonomy and social position. Like the other censored device, which I will discuss, the skirmish between Dudley and the rapist Sir Bruse sans Pitie, the masque seeks to keep Elizabeth a passive but attentive observer of male motives and desires and offers this fantasy to the purchasers of *The Princely Pleasures*.

Regardless of Elizabeth's and Dudley's inner feelings about such a marriage, the proposal is significant as a grand gesture of self-display, whether performed once at Kenilworth or perpetually in print. At a time when proposals and counterproposals of marriage were at least as interesting as actual marriages, one of the advantages of never marrying was that the proposals might continue. This was a crucial principle of Elizabeth's foreign policy, that she turn such negotiations to her advantage. In the masque, making the proposal—even one censored and thus refused— works in Leicester's favor. Whereas the censorship of the masque at Kenilworth confined Leicester's role to that of a subordinate with only limited claims to the royal person, in print it continued to advertise his position as the queen's favorite. The masque displays his proximity to her, his uniqueness among English peers (one cannot imagine any other Englishman pressing a similar suit, no matter how hopeless), and his status as a figurative equal—even, within the fleetingly imagined marriage, her superior.

A *"Military Skirmish"* and Questions of Policy in the Netherlands

The second censored entertainment that Gascoigne published has been missed because it is carefully screened as an alternative to Elizabeth's glorious moment—her rescue of the Lady of the Lake, which I will discuss in the next section. In suggesting that Elizabeth's triumph had originally been imagined differently, Gascoigne's careful introductory language simultaneously masks and identifies what he is up to: printing an abbreviated account of another censored device, a military skirmish, that places Dudley in the central heroic role usually occupied by the queen. Gascoigne introduces this touchy subject by saying regretfully that the entertainment not performed was to have been a military skirmish, which "had [it] bene executed according to the first invention, it had been a gallant shewe."Although the device was rewritten to stage Elizabeth as a magical rescuer and victor against threats to her chastity, it is clear that Gascoigne preferred the original conception:

> For it was first devised, that . . . a Captaine with twentie or thyrtie shotte shoulde have bene sent from the Hearon House (which represented the Lady of the Lake's Castell) upon heapes of bulrushes: and that Syr Bruse, shewing a great power upon the land, should have sent out as many or moe shot to surprise the sayde Captayne: and so they should have skirmished upon the waters in such sort, that no man coulde perceive but that they went upon the waves. (501)

Despite Gascoigne's claim that this device might have pleased the queen more than the device that featured her, we know that, like the marriage masque, its representations of the queen and Dudley challenge Elizabeth's desire to preserve her person and her kingdom by acknowledging the relation between the two. Specifically, the militarism of this second device makes it an argument for intervention. It presents the necessity of a male response to threat by featuring Leicester vanquishing a rapist who threatens the Lady of the Lake and also, by implication, Elizabeth herself. That the skirmish was canceled and replaced with a nonmilitary device glorifying the queen's power to overcome threat suggests that Elizabeth herself successfully read and sought to counteract the logic of Dudley's self-displays at Kenilworth.

If the queen had visited Kenilworth in 1566, 1568, and 1572, why were the entertainments of 1575 so prolonged, so princely? The answer is that in the mid-1570s the consolidation of Dudley's personal power in England coincided with developments abroad—particularly in the Netherlands—for which he repeatedly recommended that the queen choose military intervention. During the summer of 1575, although news of continued unrest in Scotland arrived to occupy Dudley[43] and the Irish campaign called for continual decisions by the Privy Council, for thirteen years Dudley had focused his economic and political attention on the Protestant cause in Europe.

Robert Dudley had been a proponent of the Normandy incursion of 1562 to 1564, whose purpose was to aid the Huguenots in Le Havre and to improve England's bargaining position for Calais. Although his elder brother, Ambrose, Earl of Warwick, had commanded in Normandy, the wound that he had sustained at Le Havre resulted in his continuing ill health in the 1570s and eventually killed him. As the queen's intimate, the younger Dudley proved the greater political and economic force. It was Leicester the privy councillor who, together with Secretary Francis Walsingham, helped lead the shifting alliance called the Protestant faction—including Francis Russell, Earl of Bedford; Edward de Fiennes, Lord Clinton; Sir Ralph Sadler; Sir Francis Knollys; and Sir Walter Mildmay—which maintained steady pressure on the queen to aid William of Orange.

In using the term "faction," I do not mean that these men represented an ever-united block of interests over the years. But there was a distinct group that lobbied hard for intervention, which was opposed at every turn by William Cecil, Lord Burghley. Cecil, the incisive analyst, had handled foreign and domestic affairs in the 1560s so carefully that the queen appointed him Lord Treasurer and created him a baron of the realm in 1571. During the 1570s, Burghley and Elizabeth agreed that overt aggression in the Netherlands would cost England its always precarious alliances with Spain and France as well as money that the treasury could ill afford.

Historian R. B. Wernham identifies three "steady purposes" in England's policy toward the Netherlands: "to get the Spanish army out of the

Netherlands; to prevent the French getting into the Netherlands; and to restore to the Netherlanders themselves, under continued Spanish protection, the ancient liberties and the measure of home rule that they had enjoyed under Philip II's father, the Emperor Charles V."[44] In addition to these diplomatic goals, G. D. Ramsay reminds us—as, indeed, does every diplomatic document of the period—that the search for economic stability formed a central concern, for only then could the Merchant Adventurers, the Crown, and even Leicester himself be assured of their principal source of revenues.[45]

In the midst of fighting a civil war in the Netherlands, the Spanish countered their fears of an English influx of soldiers and money by threatening to close the continental markets where English merchants sold England's economic mainstay, wool cloth. In striving not to offend Spanish interests so blatantly that markets remained closed, the queen and her great councillor maintained an adroit balancing act that excluded Leicester's more extreme views of English policy and, with them, Leicester himself from the center of the decision making. The report of the Spanish envoy in October 1572 conveys this sense of Burghley's power within the council: Burghley "assured me privately that he had gained over the great majority of his opponents, and especially the earl of Leicester."[46] For the earl, the question of English armed intervention in the Netherlands was both a question of control in the Privy Council and a test of his personal relationship with the queen.[47]

In the summer of 1572, covert English involvement in the Netherlands began when several Dutch cities, including Brill and Flushing, declared for William of Orange. At that time, Elizabeth sent 300,000 florins to William and allowed volunteers, including Dutch refugees exiled in England and Englishmen like Humphrey Gilbert and George Gascoigne, to travel to the Netherlands. Their goals included the support of the Dutch rebellion and the defense of key positions along the Channel. The enthusiasm for war failed to assuage the queen's concern that an intervention would both cost more than she could raise without requesting Parliament for more funds and destabilize the balance of hostilities between Spain and France.

When Elizabeth appeared at Greenwich to see off this first group of interventionists, she reportedly told Humphrey Gilbert to act "as thoughe he and his companie departed out of England thether without Her Majesties assent."[48] One Spanish observer wrote to the Duke of Alba from London that the English motivation was entirely economic. The English sought "to arrange a settlement and a re-opening of trade and the ports, with a resumption of former privileges."[49] Although trade issues were never fully resolved, the English relief of Flushing in 1572 proved to be a small holding action that continued after the St. Bartholomew's Day Massacre in September but then gradually lost impetus. One of the few English soldiers who did not come home was George Gascoigne, who remained as a soldier serving William for the next three years. Despite his complaints about the Dutch lack of firm commitment to the cause, Gascoigne doubtless hoped that the English would become more involved in the rebellion, especially in the summer of 1575 after Elizabeth was first offered sovereignty of the Netherlands.

The Dutch Protestants themselves were split between those who looked to France for support in their rebellion against Spain and those who preferred to deal with England. William of Orange chose to cultivate strong ties with the English Protestant faction, meeting and corresponding with Philip Sidney, Fulke Greville, and Leicester. During the summer of 1575, his suggestion that Elizabeth might be given sovereignty of the Netherlands in exchange for her financial and military support may well have made Dudley hope that intervention was entirely possible. Although perhaps not imminent, a military incursion in the Netherlands would be closer if Elizabeth were willing to conduct negotiations with William of Orange, even if her role, as in her relationship with Dudley, was to refuse his offers.

During the next ten years, Elizabeth remained determined to avoid a title in the Netherlands and the leadership of any Protestant alliance that would come with it, and Orange continued to be interested in the possibility of involving her through sovereignty.[50] The offer to make Elizabeth sovereign of the Netherlands was thus formally made in January 1575/1576; meanwhile, a family tree representing Elizabeth as heir to the Dutch states was drawn up.[51] Although Elizabeth was too well aware of the difficulties of maintaining a Protestant alliance to desire it, in 1575 the Protestant faction hoped to see Elizabeth's possession of the seventeen provinces as a prelude to financial support and military action.

Protestant supporters also found hope in the Spanish military and financial losses of the mid-1570s.[52] The cost of the Spanish army was sending Philip into bankruptcy. As Thomas Wilson marveled in a letter to Burghley, "King Philip and the country have been at charges within these eight years of 33,000,000 crowns, or florins of 2s. 8d. each," yet the "soldiers . . . mutiny daily in every place for want of wages."[53] By the winter of 1574/1575, Philip was ready for the talks with William of Orange, which began in March 1575 at Breda. Before, during, and after these discussions, the various letters reproduced in the *Calendars of State Papers* are filled with rumors of English support of the Netherlands, occasionally mentioning Leicester as a principal.[54] No one apparently had much hope of a lasting peace or was surprised when in the early summer of 1575 the Duke of Alba's successor, Luis de Zúñiga y Requeséns, broke off the talks to launch a new offensive. Both William and Requeséns thought that the resulting siege of Ziesikzee would determine the outcome of the entire revolt.[55]

To the Protestant faction, the summer of 1575 appeared to be a crucial and even practical time to intervene in the Netherlands. The pressure its members put on Elizabeth during these months to accept sovereignty in the Netherlands is evident in de Guaras's description the following January of Elizabeth's reaction to the news that a delegation from the Netherlands had arrived: "The Queen very loudly declared that she was against sending forces openly to Zealand and Holland. She entered her chamber alone, slamming her door and crying out that they were ruining her over this business."[56] Years later, Elizabeth recalled, while dissolving Parliament in 1593, that "in the ambition of glorie I have never sought to inlarge the territories of my land."[57] Both the rumor and the speech, although nearly twenty years apart, help explain that Elizabeth had little sympathy with the militaristic self-display at Kenilworth because she had so little sympathy for the support of the Dutch rebels that Dudley and Gascoigne championed.[58]

As was usual in the Elizabethan court and in the relationship between Dudley and Elizabeth, at Kenilworth the earl used allegorical entertainments to express the relation he perceived between events and ideology, between himself and the queen. In *The Rites of Knighthood,* Richard McCoy elucidated the history of a relationship in which Dudley "used chivalric symbolism and spectacle to advance his considerable ambitions against his many enemies at court" as he and his queen met each other through various "symbolic power struggles."[59] The military skirmish that Gascoigne describes with such regret contains the ghost of just such a struggle in an artful attempt to displace Elizabeth's strength with a battle featuring Dudley's, even if it never took place.

The skirmish's enemy, as defined in Sir Bruse sans Pitie, is a villain carefully chosen to represent male violence against females. In *La Morte Darthur,* Sir Bruse is known as a "deuourer of ladyes." He chases four women: one saved by the efforts of Gawayne and Tristram; one rescued by Dynadan; another, Dame Brangwayne, saved by Syr Launcelot; and, finally, another woman rescued by Palomydes but later senselessly killed by Bruse.[60] At Kenilworth, the allegorized threat of Sir Bruse represents a male force seeking to control, through rape, the virtue of female chastity. Within this rape narrative, however, the resolution of his threat can be counteracted only by still another strong male presence: the rescuer. Thus the military skirmish assails the royal claim to autonomy by denying that women may secure their own physical safety. Dudley's riding in full armor—made especially for the occasion (Figure 11)—to skirmish with his band would have produced a chivalrous allegory of the queen's knight riding to the rescue of Chastity. Protect the Lady of the Lake, surrounded by lecherous enemies, and protect Elizabeth; protect them, and by the military logic of threat, hegemony, and possession, protect a country ravished by an invading force. This was unacceptable to Elizabeth's foreign policy and her concomitant iconography of autonomy.

This suppressed skirmish at Kenilworth formed only an early expression of the masculinist rationale of rescuing the Netherlands. During the next two decades, sympathizers with the Protestant cause often used the age-old metaphor of the raped nation to justify intervention. Gascoigne's own *Spoyle of Antwerp,* written in 1576 while he was employed by Walsingham in the Netherlands, casts Antwerp as the injured female raped by the Spanish and features a woodcut of a woman in acute distress (Figure 12).[61]

The need for Dudley's protection of the feminized victim was publicly

Figure 11. Dudley's armor, most probably made for the Kenilworth entertainments. It is inscribed RD. (By permission of the Board of Trustees of the Royal Armouries [XI.81])

performed when in 1585 "Prince" Leicester in the Netherlands viewed an entertainment in which the allegorical female figure of Leiden was variously assaulted on stage by the Spanish. At the end, "leaping off hastily," she "hid herself under the Earl's cloak"; whereupon Leicester, in the final act of male protectiveness, "led her to his lodging."[62] The best-known literary representation of Dudley's protective role is that of Spenser's Arthur (at times, clearly the Earl of Leicester), whom Mercilla sends to act as

Figure 12. Antwerp figured as a female after her rape by the Spanish. Woodcut from the 1586 edition of George Gascoigne's *Spoyle of Antwerp*. (Bodleian Library, Tanner 42[5])

Lady Belge's champion (*FQ* 5.10–11). The first time Dudley becomes associated with this narrative of rescue is the skirmish at Kenilworth.

After the skirmish itself, Gascoigne informs us, Elizabeth's actions would have been kept to a minimum. Only after Dudley had triumphed would Elizabeth have entered the picture at all: "At last (Syr Bruse his men being put to flight) the Captaine should have come to her Majestie at the Castell window, and have declared more plainly the distresse of his Mistresse [the Lady of the Lake], and the cause that she came not to the Court, according to duetie and promise, to give hyr attendance" (501). Because "Merlin had prophecied" that only a maid better than herself might save the lady, Elizabeth would then have been allowed to release her (502). It is at this point that Gascoigne abandons the pretense that he is writing as much for Elizabeth as for Dudley: "This [armed rescue] had not onely bene a more apt introduction to *her* deliverie, but also the skirmish by night woulde have bene both very strange and gallant" (502, my emphasis). The text claims that this device would also have shown the queen to better advantage than would the device of her magical chastity, which was actually performed: "Her Majesty might have taken good occasion to have gone in [a] barge upon the water, for the better execution of *her* deliverie" (502, my emphasis).

In both these quoted sentences, "her" refers ambiguously to Elizabeth and to the Lady of the Lake, as the text avoids stating openly that Elizabeth needs to be delivered by Dudley and his knights. Instead, Gascoigne manages to imply that Elizabeth requires rescue at the same time that he downplays the distinction between Dudley's skirmish and her own device of the Lady of the Lake. After all, he says, the queen would have saved the lady in both scenarios. As a result of this fudging and the need to keep the "captain" at center stage, the queen is difficult to locate in Gascoigne's description. On the one hand, Gascoigne imagines that she would watch the battle between the captain's and Sir Bruse's forces from the lake bank in order to appreciate its staging for her. On the other hand, he imagines her as a less immediate presence, standing at the window and awaiting news of Sir Bruse's defeat.

Although Robert Dudley lost the chance at Kenilworth to stage himself at this entertainment's center, Gascoigne's text appeared at a time when its appeal to public support for the Protestant faction was particularly attractive. The conviction and detail with which Gascoigne describes the military alternative to the queen's mythology suggests his particular interest in presenting this device featuring his captain's night battle with the forces of evil, the captain's victorious address to the queen, and his speech informing her of his victory and her duty to save the Lady of the Lake as the postscript to his performance.[63] Printing what did not occur at Kenilworth—the captain's victory, followed immediately by the censored marriage masque—allowed Gascoigne to display and to argue for Leicester and for the importance of a more vigorous, militarist approach to England's problems. The text reached a far wider audience than the direct presentation of these views to Elizabeth would have allowed.

In displaying devices that could be read as personal challenges to Elizabeth's physical and political autonomy, both Dudley and Gascoigne run the risk that Edward Dyer spelled out to Christopher Hatton, that "she will imagine that you goe about to imprison her Fancye, & to wrapp her grace within your disposicion; and that will breed despite and hatred in her towards you."[64] In Kenilworth's opening and censored entertainments,

Gascoigne and Dudley refuse the feminized role that Castiglione assigned
to the courtier, to charm his sovereign, and remasculinize themselves by
publicizing a deliberate conflict with her and her policies. At the same time,
in looking outside the court for an arena of male action, they demonstrate
how right Castiglione was that the courtier is feminized by the pursuit of
ambition.[65]

"By soveraigne maiden's might"

As a sovereign in control of her foreign policy and even the most restive of
her courtiers, Elizabeth reacted, through diplomacy and spectacle, to the
revival of hostilities in the Netherlands during the summer of 1575.
Shortly before Kenilworth, she and her Privy Council supporters decided
to send envoys to the Netherlands and Spain in order to alleviate the
situation there. She sent Daniel Rogers to William of Orange in June and,
with instructions dated the week before she arrived at Kenilworth, Sir
Henry Cobham to Philip II in September. Both envoys carried her instructions to concentrate on economic matters abroad, but were authorized to
convey subtle threats of English force. Elizabeth and Walsingham personally authorized their messenger to Spain to "signify that, contrary to [the
queen's] disposition, she may be found for her own safety to be a dealer
herein . . . to preserve her own realm rather than to desire to invade
anything belonging to him [Philip]."[66]

Elizabeth's response to the combatants in the Netherlands was thus a
mixture of hard-headed economic goals, disingenuous diplomatic hopes,
and vague threats. With her government's foreign policy thus well enough
in hand, the queen could hardly have welcomed Dudley's pressure in council or entertainment to alter her policy toward the Netherlands, especially
when the performance of his views could serve as a rallying point for less
temperate policies.

The circumspection of her foreign policy contrasts markedly with the
figure she struck at home. Particularly at Kenilworth, where she had to
respond directly to Dudley's attempts to displace her authority with his
own, she and the poets serving her opted for her representation as independent, forceful, semidivine, and magical—in short, attributes that placed her
completely beyond the need for male protection. The iconography of
power that Kenilworth demanded of her was not simply wishful idealiza-
tion, but a necessary statement of her very real control of her court.

At Kenilworth, Elizabeth presented herself as a force allied with God
and nature against the male threat to chastity—in Elizabeth's iconography,
as it was developing at Kenilworth, the virtue that empowers its possessor
to mediate between heaven and earth. The skirmish would have required
the queen to validate the terms of Leicester's self-display, to be shaped in
ways that would allow him to fulfill his desires. The Deliverance of the
Lady of the Lake, as it was apparently performed, asserts the central argument of the royal mythology, that Elizabeth's virginal authority, as the

expression of God and nature, is complete unto itself, a signifier in command of its signifieds. This iconic argument, although fully developed only after the defeat of the Armada, came into being at Kenilworth through the rescue from male threat of a virtuous virgin who was in many ways a figure of Elizabeth's younger, imprisoned self. This staging of Elizabeth as Triumphant Virtue had the double advantage of developing and extending the centrality of the monarch while reducing Dudley's role to that of an observer of her power, the role that his original skirmish had assigned to her.[67]

The Dudley devices used the Arthurian myth to welcome and protect Elizabeth in terms that substantiated his claim to a nobility beyond her ability to grant or deny. The Elizabeth device subsumes the Arthurian legend within a regal cosmography whose center is not Elizabeth as guest and equal, but Elizabeth as transcendent signifier. The device, invented by Hunnis with poetry by Hunnis, Ferrers, and Goldingham, began with romantic suddenness, like many episodes in *La Morte Darthur* and, later, *The Faerie Queene*. As "the Queenes Majestie . . . passed over the bridge, returning from hunting," she was stopped by Triton, rather interestingly cross-dressed as a mermaid, who revealed in verse the "woefull distresse wherein the poore Ladie of the Lake did remaine." The text summarizes the threat to virginity as embodied in "Sir Bruse, sauns pittie," who "in revenge of his cosen *Merlyne* the prophet, whom for his inordinate lust she had inclosed in a rocke, did continuallie pursue the Ladie of the Lake: and had (long sithens) surprized hir, but that Neptune . . . had envyroned hir with waves" (498).

Triton's speech declares that Bruse "sought by force her virgin's state full fowlie to deface" (499). Like Florimell, confined in the cave "in the bottom of the maine" (*FQ* 3.8.37), the lady is imprisoned in the lake. Neptune's environing "hir with waves" only suspends the rape attempt: The description of Sir Bruse at the banks of the lake with "all the cure of cheefest Gods, Mars," at his back suggests that Bruse possesses the force to wrest the lady from her uncomfortable position of safety. The only hope for the pageant's victim lies in Merlin's prophecy that "she coulde never be delivered but by the presence of a better maide then herself." Therefore, as the gloss explains, Triton tells the queen that "Neptune had sent him right humbly to beseech hir Majestie, that she would no more but shew herselfe, and it should be sufficient to make Sir Bruse withdrawe his forces" (498–99).

> Yea, oracle and prophecie, say sure she can not stande;
> Except a worthier maide then she her cause do take in hand.
> Loe, here therefore a worthy worke, most fit for you alone;
> Her to defend and set at large, but you, O Queene, can none:
> And God's decree, and Neptune sues this graunt, O peerles
>   Prince:
> Your presence onely shall suffice, her enemies to convince.
>   (499)

Triton calls on all of nature to cooperate in this deliverance of the Lady of the Lake by Elizabeth.

> You windes, returne into your caves, and silent there remaine;
> You waters wilde, suppresse your waves, and keepe you calme
>   and plaine.
> You fishes all, and each thing else, that here have any sway;
> I charge you all, in Neptune's name, you keepe you at a stay,
> Untill such time this puissant Prince Sir *Bruse* hath put to flight;
> And that the maide released be, by soveraigne maiden's might.
>   (499–500)

Once Triton presents the situation, the Lady of the Lake's deliverance "by soveraigne maiden's might" takes place immediately and easily, even antidramatically. Stephen Orgel describes this scene's lack of suspense as a function of its focus on Elizabeth: "Dramatic interrelationships are wholly absent, and the figures of the masque do not even speak to each other. Everything is directed to Elizabeth, and the verse serves as a commentary on what happens, rather than as a vehicle for it."[68] The text says simply that "her Majestie proceeded further on the bridge." This action alone disperses the forces of Sir Bruse and frees the lady, who advances "upon heapes of bulrushes" to thank Elizabeth for subduing "mine enemies . . ./Not mine alone, but foe to Ladyes all" (500).

Until this point in her iconography, the queen's associations with God, nature, myth, and magic had been brought more cautiously to the support of her self-representation. But Dudley's challenge to her authority, with its militarist ambition and princely pretension, required a response of equal power. In assigning her the male role of rescuer and granting her magic as the means to complete the exploit, the entertainment commands its contemporary audience to see Elizabeth as the "animating center," as Clifford Geertz terms the royal position. Such an entertainment functions like "crowns and coronations, limousines and conferences" to "mark the center as center and give what goes on there its aura of being not merely important but in some odd fashion connected with the way the world is built."[69] In saving the Lady of the Lake, Elizabeth's Chastity supplies the crucial link between sovereign and God assumed in medieval political theology while giving her the power to manipulate the cosmic correspondences assumed in Neoplatonism.

After Sir Bruse's defeat, the Lady of the Lake and her ladies form an assemblage analogous to that of Elizabeth and her ladies to sing their gratitude, accompanied by a musical consort from a dolphin-shaped boat:

> Untill this day, the Lake was never free
> From his assaults, and other of his knights;
> Untill such type as he did playnely see
> Thy presence dread, and fered of all wyghts.

> Which made him yeeld, and all his bragging bands,
> Resigning all into thy princely hands. (500)

Then Proteus cleared his throat and, "in the behalfe of the Lady distressed, as also in the behalfe of all the Nimphs and Gods of the Sea," sang

> We yeeld you humble thanks, in mightie Neptune's name,
> Both for our selves and therewithall, for yonder seemely
>   dame.
> A dame whom none but you deliver could from thrall:
> Ne none but you deliver us from loitring life withall.
> She pined long in paine, as overworne with woes;
> And we consumde in endles care, to fend her from her foes.
> Both which you set at large, most like a faithful freend;
> Your noble name be praisde therefore, and so my song I ende.
>   (501)

These triumphal songs provide a retrospective view of the rescue in which Sir Bruse becomes an ever wider, more powerful threat, the lady's sufferings grow, and the extent of the queen's powers swells accordingly. God's and Neptune's request that Elizabeth deliver the lady, Triton's relay of Neptune's prophecy, and his call to nature to aid Elizabeth all suggest the cosmic import of Sir Bruse's threat to virginity. The ladies' thanks for deliverance from "all" Sir Bruse's "bragging bands" extends the influence of Malory's loner until he becomes the military threat of the originally planned skirmish. By the time the Lady of the Lake and Proteus sing their songs of gratitude, Sir Bruse has become the enthraller of the entire sea world. But Elizabeth's female virtue made active—her Chastity—disperses the threat more handily than any of the knights of Arthur or the followers of Dudley could hope to equal. In completing her subdued but effective rescue, the concluding verses make it clear that Elizabeth has restored the cosmic balance. Her own triumph appropriates the figure from Dudley's territorial welcome by effectively admitting the Lady of the Lake to the inner, female court pictured in one of the woodcut illustrations of Edmund Spenser's *Shepheardes Calender* of 1579 (Figure 13). In this way, she keeps the promise made to the Lady of the Lake, who welcomed her, that "we will herein common more with yoo hereafter."

That this was the day on which Elizabeth seized control of events at Kenilworth becomes even more evident when we consider the events that *Laneham's Letter* tells us occurred next. After the rescue of the Lady of the Lake, the queen, who was notoriously reluctant to create new knights, next pointedly staged her power to do so by knighting Thomas Cecil (who was William Cecil's older son), Henry Cobham (who, it had just been determined, would soon be sent to Philip II to inform him of the queen's continued friendship), the Catholic-leaning Thomas Tresham (who was converted sometime in the next five years), Thomas Stanhope, and Arthur

Figure 13. Elizabeth among her ladies. Woodcut from Edmund Spenser's *Shepheardes Calender* (1579). (Huntington Library RB 69548)

Basset (who presumably also represented in some way Elizabeth's decision not to intervene in the Netherlands).

Following this display of her place at the head of the chivalry of England and her pointed rewarding of non-Protestant faction members, Elizabeth completed the performance of her sovereignty by curing nine people of "the peynfull and dangerous deseaz called the King's evill; for that Kings and Queenz of this Realm withoot other medsin (save only by handling and prayerz) only doo cure it" (459), as had her Catholic sister, Mary (Figure 14). Although Elizabeth was the sovereign who ended the practice of giving "cramp rings" she had handled to epileptics, at Kenilworth she felt the need to substantiate her royal power in the spectacle of cosmic harmony as well as in the spectacles of her ability to raise up or heal her subjects by the touch of her sacred hand. William Took describes how before she began healing the sick, Elizabeth publicly prepared herself "prostrate on her knees, body and soul rapt in prayer."[70] Because healing the sick involved making a spectacle of her piety, it must have made it an appealing way to round out the day that, for a change, focused on her powers.

The feminine was in the ascendant in the final days of Kenilworth. These allegorical, magical, chivalric, religious, and medical assertions of Elizabeth's autonomy were followed the next day by the presentation by some Coventry men of an ancient play called *Hocks Tuesday,* which humorously enacted the destruction of the Danes by King Ethelred and fighting English women (*Laneham's Letter,* 447). Another contemporary source tells us that this entertainment "pleased the Queen so much, that she gave them a Brace of Bucks, and 5 Marks in Money, to bear the Charges of the Feast."[71]

Figure 14. Queen Mary exercising the royal touch, as seen in a manuscript (ca. 1555) attributed to Levina Teerlinc. (Courtesy of Westminster Cathedral)

Elizabeth, Dudley, and the Competition for Representation

The foregoing analysis of the entertainments has followed my recon-
structed chronology of the events at Kenilworth. At first, Dudley controlled the queen's welcome and a variety of entertainments arranged far in
advance of her arrival, including the celebratory fireworks, bearbaiting, and
the ambiguous bride dael. Then, Elizabeth censored the masque and skirmish, featuring Dudley's pretensions, replaced them with her own apo-
theosis as the rescuer of Chastity in the person of the Lady of the Lake,
created knights, and cured the King's evil.

In Gascoigne's text, however, these events either are missing or follow a
very different chronology. Instead, Gascoigne first provides the text of
Elizabeth's rescue of the Lady of the Lake and follows this with the regret-
ful description of how splendid the military skirmish with Sir Bruse would
have been. Then Gascoigne prints the marriage masque. Although the
censorship of Dudley's central self-displays must have occurred *before* Elizabeth could replace them with her own performance, Gascoigne has them
appear *after* Elizabeth delivers the Lady of the Lake, a placement that
invites the reader to compare feminine and masculine responses to
threat.[72] Moreover, the placement of the censored texts after Elizabeth's
restructured rescue allows Gascoigne—and, through him, Dudley and the
Protestant party—the last word in the competition for the representations
at Kenilworth in his description of a military response to Sir Bruse.

What was performed at Kenilworth was subject to the queen's revision,
but the published text reveals that she did not exercise the same control
over printed material. Elizabeth's presence inevitably limited what might
be performed for her and the court audience, but what was printed and
read by a wider audience—if it were carefully worded—was difficult for her
to control. Although registering these challenges to Elizabeth's policy and
its representation, *The Princely Pleasures* could not be contained or, finally,
suppressed because it was far more than a court document.

Gascoigne's text, for once, was not suppressed, perhaps because by the
time it appeared, its increasingly popular point of view was shared by many
members of the government. The text, like the interplay between Dudley's
interests and the queen's throughout the July 1575 entertainments, was
only part of an ongoing struggle for control of the queen's ear, for power
in the Privy Council, for the shape of English–Dutch relations, and for the
representations of conceivable resolutions to complex questions of policy
raised by gender, religion, and economics. Dudley's part in this competition was dictated by his ambition, whether voiced in Privy Council meetings or in elaborate allegorical declarations. This ambition might be momentarily stifled, as at Kenilworth itself, but it reappears—in this case,
gaining a second life through the dissemination of Gascoigne's text.

Not only did the text of *The Princely Pleasures* record Dudley's ambition,
but its unfolding of Elizabeth's response to his militarist, hegemonic policies anticipated the events of the next few months and years. In 1576, the

Netherlands moved closer to an English alliance as it became apparent that Don John of Austria would replace Requeséns as the Spanish governor. In January 1576/1577, Thomas Wilson voiced the underlying assumption of the Kenilworth entertainments, that Dudley was the most logical leader of an English force—in this case, the best way to meet Don John: "It shall not need to send any man of quality hither to appease things, if the Prince [of Orange] be once received, except it be to send a general over an army of our nation in aid of the States, which I wish were my Lord of Leicester, if the Duke of Guise or other foreigners should invite Don John."

Also at this time, Dudley himself apparently wrote to the Dutch States General to offer himself as commander, for "the States General wrote directly to the Earl declining his offer to lead an army into the Low Countries."[73] Between 1575 and 1585, a variety of factors enabled intervention in the Netherlands—and the consequent break with Spain—including the increasing independence of English merchants from Spanish-controlled markets and inept diplomacy in the service of both England and Spain.[74] Moreover, the sweeping victories of the Prince of Parma's army in the Netherlands and the organization of the Catholic League threatened English interests and England itself.

In 1584, the death of Anjou and the assassination of William of Orange also drove Burghley and Elizabeth to agree to aid the Netherlands in the treaty concluded at Nonesuch in August 1585. At Nonesuch, Elizabeth openly promised money and six thousand soldiers for the Protestant Lowlands. When she selected Dudley as their commander, he experienced a momentary and precarious triumph, the result of all the lengthy negotiations and personal expenditures, of which the Kenilworth entertainments were a part.

In December 1585, Dudley entered the Netherlands to head the assembled Dutch and English force of eight thousand with a princely entourage, to a series of triumphal entertainments that Roy Strong and J. A. van Dorsten describe as representing "the conscious fulfillment of a project which had been in existence for over a decade." Interestingly enough, the preliminary spectacles that greeted Dudley represented a symbolic marriage with Elizabeth in which their personal impresae were joined with the inscription "Quos Deus coniunxit homo non separet"—Whom God hath joined together, let no man put asunder.[75] The political "marriage" advocated in the masque of Diana and Juno was represented as complete when at last Dudley arrived in the Netherlands on his queen's behalf and also on his own.

This marriage of their political interests could never really exist, however, largely because upon his arrival Dudley was not as interested in cooperating with his sovereign as in ruling the Netherlands. Even as Dudley was hailed as the Prince of Orange's successor, maintained the entourage of a prince, was named as prince in legal documents of the States General, assumed the title of excellency, and viewed repeated entertainments addressed to him as "princeps," he and Elizabeth once more fell out over the issue of the relation between Dudley's ambition and Elizabeth's authority. When Dudley arrived in the Netherlands to help create a powerful central government with the help of the States General, the nature of that government and its relation to England had not yet been negotiated. Dudley's ambition to be governor-general conflicted with Elizabeth's understanding that he was to serve as captain-general; Elizabeth interpreted his function as military, whereas Dudley, the States General, and even Walsingham and Burghley saw his role as equally and necessarily political. If Elizabeth herself refused to rule the provinces, it seemed logical that Leicester would.

These differing opinions about Dudley's role led for a time to Elizabeth's alienation from both Dudley and her entire Privy Council, including Burghley and the Dutch States General. It became clear through Elizabeth's subsequent negotiations with Spain from 1586 to 1588 that she did not intend to fund or fight an all-out war with Spain. Instead, the goal of her policy remained to return to the Netherlands of 1566, with the seventeen provinces again under the rule of the king of Spain. But the northern provinces and her own Privy Council disagreed with her, siding with the war party to a nearly treasonous degree and supporting Leicester's ambitions in the tenuous hope that his military victories, his popularity, or his commanding leadership would prevent her from undermining his position.

For a time, the entire Privy Council, including Burghley, kept Elizabeth in ignorance of Dudley's growing political power abroad.[76] The governorship was his, however, only as long as her Privy Council conspired to keep Elizabeth in the dark. Once she discovered what was happening, she responded with rising anger. As she wrote the States General, she "found their proceedings verie strange, and greatly tending to her dishonor" that they would offer such a position to her subject "without making her acquainted with the same . . . as though she wanted judgement to accept or refuse what was competent."[77] The whole affair served to publicize the weaknesses of both Elizabeth and Dudley, revealing the queen to be reliant on the information provided her and the earl as no more than her "creature." As such, the attempt to take away Elizabeth's control of English policy in the Netherlands exposed the gap between the representations of their power and their actual degree of control.

Although, as Elizabeth wrote Dudley, she considered herself to have been "contemptuously . . . used"[78] by him, as long as he remained in the Netherlands the earl continued to be widely referred to as a prince and repeatedly addressed as "your princely grace." Lavishly entertained during his two progresses, he saw himself allegorized in the terms that the Kenilworth entertainments had claimed for him. As "Arthur," he was represented as "aloft vpon a scaffold, as if it had beene in a cloud or skie."[79] The verse that accompanied one such device at his entry into The Hague on 6 January 1586 (Figure 15) proclaimed: "Mighty Arthur, ruling Britain, drove out those who persecuted the people, with an eternal honour which

Figure 15. Dudley as Arthur. From Hendrik Goltzius's *Delineatio Pompae Trium-phalis* (1586), an engraved book that unfolds to present a continuous, horizontal picture of Leicester's entry into The Hague, on 6 January 1586. (British Library)

does not fade, and protected the orthodox of his time, for he is remembered as a glorious prince: we hope that you will be a second Arthur."[80]

Spenser later extended his own Arthurian allegory by figuring Dudley as his Arthur in book 5, canto 10, of *The Faerie Queene*. But Spenser repressed the complex circumstances that resulted in the queen's insistence that Dudley relinquish the title of governor-general of the Netherlands and return home. The Earl of Leicester returned to find his reputation damaged beyond repair. He had raised the hopes of the Dutch that England would fund an all-out war, but had secretly been forced to carry out Elizabeth's policy of not angering the Spanish. When he moved too quickly and grandiosely into position as governor-general, the queen's investigation and publicly reported indignation seriously undercut his credibility. She did not, however, consider the result a victory. As she wrote to him: "It is always thought . . . a hard bargayn when both parties are l[o]sers, and so doth fall out in the case betwene us two."[81]

Elizabeth's speech dissolving Parliament in 1593 harks back to this period when it seemed to many of her subjects that England could possess the

Netherlands. She stated that "manie wiser princes then my selfe you have had but [none more careful over you]." If "I have never sought to inlarge the territories of my land nor thereby to Advance you," this was because "I have vsed my forces to keepe Warres from you." She evokes her male sovereign body repeatedly in this speech in order to restate her policy of passive defense as the expression of "A Prince that nether careth for any particuler no not for life, but to live that you may flourishe."[82] For a moment, though, this speech verges on regret that she did not give Dudley more power, although even he finally acknowledged he had made a hash of things.

Dudley returned home in 1586, his wealth depleted, his detractors louder than ever, and his friends quiet. Even the tract published to justify his behavior in the Netherlands, *A Briefe Report of the Militarie Services done in the Low Countries, by the Erle of Leicester,* forms at best a meek defense.[83] But the queen once again forgave his ambition, and his service in the Netherlands was just credible enough that the Privy Council sent him back through 1587. Shortly after his second return to England, in 1588, he was commissioned as Her Majesty's Lieutenant Against Foreign Invasion, although with his powers strictly limited owing to a lack of both funds and trust. To his frustration, he was permitted to assemble an army only when the Armada was sailing up the Channel. After giving the Privy Council scathing reports of his fellow officers, the poor conditions, and the disorganization that prevailed at Tilbury, Dudley left London for Rycote, where he died.

As in London's coronation entry for Elizabeth, the allegorical representations of the queen at Kenilworth failed to stifle her self-assertion. In 1559 and again in 1575, spectacle generated gendered images of the queen and those who entertained her that, when published and disseminated, became part of the semiotics of culture. The images must have to some extent been supplanted by the queen's considerable administrative, financial, and diplomatic powers, but as published texts they remained in currency. Despite the frustrations and failures of a political and military career built on his relationship with Elizabeth the queen, the view of Dudley's abilities published in the *The Princely Pleasures at the Courte at Kenelwoorth* anticipated and helped shape England's foreign policy during the next decade. Not Elizabeth's insistence to the Lady of the Lake that Kenilworth was hers, the suppression of Dudley's daring self-displays, or, a decade later, the queen's fury at Dudley's acceptance of princely titles in the Netherlands could stop him from seeking other fields for his ambition. In the 1570s and 1580s, Queen Elizabeth I's power was at its height, and she retained as much control of her iconography as she ever had at the same time that she helped shape her public image as increasingly divine and magical. Nevertheless, in a world in which military threat inspired military response, the allegory of the queen's autonomy failed to control even her closest male associates and advisers.

3

Engendered Violence: Elizabeth, Spenser, and the Definitions of Chastity (1590)

The rape of a female by a pen occurs and recurs toward the end of *The Faerie Queene*'s book 3, in the poet-magician Busirane's masque of Amoret's impaled heart. Britomart observes the horrific masque, discovers that Busirane is "penning" Amoret by writing the entertainment in her blood, and then defeats him. The poem's narrative seems to condemn the assault on Amoret, who appears as a figure of vulnerable Chastity, and then allows Britomart's more militant Chastity to rescue her. Nevertheless, the "torture"[1] of a figure of Chastity reverberates beyond the poem, as is evident in the many discussions that seek its containment through interpretation.[2] The poem's simultaneous address and assault of a Chastity figure inaugurate the sophisticated reworkings of the queen's image that characterized the decade of the 1590s while anticipating the violent extremes that the social and political relationships contested through Elizabeth's body would reach by 1600.

In the first two chapters of this book, I discussed how the London elites of 1559 and, fifteen years later, Leicester and the Protestant faction sought to "entertain" Elizabeth through performed and printed representations that attempted to define her within their anxieties and concerns. I also considered how through economic cooperation, verbal self-presentation, spectacles of magical chastity, and claims of divine approval, Elizabeth

97

could be seen constructing her active, self-defining virtue in response to essentialist expectations that she marry, have children, or at least defer to militant advisers. In this final chapter, I examine a selection of material and discursive practices from the 1590s, rather than a single occasion or year, in order to demonstrate the ways in which Elizabeth sought to control her representation in response to—and as the means to shape—political events during the demanding final decade of her reign. During this period, Elizabeth engaged in a variety of practices that related the autonomy of her physical body to the authority of her political self, an autonomy represented allegorically as the virtue Chastity.

In the 1590s, the aging of the queen and the widespread anticipation of her death left her vulnerable in new ways to material and figurative tests of her authority: Essex's rebellion at the end of her final decade as much as Spenser's encomiastic challenge of her self-definition published in 1590, book 3 of *The Faerie Queene*. Her response was to shield herself physically and psychologically from the escalating threats while representing herself as the youthful figure at the summit of her society's social, religious, and political hierarchies. The very strategies that worked to preserve her power created a figure so remote in her material and discursive autonomy—so *chaste*—that penetrating that chastity attained enormous value.

Turning Sixty in the 1590s

As Queen Elizabeth I entered her sixties, she remained both physically vigorous and articulate in the defense of her right to make her own decisions. Roland Whyte, Robert Sidney's able agent whose nearly three hundred letters written from 1595 to 1600 form an invaluable insider's view of the court, observed during the summer progress of 1600 that "this gracious souverayne of ours is very well, and meanes to kill many staggs and buckes er she remove from these hunting cowntreis. Her body endures more travell than they can that attend her."[3]

This was a queen who continually journeyed on short progresses from Windsor to Oatlands to Nonesuch to Hampton Court or Whitehall; who, after hearing Bishop Rudd preach that according to biblical sources death was imminent at the age of sixty-three, called out loudly that he should keep his arithmetic to himself; whom her old enemy's son, Philip III, reportedly adjudged "so able a sovereign that she required no advice and was quite competent to manage her own affairs." She knew that her death was widely anticipated. As she wrote to James VI of Scotland after an attempt on *his* life, "though a King I be, yet hath my funeral been prepared (as I hear) long." She pointedly tells her anticipated successor that she hears of the preparations for her premature funeral "daily as I may have a good memorial that I am mortal," "whereat I smile" to think they "may be readier for it than I."[4]

Only in the final two years before her death in 1603 could Elizabeth be seen to falter. In a letter from this period, Robert Sidney wrote to the queen's godson, John Harington, that "I do see the Queen often; she doth wax weak since the late troubles." She had visited him at Penshurst wearing "a marvelous suit of velvet borne by four of her first women attendants in rich apparel," but such gorgeous self-display now took its toll: "At going up stairs she called for a staff" and "was much wearied in walking about the house."[5] Shortly before Elizabeth's death, Harington himself entrusted his wife with the details of the queen's degeneration. "Bidden to her presence," he "founde her in moste pitiable state." When Harington read her "some verses," she "smilede once" but declared that "I am paste my relishe for suche matters; thou seeste my bodilie meate dothe not suite me well."[6]

Although Elizabeth was physically frail only in the final two or three years of her life, throughout the 1590s her aging made her vulnerable. Her most trusted friends and advisers who had aided her move from a disempowered, even imprisoned woman to an active ruler, were also growing old. Leicester's death in 1588, Walsingham's in 1590, and Burghley's in 1598, together with the deaths of intimates in the privy chamber like Mistress Mary Ratcliffe, whom Elizabeth buried as a nobleman's daughter in Westminster Abbey in 1599, depressed her personally while having profound political consequences. As she wrote in a prayer, "I need good advice, wise counsels, and ready help at all times, especially should I come to be attacked by the violent winds and fierce tempest with which thrones are assailed."[7] The young queen who had complained to Guzman de Silva in 1567 that she was "left alone" and "grieved thereat, magnifying to me the peril in which she had been, and the pertinacity and disrespect of many towards her,"[8] in the 1590s was anxious that she might be left outside her own government's decision-making process as she aged. Roland Whyte reported that Elizabeth responded to the "many rumors . . . bruted" of her demise, "which troubled her Majestie a litle, for she wold say, *Mortua sed non sepulta*"—[I prefer] death to being consigned to obscurity (literally, burial).[9]

Thus in the 1590s, Elizabeth took special care to retain control of decision making. Retaining a measure of control over the interlocking organizations of court and Privy Council meant ensuring that her courtiers sought money, position, and employment that only she could deliver. When she authorized the raid on Cadiz and the disastrous invasion of Panama or agreed with the Privy Council that a force of sixteen thousand should be sent against the rebel Tyrone in Ireland, she exercised her power to grant her most powerful courtiers their desires and the opportunity to attract and reward a large body of followers. Writes Whyte, "The factions [were] never more malicious yet [are] well smothed outward . . . she whom it most concerneth doth rather use her wisdom in balancing the weights, then in drawing all to one assize."[10] Although late in her reign Elizabeth sometimes reluctantly allowed Drake, Essex, Howard, Ralegh, Cobham, and Cumberland more scope abroad, ambitious courtiers found that Elizabeth guarded the placement of her immediate advisers with greater care. Essex, jostling for position among the other later favorites, found that even though his personal revenues soared and his military responsibilities increased, he was unable to expand his sphere of influence in the government by providing his clients with proportionate gains. In attempting to find positions for his men, Essex found himself particularly obstructed by the power and influence of the Lord Treasurer, William Cecil, Lord Burghley, the cautious negotiator between foreign and domestic priorities who had positioned his younger son Robert to succeed him as Elizabeth's chief adviser.

In the interest of maintaining a balance among the special-interest groups closest to her person, the queen deferred making most of her domestic appointments. Concerning suits for the position of vice-chamberlain, Whyte tells us that "there have been so many suitors, that her Majesty will be hardly drawn to bestow it, and she will not discontent many. . . . Besides, there is in her Majesty no great inclination to bestow any place that falles, unles meere necessity occasion it for the good of her service." For six years, she purposely declined to replace her able secretary, Francis Walsingham, because Essex favored Francis Bacon and Burghley preferred his son Robert for the post. Such deferrals could be maddening. Whyte, frustrated when his own ambitions were limited by Essex's inability to advance Sidney, concluded "I doe observe the fashions of the Court and . . . find the way to preferment very difficult."[11]

Although more militant policies abroad and deferred appointments at home helped Elizabeth maintain immediate control of the most ambitious and thus dangerous men in her kingdom, these tactics could not entirely counteract the queen's greatest liability, her own aging female body. In 1593, Elizabeth was sixty in a society whose attitude toward older unmarried women Erasmus baldly summarized in his *Courtship* colloquy: "A maiden is something charming, but what's more naturally unnatural than an old maid?"[12] Writing from the Tower while awaiting execution, the young Earl of Essex imagined himself as an old woman in terms suggesting not only his society's attitude toward the aging female, but also something of his own way of reading Elizabeth's situation in her older face:

> [I will] in sorrowing spend my breath,
> And spot my face with never-drying teares,
> Till aged wrinckles, messengers of death,
> Have purchasde mercy and remov'd my feares.[13]

Although Elizabeth frequently admitted the consequences of her aging, her iconographic response to the fear of premature burial was to claim herself ageless. The inherent claim was that her active virtue, so often particularized as her virginity or chastity, protected Elizabeth from the normal aging process, helping preserve her metaphoric fertility in the guise of a continuing physical fertility. Her represented denial of old age was an assertion of her political viability, an attempt to transcend her society's tendency to disparage and ignore any woman past childbearing age— without, however, challenging that prejudice. As usual, Elizabeth's self-representations made no claim for women as a whole, but, rather, sought to distance her from normative constructions of the feminine.

On May Day in 1600, the Earl of Cumberland directly addressed the issue of loyalty to an aging queen during a "shew on horseback," which except for the recorded song was apparently a tournament showcasing his knightly virility.

> Time's young houres attend her still,
> And the eyes and cheekes do fill
> With fresh youth and beauty

runs the song, whose reassurances touch on the fear that men may desert an aging queen:

> All her lovers olde do grow,
> Cut their hearts they do not so
> In their loue and dutie.[14]

In Cumberland's entertainment, the allegory of a youthful virgin represents Elizabeth's political vigor while allowing those who served her to continue expressing their desire for her favor as a desire for her person.

Despite the visible dissonance between the figured queen and the queen's aging body, the fiction of Elizabeth's youth sought to deflect the questions that her aging evoked about the succession and the loyalty of subjects who had begun looking past her to James. Two portraits of the 1590s suggest both how Elizabeth preferred to view herself and an anxiety that her view be treated as sacrosanct. In the "coronation" portrait (Figure 16), which John Fletcher dated to around 1600 using the tree rings of its oak panels,[15] the youthful face, so like Levina Teerlinc's early portraits of the queen, appears encased in the visual iconography attending the medieval political theology of divine right. The effect is simultaneously that of the youthful virgin queen and a gilded icon of neomedieval orthodoxy, as if flattening perspectives might obviate alternative points of view.

Perhaps the best-known portrait of the last decade is the "rainbow" portrait, which portrays a radiantly youthful queen in fantastical dress. Although the queen's face and body have a more three-dimensional quality than they do in the "coronation" portrait, it contains no less a claim to youthful virginity. Both young queens wear their hair down, in the style of an English maiden. In the "rainbow" portrait (Figure 17), the coronation robes are replaced by a low-cut bodice, again signifying maidenhood; the masquelike headdress is surmounted by the crescent moon in reference to the virgin goddess Diana; pearls—further emblems of chastity—dangle from her headdress, hair, ears, throat, and wrists; and the bejeweled serpent of wisdom winds around itself on her sleeve. The only unfamiliar iconographic element is the mantle, whose sumptuous folds—covered with ears, eyes, and mouths—suggest the figure of Fame, whose less savory double is Rumor. In her right hand, Elizabeth is holding a rainbow: Both the illumination of her face and chest and the inscription "Non sine sole

Figure 16. The stylized, youthful queen in her coronation robes, painted around 1600 by an unknown artist. (National Portrait Gallery, London, No. 5175)

iris" (No rainbow without the sun) make clear that Elizabeth represents the sun.

Taken together, the "coronation" portrait and the "rainbow" portrait constitute two different but related strategies of Elizabeth's claim to youth. The first portrait attempts to connect the aging queen's right to the throne with the medieval past in the iconlike tradition of the portrait of Richard II—a claim carrying its own contradictions, given his early deposition and murder. The second depicts an assemblage of iconographic elements that claim the queen's chaste body as the center of the Ptolemaic universe while wrapping her in a mantle whose open mouths, ears, and eyes form a

Figure 17. The "rainbow" portrait (ca. 1600–1603), attributed to Marcus Gheeraerts the Younger. Elizabeth is depicted as the sun who makes possible the rainbow. (By courtesy of the Marquess of Salisbury, Hatfield House)

disquieting suggestion of vaginal openings combined with a sense of governmental surveillance. These portraits form two of the most luminous representations of the queen left to us. Viewing them, it is difficult not to believe for a moment in the connections they assert among Elizabeth's chastity, youth, and power. No representation, however, could efface the inevitability of Elizabeth's death.

Just as the succession question had surrounded the body of the young and potentially fertile queen, so now it appeared again in more violent modes as supporters of the various claimants to the throne attempted to hasten the transition of power. Her potential heirs included the infanta of Spain, who claimed her right through Henry III of England; James VI of

Scotland; Arabella Stuart, descended from Henry VII; and Robert Devereux, Earl of Essex, who tested the waters for a popular coup. Apparently the number of plots on Elizabeth's life increased as she aged; certainly the suspicion of such plots increased.

In the diplomatic correspondence—which throughout the reign betrays a keen interest in rumors like de Guaras's of the assassination attempt at Kenilworth—likewise reports increase of attempted shootings and attempted poisonings by gloves, chairs, saddles, and even a Bible. Unlike William of Orange of the Netherlands and Henry III of France, Elizabeth survived. But that survival was used to justify the imprisonment and interrogation of suspected dissidents and assassins, who were tortured, as Burghley pointed out in his published defense of the practice, in those cases in which treason "was first knowne and evidently probable."[16] Torture was probably the fate of the queen's physician, the Jewish Portuguese Dr. Lopez, whose confession Essex extricated in the competition with the Cecils to provide the queen with information and which he used to see him executed. Elizabeth later saved Essex himself from the routine violence of his sentence to be publicly hanged, taken down alive, castrated, disemboweled, drawn by four horses, and quartered. Instead, his own attempt to control the succession ended with the three ax strokes it took to sever his head from his shoulders in the inner courtyard of the Tower.

The Queen's Presence

Another way in which Elizabeth worked to show herself "worthy the place" of a sovereign by steering "a steady course held to make [herself] loved and feared"[17] was to construct herself as a figure of nearly inaccessible power. The significance assigned to the physical space surrounding her body, for example, became highly important. In the 1590s, Elizabeth continued to take care to make public appearances at progresses, parliaments, cities, towns, and great estates. Even as her voice proliferated in published speeches and proclamations and her image appeared in paintings and popular engravings, as she grew older she became a more physically remote figure, one who carefully guarded access to the body she had situated at the center of the integrated networks of decision making and representation.

In 1558/1559, the Venetian ambassador in France had heard that Elizabeth gained power by "frequently showing herself in public, giving audience to all who wish for it, and using every mark of great graciousness towards every one."[18] By the 1580s, a growing sense of the queen's inaccessibility within the privy chamber (Figure 18) resulted from several factors. As the threats on her life mounted, the queen was increasingly prevailed on to stay where she was safe. In addition, having proved herself as a ruler and a patron, she became more than ever the desired audience of every ambitious person in an era that offered few outlets for individual talent. She seems also to have preferred the pleasures of her life in the

Figure 18. Elizabeth receiving two Dutch emissaries in a privy chamber, around 1585, in a composition that juxtaposes their figures with that of Mary Queen of Scots, who is seated at the left. (Staatliche Kunstsammlungen, Schloss Wilhemshöhe)

company of selected women. Regardless of the many reasons for her privacy, the scarcity of her personal appearances gave her body a value that her contemporaries increasingly characterized as "sacred."

Her intimates reinforced Elizabeth's inaccessibility, of which Roland Whyte again provides our best picture as he explains the difficulty of getting either verbal messages or Sidney's letters delivered to a queen who became impatient at his repeated requests for leave to return from Flushing and for further appointments. Nearly every letter for five years describes Whyte's attempts to find a female confidante like Lady Huntingdon, who "governes the Queen, many howres together very private," to fulfill promises to act as intermediaries or to represent Sidney directly. In 1599 Whyte and Sidney tried another tactic, prevailing on Barbara Sidney to petition the queen for her husband's leave from Flushing, although she, in advanced pregnancy, was reluctant to leave Penshurst. Once at court, it was only through the auspices of Lady Huntingdon, with whom she was staying, and Frances Walsingham, Lady Essex, who came "at Court of purpose to help her to privat access to the Queens presence," that she was allowed to move her suit in person, albeit unsuccessfully.[19]

From the time of her accession, Elizabeth lived sequestered at her palaces in the privy chamber, in which space and personnel were organized according to her immediate needs for shelter, clothing, entertainment, and a place to fulfill the most immediate bodily needs to sleep, eat, and evacuate—hence, as David Starkey pointed out, the intimate physical relations between sovereign and aristocratic attendants signified by the term "privy."[20] Elizabeth inherited the organization of this court within a court in large part from her father, but her sister, Mary, also had adapted it to meet a queen's need for female attendants. The inner apartments occupied by Elizabeth and her chosen intimates were reached by passing through the presence chamber or chambers (there were two at Hampton Court) and through a set of guarded doors to even more interior spaces.

Elizabeth spent so much of her life in these privy spaces that by the 1590s, descriptions of her body become entangled with the rooms that housed her. Thus Whyte plays with the double meaning of "presence" in his report that "at Court her Majesty hath graced the daunsing and plaies with her own presence . . . and plaied at cards in the presence." Thomas Churchyard, composing "A Pleasant Conceit" as a New Year's gift to Elizabeth in 1593, describes a painter called on to decorate her palace: At the "Presence Chamber doore: / And peeping throw the same" the poet-painter sees the ladies in waiting "dancing" in the "Presence"—the word for both the queen's body and the room designed to display that body to the intimates of her power.[21]

When Essex returned, against strict orders, from Ireland in 1599, his campaign at the head of an expensive army of sixteen thousand resolved in a truce with the Irish rebel Tyrone that granted the Catholics religious toleration, he hastened "boldly to her Majesties presence" to plead his return against orders. Having "made all hast up to the presence, and soe to the Privy Chamber, and staied not till he came to the Queen's bed chamber," he found "the Queen newly up, the heare about her face; he kneeled unto her, kissed her handes, and her faire neck, and had some privat speach with her." Although momentarily relieved that she was so receptive, in the end this intimate intrusion on her sovereign body in its private spaces worked no magic. They spoke again, later in the morning, when the queen questioned him before the court about the truce in Ireland, the knighthoods he had created, and his return to court against orders. By that afternoon, he was summoned before the Privy Council to explain himself.[22] She never allowed him in her presence again and in the next year permitted his licenses, including the lucrative monopoly on sweet wines, to lapse. During that year, Essex's easy grace and courtly demeanor dissolved before the dishonor of house arrest, impending financial ruin, and his dismissal from court, which obviated his pleading his own case in her privy chambers.

The result of this exclusion from Elizabeth's presence was the event that came to be known as Essex's rebellion. According to the retrospective accounts of his confederates, the insurrection suffered from his having three conflicting goals: to make himself king, to hasten James VI's installation, and (more modestly) to secure the court so that he could gain the queen's presence in order to make his case. Essex himself testified that his "purpose" was to have come with eight or nine honorable persons . . . and so by petition, prostrating ourselves at her majesty's feet, to have put ourselves unto her mercy. And the effect of our desires should have been, that she would have been pleased to have severed some from her majesty, who, by reason of their potency with her, abused her majesty's ears with false informations; and they were Cobham, Cecil and Raleigh.[23]

The reasons that Essex's treason never prospered lay not only in the excluded earl himself, but also in the interplay of the queen's self-representation as an autonomous decision maker with the material reality of its force. London's elites stood solidly behind the queen with the help of "trained bands of Essex, Hertfordshire, Buckinghamshire, and Surrey . . . called up to London,"[24] while the aristocracy and the judiciary supported her. Essex's failure was the final proof of the success of Elizabeth's diverse strategies to identify her needs with those of the elites of England, a victory that once again won her the right to determine the ownership of her body and whatever degree of political agency she could achieve as a result. The resounding defeat of Essex earned her the right to the final political act of which her body was capable, the right to die on the throne.

Elizabeth's Later Strategies of Self-representation

In order to preserve her body as inviolable—virginal, unassaulted, sanctified—Elizabeth perpetually had to negotiate control of as much of the material world as she could muster, from her palaces and privy chamber to the streets, stages, and printing presses of London. As her aging body re-excited and reshaped anxieties about the succession, she used several strategies to counter the mounting challenges to her authority. She guardedly appointed her closest advisers, exercised control of her Privy Council, maintained access to the Cecils' information-gathering network, and isolated herself so that when she did grant an audience or appear in public, she created a sensation.

When Elizabeth made self-protective decisions that helped ensure her physical and psychological seclusion, she employed complementary language and imagery. She increasingly represented herself and was represented in discourses that positioned her as powerful because she was remote, self-sufficient, and desirable—"chaste," according to her own redefinition of the word. In her attempt to place herself beyond the control of others, she relied on a shrinking circle of advisers and located herself in the inner rooms of Hampton Court, Whitehall, Hatfield, and Windsor. She articulated this withdrawal through three discourses that I will examine in this section: Petrachism, Neoplatonism, and medieval political theology. In their different but convergent ways, these three discourses describe the cosmos as hierarchical and were useful to the extent that they describe what is desired as a long way off. The first two discourses are of particular interest not only because Elizabeth used them, but also because courtiers used them in their attempts to penetrate her isolation, to address and persuade her.

The first discourse through which Elizabeth structured her inviolability in the 1590s was Petrarchism, which negotiates the relation between subject and audience as the territory to be traveled between desire and consummation.[25] In imitating Petrarch, a male author generally strives both to attain a high position in the cosmic hierarchy through the aestheticized contemplation of the female subject and to attract the notice of his peers and the patronage of his betters. As has long been recognized in studies of Elizabeth's court, Petrarchism provided a ready means of expression for courtiers addressing a queen whose distance was quite real. The extent to which Elizabeth's interests were served by Petrarchist discourse and the ways in which Elizabeth herself used Petrarchism are, however, new subjects.

At Elizabeth's court in the 1590s, the lyric of distance was of distinct service to her self-representation. Of the numerous poetic requests for Elizabeth's favor that helped her maintain her position as the desirable inviolate, none was more witty than John Harington's plea of the mid-1590s that since she had

> . . . read a verse of mine a little since,
> And so pronounst each word, and euery letter,
> Your gracious reeding grac't my verse the better,

she should

> Let my poore Muse your paines thus importune,
> To leaue to read my verse, and read my fortune.[26]

The meanings of "importune" in the sixteenth century were not so much "to request" as "to solicit pressingly or persistently; to beset with petitions; to ask for a thing urgently and persistently" (OED). The politics and the urgency of desiring "love" as material reward in Elizabeth's parsimonious court reside in this word "importune." Harington petitions Elizabeth to look into his verse and, in so doing, to gauge his worth and then tell him the fortune she is willing to grant him as a result. But the final couplet modestly backs away from its own request. Harington displaces his desire to address the queen directly by having his "poore Muse" (instead of himself) "importune" her labor (instead of her). By "labor," he means the "paines" she must take to "read" him. The infinitives "to leaue" and "to read" further displace agency, and his clever play on reading his verse and reading his fortune grants her the power to both read and reject him. These several displacements in the poem's final two lines define the distance between Harington and Elizabeth as a function of her power.

One of Elizabeth's own Petrarchan lyrics emphasizes this self-sufficient distance from her own point of view. Its speaker describes the sheer number of suitors she has rejected as the means to accentuate the isolation created by her virginity—in this poem, as at Elizabeth's court, a condition as physical as it is political. As in Harington's verse, the verb that negotiates the connection between the woman and the prince, the courtier and the woman is "importune."

> When I was fair and young, and favor gracèd me,
> Of many was I sought, their mistress for to be;
> But I did scorn them all, and answered them therefore,
>   "Go, go, go seek some otherwhere!
>   Importune me no more!"
>
> How many weeping eyes I made to pine with woe,
> How many sighing hearts, I have skill to show;
> Yet I the prouder grew, and answered them therefore,
>   "Go, go, go seek some otherwhere!
>   Importune me no more!"[27]

In the next two stanzas, "Venus' son" plucks "her plumes" so that a "change grew in my breast / That neither night nor day since that, I could take any rest." The speaker's unapproachable stance does not, however, alter with her ambiguous regrets. The final stanza, in which she admits, "I did repent that I had said before," still repeats the refrain and, with it, the isolation that gives her the authority to speak so peremptorily. The repetition of "go," the lines' emphatic tone, and the command "Importune me no more" form the boundary between the female sovereign and her suitors. In the queen's life, it was a line that frequently had to be redrawn: Lady Essex reported that one day, after hearing several petitions from her privy chamber suitors, Elizabeth protested, "What shall I doe with all these that pretend to titles? . . . I am importuned."[28] In her poem, Elizabeth is able simultaneously to control her distance from her courtiers and to construct herself through their amorous gaze because she occupies the position of both author and female subject.

Ann Rosalind Jones observed that women poets in the sixteenth century found that the Petrarchan mode could be "regendered to guarantee the chastity of a woman poet." Because the poetry of male Petrarchans "dramatized involuntary separations from their ladies" as "the occasion for their poems," women found that through Petrarchism they could write from a perspective in which the male's absence "guaranteed the speaker's purity."[29] In Elizabeth's case, I would describe her endeavor as "engendering" rather than "regendering" masculinist discourse, because the queen, as she so often prefers to do, straddles both the masculine and feminine positions, gaining power from both and from her claim to both. Her courtiers' expression of their desires and needs as their "love" for her[30] substantiated her chaste self-possession by emphasizing the distance between them. When the speaker describing the poem's emotions is also the desired female, the gender assignments of Petrarchism are confused as she turns her gaze back across the ever-so-long distance to the males surrounding her, a strategy that restates the distance—the expression of her position in the hierarchy—between her power and that of her suitors.

In examining Elizabeth's verse, we must, as always, exercise caution when reading poetry as biography. But Harington's lines as well as the letter to his wife mentioned earlier recall how Elizabeth and he often read his poems aloud. This suggests that having composed her own verse, Elizabeth would likely have read it publicly, if only to a private audience. If we imagine further that her court audience would be composed of her primary petitioners, then the poem can be read as more than the reification of the gap between the queen and her court. It may be the record of a moment of Elizabeth's public self-representation in the Petrarchan mode that sent a clear if ironic message to her "suitors" to leave her alone.

The second discourse to which Elizabeth increasingly turned in the 1590s was Neoplatonism. Like its closely associated discourse, Petrarchism, Neoplatonism was not created for princes, but for people not possessing direct power. When Sir Thomas Hoby's translation of Baldassare Castiglione's *Book of the Courtier* first became widely available in 1561 and in several subsequent reprints, its Neoplatonist discussions of appropriate court behavior strongly appealed to the male courtier or gentleman who sought empowering conceptualizations of his relatively powerless—even feminized—position in relation to his prince.[31] Castiglione's text, whose "worke" Thomas Sackville's dedicatory sonnet says outshines the "pallace tops" of "royall kinges,"[32] proposes the explicit power of the male courtier to fashion both princes and women at the same time that its dialogue debates the means to gain their favor.[33]

In his own search for self-definition, the courtier's relation to both women and the prince turns on a politicized definition of love. Castiglione, Joan Kelly reflects, "used the love relation as a symbol to convey his sense of political relations."[34] The idealized "stayre" toward heaven that Peter Bembo imagines as the "most sweete bond of the world, a meane betwixt heavenly and earthly thinges" that "with a bountifull temper [sway] bendest the high vertues to the government of the lower" (321), functions aesthetically as a breathtaking vision of human possibility and ideologically as an image of the courtier's ability to use the power relations expressed through love to attain his own desires.

For her courtiers and Elizabeth alike, Neoplatonism became the means to conceptualize the universe as a hierarchy of love that individuals might manipulate to suit themselves. This "love" is a political conception in Neoplatonism that helps explain how love functions as a metaphor for the give-and-take of the patronage system and also how love can be considered synonymous with magic.

In Neoplatonism, the bond of love forms a correspondence among all things, a "common relationship" that allows the equation of love with magic. As Ioan Couliano states, the relation between love and magic depended on the analogous relation between microcosm and macrocosm, the "structure of cooperation" between "the world's parts." Marsilio Ficino writes in his *Commentary on Plato's Symposium on Love* that "from this common relationship is born a common love; from love, a common attraction. And this is the true magic."[35] Extending Couliano's discussion of the relation between love and magic in Italian Neoplatonism to include its implicit political dimension makes it possible to envision the manipulation of the cosmic hierarchy from the middle of the social ladder. In other words, the Neoplatonism of both Castiglione and Ficino suggests that the courtier may control the prince through "love," the representation of their interconnection that he hopes to turn to his advantage.

To Arthur Marotti's ground-breaking discussion of Elizabethan "love poetry as a way of metaphorizing [courtiers'] rivalry with social, economic, and political competitors, converting . . . self-esteem and ambition into love,"[36] I would add that the impetus to discuss personal ambition and complex social relations as "love" derives both from the tradition of courtly love combined with Elizabeth's position as an unmarried female and from Neoplatonism's attempt to codify love as the means to express and attain the courtier's ambition. Elizabeth responded to the social and political relations expressed in the discourses of both Petrarchism and Neoplatonism by using their codes—especially their definition of love—to assert both her interconnection with her subjects and her supremacy and isolation. As John Harington observed after her death, "We did all love hir, for she saide she loved us, and muche wysdome she shewed in thys matter."[37]

Because Elizabeth adapted Neoplatonism to self-representation, her use of the word "love," the "most sweete bond of the world," took on the associations with magic that Marcilio Ficino described in his *Commentary on Love*. Representations of Elizabeth's sovereign Chastity contained the magical assertion (with its distinctly religious overtones) that the queen occupied an intermediary position between God and her subjects as well as between nature and mortals as the means to assert her divine power. And on occasion, she was not simply an intermediary, but pictured as God himself (Figures 19 and 20).

In her representation as a heavenly intermediary, Elizabeth's restructuring of Neoplatonism merges with the third of the discourses to which the Crown turned in the 1590s. Medieval political theology stated the relation between the king and God with an appealing simplicity. Legal conceptions like "the power of the king is the power of God"[38] had appealed to other Tudor monarchs—both Henry VIII and Mary had used them. Early in her reign, Elizabeth only cautiously invoked divine right, a doctrine that at first raised disturbing questions about God's wisdom in choosing a woman and was never popular with her reformist clergy.[39] But the sheer length of Elizabeth's reign, a rising sense of empire attendant on expanding trade and English exploration, together with the "defeat" of the Spanish Armada, made more acceptable the claim that God approved her chastity. As she aged, Elizabeth herself and those who developed her iconography

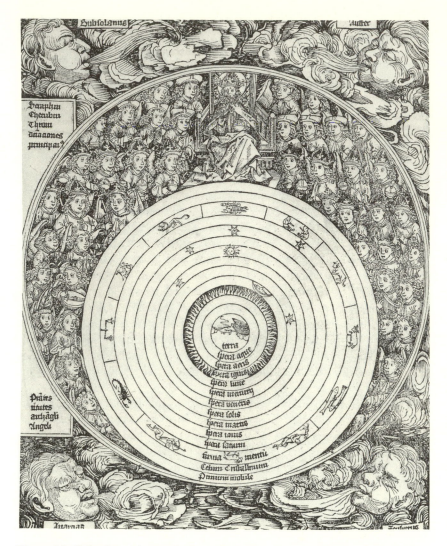

Figure 19. "The Seventh Day." From Hartmann Schedel's *Nuremberg Chronicle* (fifteenth century). God is at the head of the concentric correspondences of the Ptolemaic universe. (British Library)

increasingly claimed Elizabeth's connection with God via her virginity. "Praised be Dianas faire and harmless light," wrote Walter Ralegh in a poem published in *The Phoenix Nest* in 1593. "In heaven Queene she is among the spheares . . . In hir is vertues perfect image cast."[40]

In speeches delivered between 1593 and 1601, Elizabeth politicized her position as intercessor between God and her subjects by concentrating on their loving relationship. Her Latin oration that developed the terms of this love, delivered to the members of Oxford University in 1592, makes clear that "your love for me" is more important than learning. Their love, she explained, "is of such kind as has never been known or heard of in the memory of man. Love of this nature is not possessed by parents; it happens not among friends, no, not even among lovers." Her subjects' love constitutes their political function in the commonwealth: "It is of this that your services consist, and they are of such kind I would think they would be eternal, if only I were eternal."[41]

In her final speech concluding the brief Parliament of 1601, Elizabeth made it clear that if love formed the connection between herself and her subjects, her chastity defined her as necessarily remote from them. She addressed the members as her "louing subiectes" who had "so fully and

Figure 20. "Sphaera Civitatis." Preface to John Case's *Sphaera Civitatis* (1588). From the position of God, Elizabeth embraces political virtues that parallel those of the Ptolemaic universe. (Huntington Library RB 46631)

effectuallie deuoted yor vnchangable affection"—in particular, by granting her needed subsidy on condition that she reform the system of monopolies. "I haue diminished my owne revenewe that I might add to yor securitie," she reminded them, and continued, "and [I have] bene content to be a tapere of trewe virgin waxe to wast my self and spend my life that I might giue light and comfort to those that liue vnder me."[42] Her self-representation as a candle of virgin wax[43]—that is, pure white—manages simultaneously to suggest the power of her chastity, which enables her to shed light; her height above "those that liue vnder me," which her chastity helps create; and the relation between the chaste queen and her subjects, which was necessary for their continued light and warmth. In claiming from her people a sacred, binding love that acknowledges her chaste isolation, the queen creates herself as a figure standing, as in the Ditchley portrait of 1592 (Figure 21), between England and God.

Spenser and the Definitions of Chastity

These larger-than-life images—the candle of virgin wax towering above her subjects, Elizabeth as the divine intermediary in the Ditchley portrait—formed the Crown's response to real and incipient challenges to her authority. The strategies of sequestering her body, representing herself as politically viable through the images of youthful virginity, and distancing herself from her subjects through the discourses of Petrarchism, Neoplatonism, and medieval political theology while using "love" to define connections with her subjects were the means by which she competed for control of her representation in the 1590s.

Among those who challenged her authority by attempting to rewrite these representations was Edmund Spenser.[44] I focus on Spenser because book 3 of *The Faerie Queene* directly addresses Elizabeth's Chastity. In doing so, Spenser focuses on the representation that figured her genuine power over his life. As I have attempted to show, Elizabeth's Chastity allegorized her very real—although always conditional—control of the court and government, a control that gave her the power to deal with other controlling elites like powerful aristocrats and London merchants. Her Chastity was also the representation to which Elizabeth was most vulnerable, because it spotlighted her claims to both male and female attributes in ways that threatened accepted gender distinctions.

Spenser's response to Elizabeth's Chastity is to redefine it according to the patriarchal definition of chastity as "purity from unlawful intercourse" (OED), which assumes that a "chaste" woman acquiesces to the roles first of virginal daughter and then of wife and mother, as defined by the masculinist codes of English law.[45] In redefining Chastity, however, book 3 unleashes the frustrations and violence that Elizabeth's material and discursive strategies had generated in Spenser and in figures as diverse as Roland Whyte, Philip Sidney, and the Earl of Essex. The result of these conflicting definitions of chastity is that book 3's concluding cantos feature a figure of

Figure 21. The Ditchley portrait (ca. 1592), by Marcus Gheeraerts the Younger. Elizabeth stands on Oxfordshire. The verse cannot be read in its entirety, but reads in part "The prince of light. The Sonne." (National Portrait Gallery)

Elizabeth that is simultaneously imprisoned, entertained with spectacle and poetry, and raped.

Before entering Spenser's text, let us consider these conflicting definitions of chastity in more detail in order to understand what is at stake. Elizabeth's own redefinition of chastity was necessarily shaky. In asserting that Elizabeth's position as a magical or divinely approved virgin had imposing precedents in the Hebrew, classical, and Marian traditions, her images did not succeed in silencing other points of view, nor did they form a dominant discourse, especially since their conceptualizations of Elizabeth's sexuality ran disturbingly counter to prevalent definitions of the feminine.[46] The queen's conception of herself as an autonomous female body was, Maureen Quilligan found, at odds with the social construction of the female: "The queen's virginity conflicts with the broad sweep of the Protestant redefinition of the family—and therefore of women and of sexuality itself."[47] The conviction expressed in Castiglione, Vives, and derivative texts like *The Mothers Counsell, or Liue within Compasse* that "if chastity be once lost, there is nothing left prayseworthy in a woman" is founded on a desire to ensure bloodlines and to contain women in socially sanctioned roles. The opposite of Chastity, *The Mothers Counsell* makes clear, is Wantonesse, which "maketh a woman covet beyond her power; to act beyond her nature, and to die before her time."[48] Death threatens unchaste women because "wantonesse" is defined as a woman's seeking alternative self-definition "beyond her nature."

"Chastity" was so central a term in describing men's desire to control women's behavior that by the end of the sixteenth century the social institution of marriage may be said to rest on it. The ideology of the companionate marriage based on lawful chastity and articulated in Erasmus's *Colloquies* was not only emergent but even dominant by the close of the century. Margo Todd and Valerie Wayne, who wrote more specifically about the discourse of marriage in England, elucidated the importance of this ideology.[49] Long before Elizabeth's iconography raised the challenge of self-possessed female virginity, the colloquy *Courtship* attempted to redefine it. When Maria, the text's young woman, argues for her virginity and against marriage by protesting, "But they say chastity is a thing most pleasing to God," Pamphilus, who wants to marry her, firmly incorporates the sanctity of chastity into the bond of matrimony: "And therefore, I want to marry a chaste girl, to live chastely with her. It will be more a marriage of minds than of bodies. We'll reproduce for the state; we'll reproduce for Christ." Such bondage as exists in marriage is like "your soul imprisoned in your body . . . like a little bird in a cage." One might "ask him if he desires to be free. He'll say no, I think. Why? He's willingly confined."[50]

Spenser's poet uses similar assurances in the *Amoretti*, particularly in sonnet 65:

> Sweet be the bands, the which true love doth tye,
>   without constraynt or dread of any ill:

> the gentle birde feeles no captivity
> within her cage, but sings and feeds her fill.

Through her captivity the male speaker attempts to reassure his fiancé that "The doubt which ye misdeeme, fayre love, is vaine, / That fondly feare to loose your liberty"; for in such a marriage,

> . . . simple truth and mutuall good will
> seekes with sweet peace to salve each others wound.
> There fayth doth fearlesse dwell in brasen towre,
> and spotlesse pleasure builds her sacred bowre.

Similiar expressions abound during this period. The Catholic William Byrd's song of marital chastity suitable for wedding parties asserts, for example,

> Sound is the knot, that Chastity hath tied,
> Sweet is the music, Unity doth make,
> Sure is the store, that Plenty doth provide.[51]

The question of the control of female sexuality that resides in the definition of chastity is central to Spenser's probe of its meanings, a probe that took place within an ongoing inquiry into the most appropriate representations and roles for the queen. Despite all of Elizabeth's efforts to use her virginal chastity as the means to explain and to exercise power, at court and in the literature that reproduces the language of the court, chastity underwent constant if sometimes subtle redefinition. In particular, court entertainments offered an opportunity to assert and appropriate the queen's represented body in relation to the political moment.

At Kenilworth, the rescue of the Lady of the Lake from the lustful Sir Bruse sans Pitie emphasized Chastity as a cosmological force, with the queen's rescue the act of a mediator between heaven and earth, nature and humanity. The entertainment that Philip Sidney helped compose, *The Four Foster Children of Desire* (1581), in turn appropriated this cosmological association to make the Protestant faction's political point, that Elizabeth's virtue precluded her marrying the Duke of Anjou—when Anjou's ambassadors were in the audience.[52] The message contained in *The Four Foster Children* reminds us of two important aspects of Elizabeth's iconographic Chastity. First, her Chastity was conceivably the property of any individual or group that found it useful, and second, the images of Elizabeth that these entertainments enacted were not only for her. Narratives of rescue, in both the pageants and *The Faerie Queene*—narratives constructed by males in part for a male audience and not just for the queen—are also narratives of captivity. These and other similar entertainments at Woodstock and Bissam construct Chastity as powerful and independent through a repeating narrative in which one Chastity figure delivers another.

Although book 3, cantos 11 and 12, of *The Faerie Queene* is part of a

lengthy poem written far from the court in Ireland in the 1580s, it corresponds in several ways to the court entertainments enacting Chastity's
rescue by Chastity. Like court spectacles, many of which were published,
and Spenser's first great courtly work, *The Shepheardes Calender* (1579), it
simultaneously addresses the queen, the courtiers surrounding her, and a
larger public audience. In writing *The Faerie Queene* as an allegorical romance cast as a stupendous court entertainment—rather like the Kenilworth entertainments and the Accession Day tournaments combined—
and in appropriating the Chastity primarily developed in the pageant genre
of the rescue of Chastity by Chastity, Spenser not only claimed the queen
and her court as his subject and his audience, but openly participated in
that most courtly activity, the competition to redefine the queen's iconography.

The allegory organizing the House of Busirane, and indeed all of book
3, as Spenser specifies, is Chastity, an allegory whose variant meanings
record the struggle for representation between a queen and her courtiers.
Spenser's text is also courtly in that it screens the poet's own concerns with
his praise.[53] In fact, all of book 3, particularly its final two cantos describing the captivity and rape of Amoret at the hands of Busirane, provides a
text through which to examine the ongoing attempt to confine the queen's
self-sufficient Chastity within male control—if not the control of a father
or husband, a courtier or faction, then the control of a masculinist poetics
formulated through the conventions of humanism, Petrarchism, and Neoplatonism.[54]

Spenser's exploration of the range of policy encoded in Chastity assumes
his reader's knowledge of its court forms. From the outset, book 3 plays
against the reader's familiarity with court-defined Chastity, as Spenser first
asserts and then denies the queen's correspondence with Britomart. Book
3's title, "The Third Booke of the Faerie Qveene Contayning, The Legend
of Britomartis. Or of Chastitie," stands juxtaposed with the proem's opening stanza about Elizabeth's Chastity, implying at least at the outset that
Britomartian Chastity directly corresponds to the queen's and that the
poem will observe the forms of court Chastity. These first lines seem to
make Chastity's whereabouts explicit: Elizabeth is the source of the Faery
virtue. Yet in the following lines addressed to his queen, the speaker asks a
puzzling question:

> It falles me here to write of Chastity,
>   That fairest vertue, farre aboue the rest;
>   For which what needs me fetch from *Faery*
>   Forreine ensamples, it to haue exprest?
>   Sith it is shrined in my Soueraines brest,
>   And form'd so liuely in each perfect part,
>   That to all Ladies, which haue it profest,
>   Need but behold the pourtraict of her hart,
> If pourtrayd it might be by any liuing art. (3.proem.1)

For the speaker to ask himself the question "What needs me fetch from *Faery*/Forreine ensamples, it to haue exprest?" is to ask: Why create a Britomart, or other figures of Chastity, when I have sovereign Chastity? Why, indeed, if the "pourtraict of her hart" is sufficient? In asking, the speaker points to the discrepancy between sovereign Chastity and the Faery virtue, between the sovereign Chastity—militant, compelling but unapproachable, as repellant as inspirational—and a vulnerable, male-assaulted and -protected virtue repeatedly realized in the poem.

The proem's playful identification of Faery Chastity with Elizabeth and its failure to explain why Spenser needs the "forreine ensamples" of Chastity for his poem provide a canceled association through which Britomart acquires all the regal, virtuous, and court-validated qualities necessary for an entertainment. At the same time, Britomart remains Spenser's creation, subject to an exploration of the sexuality implicit in either form of Chastity.[55] It is not Spenser's project to answer his question openly, as he works within and also alters the meanings of Elizabeth's Chastity.

As book 3 progresses, it becomes evident that Britomart's self-sufficiency is of the regal kind, if only insofar as it continually inspires attempts to control her. She appears in the first canto as an admirably independent figure who defeats the previous book's problem hero, Sir Guyon, and then six of Malecasta's knights. Nevertheless, Britomart is a figure whose femininity exists within social prescriptions, as figured in the male threats surrounding her during her search for an eventual mate. The Britomartian narrative of book 3 moves in and out of courtly Chastity, skirting allegorical dangers as well as the queen's active displeasure, simultaneously nodding at Elizabeth's independence and affirming her assailable sexuality. Britomart triumphs in battle against Malecasta's knights, only to be exposed to Malecasta's attempt to share her bed, after which Gardante gores her side.[56]

Faced with these assaults, Britomart does not possess—as does Thomas Churchyard's 1578 figure of an autonomous, militant Chastity played for the queen—a "heart of stone/That none can wound, nor pearce by any meane."[57] Instead, Spenser's vulnerable Chastity is attacked in Castle Ioyeous and again in the House of Busirane. It is important to note that even an unsuccessful assault transforms the royal iconography. Through analogous threats to other female figures like Florimell, whom Proteus confines in the sea, the text establishes Britomart's vulnerability as part of its redefinition of Chastity. Belphoebe herself, the "mirror" of Elizabeth, "To whom in . . . spotlesse fame/Of chastitie, none liuing may compair" (3.5.54), on perceiving Timias's wound knew "unwonted smart" when "the point of pitty perced through her tender hart" (3.5.30).

The landscape of book 3 presents an array of youthful, procreative Chastities. The prankish exposure of Britomart indignant in her nightclothes gives way to the celebration of fertility in the Garden of Venus and Adonis. Even through chaste Belphoebe, as Louis Montrose demonstrates in his analysis of Belphoebe's vulnerability to the reader's gaze, Spenser "repeatedly insinuates a current of sensuality and erotic arousal into its encomium of militant chastity."[58] Florimell's chaste wanderings succeed Venus's sensuality, but are interrupted by the lustful Geauntesse Argante. Argante, while carrying the Squire of Dames to sexual slavery, is forced to drop him when Pallidine, the other female knight in book 3, intervenes (7.52). Like the other narratives, including that of Malbecco and Hellenore's marriage of jealousy and adultery, the Squire's quest to find three hundred women too "chaste" to yield to his wooing continues the book's quest to define chastity in terms of fertility and morality. The final cantos' manipulation of Elizabeth's allegorized sexuality into its captivity and abuse simply provides the definition of chastity toward which these episodes point.

Love, Magic, and the Female Audience

What about Britomart, the titular subject of book 3? Britomart's strengths and behavior allude to Elizabeth, but these strengths are perpetually undermined by circumstance. Although Britomart seems to act freely, she is not as self-possessed as her militant figuring of Chastity suggests. Even as Britomart retains the advantages of self-defense, disguise, and mobility inherent in dressing up as a knight, her strength is mitigated by the attacks on her person. The reader also knows that her taking up arms is no final evidence of autonomy, but is, rather, the means to find her future husband, Artegal, whom she has seen in Merlin's mirror. When Britomart discovers this mirror registering the figure of her destined mate in her father's closet, the poet-narrator becomes a matchmaker, magically producing an appropriate object for her desire.

The poet as magician is certainly an implied role for Spenser in his relation to the queen. Christopher Highley wrote that through Merlin the powerful poet-magician, "Spenser covertly advertis[es] his utility to Elizabeth," offering his poem to her in the same way in which Merlin offers his "glassie globe" to Britomart as the means to read herself (3.2.21).[59] Book 3's proem, for example, ends by offering, even insisting, that Elizabeth look into the mirror of his poem in order to see how he has figured her: "Ne let his fairest *Cynthia* refuse, / In mirrours more then one her selfe to see" (proem.5). Unlike the more tentative lines by John Harington, which ask the queen to look into his verse and read his fortune, Spenser's lines narrow the gap between his sovereign and himself. By inviting his female audiences to step close enough to read their own narratives in his mirrors, Spenser declares his supervision of the figurative past, present, and future in which they situate their lives. Spenser shares Merlin's power, just as Merlin expresses his, and the power is considerable: Through his "Magicke," Merlin gained "more insight, / Then euer him before or after liuing wight"(3.3.11). Spenser also assumes the role of poet-magician in sharing his insight with his female audiences through the mirror that his words create. Thus the poet asserts his ability to control subject or audience through the correspondences among words, pictures, and love itself, correspondences figured in his elaborate allegories of Elizabeth's allegories. Spenser places himself as the creator of a web of echoes and analogues between figures and narratives, the text and the court, a cosmos like Peter Bembo's in which love, "the sweete bond of the world," can be invoked as a force that "bendest the high vertues to the government of the lower" and so allows him to address his queen through his figures of her.

Thus Spenser as poet-magician recalls the Neoplatonic conception of love as a binding force consonant with magic. As has long been recognized in Spenser scholarship, the poet was deeply indebted to Marcilio Ficino, possibly Giordano Bruno, and other Neoplatonists like Castiglione for his Neoplatonic theories of the ascent of love and related theories regarding generation, friendship, numerology, demonology, psychology, and the soul. Spenser's assumption of the role of poet-magician is in many ways an expansion and exploration of Neoplatonist theories of the relation between love and magic like those of Marcilio Ficino. Spenser, however, was not a programmic thinker, and his Neoplatonism is heavily influenced by English folklore and his own sociopolitical situation.

Spenser's debt to Neoplatonism in general and to Ficino in particular is visible in book 3, canto 6, of *The Faerie Queene,* in which the world is perpetually created through the lovemaking of Venus and Adonis, and in the *Amoretti* and *The Fowre Hymns,* which celebrate the ascent of the soul through love. Like Elizabeth in her portraiture and speeches, Spenser repeatedly situates himself as controlling the forces of Neoplatonic correspondence. Instead of creating a love marked by distance, a love made possible by a virginity that situated Elizabeth in a divine or semidivine position of unapproachable authority, Spenser acts through language to naturalize the more dominant ideology defining female chastity in terms of marriage and human reproduction. His Neoplatonism routinely deviates from and elaborates that of Italian humanism while using its frequently homoerotic imagery to picture the procreative bliss of a companionate marriage.

The first stanza of book 3's third canto, which features Merlin's encounter with Britomart, invokes love as a Neoplatonic force:

> Most sacred fire, that burnest mightily
>   In liuing brests, ykindled first aboue,
>   Emongst th'eternall spheres and lamping sky,
>   And thence pourd into men, which men call Loue. (3.3.1)

Because of love's power, particularized as the "dread darts" planted in Britomart, she will seek her mate, Artegal, in order that Elizabeth will some day spring from their "two loynes" (3.3.3). In sum, book 3 joins eros and magic in ways that empower the poet-magician while covertly disempowering the political love and the iconographic magic commanded by the queen.

What Britomart sees in the magic mirror—placed in the textual "mirror" that Spenser has offered his queen in the poem—is her destiny as a married

Chastity naturalized through the will of God. "Eternall prouidence," Merlin tells her, has "guided thy glaunce, to bring his will to pas." Speaking as the voice of that providence, Merlin enjoins Britomart, "Therefore submit thy wayes vnto his will,/And do by all dew meanes thy destiny fulfill" (3.3.24). Merlin's use of language to control Britomart's destiny recalls the importance of the arts in Ficino, through which "men charm and win" the beloved "through the powers of eloquence and the measures of songs, as if by certain incantations."[60] Language in this congruent logic is a means to use the relationships among all things. Britomart is calmed by Merlin's explanation of her relation with Artegal, Spenser's narrator tells us, because his "words are like to Magick art" (3.2.15).

If Spenser-as-poet and Merlin correspond at some points and, as James Nohrnberg pointed out, Spenser and Archimago coincide to some degree, what is the relation between Spenser and Busirane? There is a particularly nefarious side to magic in book 3's final cantos that prompts an examination of the implied connection between Spenser and its less beneficent poet-magician, Busirane.[61]

In reading the end of book 3, literary critics have long sought to illuminate the source of Busirane's house, the masque, and Amoret's ordeal.[62] In what proved to be an enduring reading, Thomas P. Roche, Jr., concluded in 1961 that the violence directed against Amoret formed "an objectification of Amoret's fear of sexual love in marriage." There have been many other suggestions: In 1970, Maurice Evans read book 3 as a narrative about "Britomart's growth to sexual maturity" and her encounter with Busirane as central to this growth. Harry Berger's complex readings have undergone subtle redefinition; one article first published in 1971 centers on "the masculine mind wounded first by desire and then by jealousy and envy," as allegorized in Busirane. In 1983, though, Robin Wells saw Scudamour as responsible for the violence "because it is his own lack of faith in her [Amoret's] ability to withstand temptation which is the real cause of her torture." Most of the criticism in the 1980s saw Spenser as using Busirane to expose the violence and misogyny in Petrarchism, but envisaged Spenser as standing outside the horror, not implicated by its use of court structures and discourse, its attack on female figures openly linked with the queen, and its attempts to tell us that in the end no violence has actually been committed.

One way to address directly the text's representation of the feminine while resolving the issue of agency is to contemplate Busirane as the figure of all the displaced frustration and violence that Spenser feels toward his queen. Book 3's narrative of Chastity authorizes this displacement of the queen's sovereign virtue by bringing together Britomart and Amoret, two figures whom the text suggests we associate with Elizabeth, to be the audience of Busirane's brutal enactment of the relation between the poet-magician and the feminine. As such, the Busirane episode anticipates the repeated assault or undermining of the figures of the queen in Spenser's later books, including the much-discussed proem to book 4, in which

Spenser expresses his frustrations toward Elizabeth's court in general and possibly Burghley in particular. Judith Anderson stated that "books IV to VI are bedeviled by recurrent images of revilement and public infamy. . . . Most of these glance at the Queen, the Queen's court, or events impossible to disassociate from the Queen."[63]

Amoret, too, is a figure for Elizabeth because she is the twin of the Amazon Belphoebe; Amoret, Belphoebe, and Britomart "mirror" the queen's "rare chastitee" (3.proem.5). The relation between Britomart and Amoret, figures of Elizabeth who also become figures of procreative chastity, epitomizes the complex interactions that Spenser's text achieves in the process of redefining Chastity. Britomart is in the midst of Merlin's quest when she encounters Amoret, imprisoned in the house possessed by Busirane, in which she witnesses and participates in scenes that further set the seal of lawful Chastity upon her. In allegorical narratives and the successive tableaux of figures that compose them, the meanings embodied in one figure are amplified and subtly altered by its juxtaposition with others.

What happens when Britomart and Amoret come together? To the extent that they participate in the queen's chastity, they are targets. And to the extent that they participate in the patriarchal definition of chastity, they are vulnerable. In the House of Busirane, Britomart's role is to rescue Amoret, the captive of the poet-magician Busirane. At first, Britomart seems strong and Amoret seems weak. But, in fact, they are equally vulnerable. Thus for a time, in canto 12, stanzas 33–38, the distinction between Britomart and Amoret is not complete. Busirane's wounding of both Britomart and Amoret suggests their kinship as victims of the violence they exist to view.

The profusion of singular feminine pronouns referring one moment to Amoret and the next to Britomart serve to conflate them into a single unstable feminine figure who, whether rescuer or rescued, is also an unwilling audience. When, for example, Amoret prevents Britomart from killing Busirane because only he can undo the spell that keeps a knife in her heart—the only time she speaks—the two females become one as they listen to his voice: Busirane read

> . . . and measur'd many a sad verse,
> That horror gan *the virgins* hart to perse,
> And *her* faire lockes vp stared stiffe on end,
> Hearing him those same bloudy lines reherse. (36, my emphasis)

The "virgins" and "her" signify Britomart or Amoret, as well as Britomart and Amoret. Although lack of familiarity with the spell may explain why Britomart's hair stands on end, "she" hears the "same" lines—and only Amoret could have heard the spell before.

Like the Elizabethan court spectacles featuring Chastity, the House of Busirane defines the chaste captive and the chaste rescuer by pairing them: The captive and the rescuer may seem to fulfill opposite roles, but in this device neither can exist without the other or as the other. The very similarities between Britomart and Amoret with which book 3 concludes serve to revise the royal claim to female independence by locking up Amoret, or the marriageable form of Chastity, and sending Britomart, the other embodiment of marriageable Chastity, to her rescue. In this way, the representations of the queen's independent Chastity present in similar court spectacles as powerfully feminine, even cross-gendered or androgynous, are transmuted into the two fertile, marriageable figures of Amoret and Britomart.

Because in allegorical terms Britomart and Amoret are, for the moment, mutually constitutive and even symbiotic, the triangle they form with the poet-magician who addresses them becomes especially worthy of attention. Busirane rapes and tortures Amoret—the male threat exposes the female as vulnerable—and until the moment when she acts, Britomart must watch. Thus the text's violence exists in its relation with its author, and it is difficult to distinguish that elusive poet-magician, Spenser, from his creation, Busirane; its narrator, who provides and withholds descriptions and interpretation; and its audience, whether Britomart, Amoret, Elizabeth I, or ourselves. The text's exhibition of the poet's power to turn the celebration and entertainment of his audience into captivity, and the rhetoric of desire into rape, results in a horror so deep, an anxiety about the relation among sexuality, persuasion, and control so pervasive, that the text attempts to dissociate Spenser from Amoret's abuse.

The Topography of Threat and Rape

Threat, rape, and captivity are the interconnected strategies that Spenser's text uses to enforce its definition of Chastity. The threat of violence had always been implicit in attempts to represent the queen's virtues to herself—from the device titled the Seate of Worthie Governance in her coronation entry, which insinuated that if Elizabeth did not conform to the city's ideas of virtue, she could expect to lose her "seat," to Leicester's desire to enact his queen's virtue as requiring his protection from the rapist Sir Bruse sans Pitie, to the assumption underlying *The Four Foster Children of Desire* that only Elizabeth's chaste beauty could disarm the threatening lances of the knights.

As Britomart's entry takes her into the world of women imprisoned by the masculinist structures of desire, the House of Busirane containing Britomart and Amoret locates the male threat spatially. In effect, the text's first assault on female self-possession resides in the topography of tyranny and pain that Britomart must traverse to reach Amoret. Busirane's three rooms open sequentially, like Elizabeth's presence chambers at Hampton Court (Figure 22), described in 1598 as "adorned with tapestry of gold, silver, and velvet, in some of which were woven history pieces."[64] If we also consider the political implications of the verb "love," then the enter-

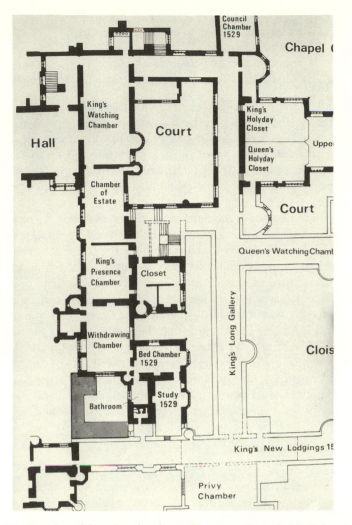

Figure 22. The plan of the privy chamber at Hampton Court in 1547 showing the presence and privy chambers opening into one another. (Copyright Simon Thurley)

tainment that Spenser's poet-magician presents to his two Elizabeth figures can be said to occur in his own courtly territory of presence and privy chambers.

The first room is hung with tapestries illustrating Jove's adventurous metamorphoses in which the full extent of Cupid's power turns on the orthographic pun of Iove/love. The speaking pictures show that "Iove" dominates the cosmos to the extent that the social hierarchy of humankind collapses beneath his power:

> Kings Queenes, Lords Ladies, Knights & Damzels gent
>> Were heap'd together with the vulgar sort,
>> And mingled with the raskall rablement,
>> Without respect of person or of port,
>> To shew Dan *Cupids* powre and great effort. (11.46)

The bloody borders surrounding and uniting these stories of gods and men suggest the violence existing in the conception of love. Seeing the house's courtly tapestries, friezes, and statuary takes Britomart ever closer to the poet-magician composing them as she moves through the house whose artwork conveys pain and whose structures—the frames, the walls, the verse itself—communicate the message that love is a form of possession and control.

When the inner door of the third room flies open to reveal a processional masque (for a contemporary example, see the wedding masque of Cupid from *The Life of Sir Henry Unton* [Figure 23]), the entertainment presented for our view physically confines the central female, Amoret, among the animated forms of masculinist love poetry, the courtiers of a horrific court that articulates the relation between patronage and hierarchy as "love." Two by two the courtly players step forth—Fancy and Desyre, Doubt and Daunger, Feare and Hope, Dissemblance and Suspect, Grief and Fury, Displeasure and Pleasance. The first six couples emerge slowly enough for the narrator to provide a lengthy description of each costume's allusive iconography, although he fails to explicate the scene as a whole. Trailing behind the six couples, defined by their physical and metaphoric proximity, walks Amoret, the centerpiece of the masque and, as we later discover, the interior audience of its rhetoric. She holds her heart in a basin, removed and pierced.

> Her brest all naked, as net iuory,
>> Without adorne of gold or siluer bright,
>> Wherewith the Craftesman wonts it beautify,
>> Of her dew honour was despoyled quight,
>> And a wide wound therein (O ruefull sight)
>> Entrenched deepe with knife accursed keene,
>> Yet freshly bleeding forth her fainting spright,
>> (The worke of cruell hand) was to be seene,
> That dyde in sanguine red her skin all snowy cleene.
>
> At that wide orifice her trembling hart
>> Was drawne forth, and in siluer basin layd,
>> Quite through transfixed with a deadly dart,
>> And in her bloud yet steeming fresh embayd. (12.20–21)

The masque's "pourtraict of her hart" is repeated on the next night, as it has been for the past seven months and would have been on the following night. But before the masque concludes a second time, Britomart dispels

Figure 23. Processional wedding masque similar to that described in Spenser's *Faerie Queene* (book 3, cantos 11–12). Detail from *The Life of Sir Henry Unton* (ca. 1590). (National Portrait Gallery)

the players by striding into the third room. There Britomart finds the "real" figure of Amoret, whose captivity has been effected through the love metaphors embodied in the masque:

> . . . both [her] hands
> Were bounden fast, that did her ill become,
> And her small wast girt round with yron bands,
> Vnto a brasen pillour, by the which she stands. (3.12.30)

Her breast is cut open, and instead of being in a basin, her heart here is pierced but unremoved, because the Amoret of the inner room has resisted being persuaded or "moved." In a moment of insight rare in these cantos, the narrator explains that Busirane has been writing these pageants—the tapestries, the musicians and their lay, the masquers, the house itself—in the blood flowing from Amoret's wound.

> And her before the vile Enchaunter sate,
>   Figuring straunge characters of his art,
>   With liuing bloud he those characters wrate,
>   Dreadfully dropping from her dying hart,
>   Seeming transfixed with a cruell dart,
>   And all perforce to make her him to loue. (3.12.31)

Like Merlin, also an "Enchaunter" (3.3.17) who writes "straunge characters" (3.3.14), the poet-magician Busirane creates his spell to instill certain pictures in his audience. The picture created for Britomart and Elizabeth is Busirane's suit, here effected as the rape of a female through the spell of words written in her blood.

The assertion that Busirane tortures Amoret, "and all perforce to make her him to loue," has been largely ignored in interpreting Amoret's situation, although it provides the narrative explanation for this house, these pictures, this masque, and Amoret's pain. Just as Harington loves Elizabeth, Busirane loves Amoret and writes with her blood his rape of her, the processional masque with herself at the center. The narrative's explanation is only the place to start tracing the origins of this horror. Larger questions about the need for this violence exist, as the text itself recognizes, if only to pose them at the beginning of the Busirane episode.

"So cruelly to pen": Denying Rape and Having It, Too

To the extent that anything may be said to begin in *The Faerie Queene*, the House of Busirane originates in Britomart's discovery of Scudamour, who is bewailing the absence of values in this corner of Faeryland.

> If good find grace, and righteousnesse reward,
>   Why then is *Amoret* in caytiue band,
>   Sith that more bounteous creature neuer far'd
>   On foot, vpon the face of liuing land?
>   Or if that heauenly iustice may withstand
>   The wrongfull outrage of vnrighteous men,
>   Why then is *Busirane* with wicked hand
>   Suffred, these seuen monethes day in secret den
> My Lady and my loue so cruelly to pen? (3.11.10)

As in book 3's proem, the speaker's unanswered question reveals problems that the text subsequently mystifies: Why a victim? Who permits this suffering, this penning? Who holds the "pen"—the pun signaling the relation among authorship, penis, and captivity?[65]

The holder of the pen was once literally Edmund Spenser, whose text simultaneously recognizes and denies, in the words of Lynn Higgins and Brenda Silver, that "the politics and the aesthetics of rape are one."[66] It is all too easy to accept the opportunities that the text offers us for forgetting what we are told happens. The scene of Amoret's rape that we observe with Britomart attempts to enforce several modes of reading that help ensure erasure, including innocence, ignorance, and denial. Britomart takes up Scudamour's quest for Amoret and seems to be one figure in some kind of control. Obliged, however, to rescue a passive version of herself, she is not interested in answering such questions. As the text presents her, Britomart never understands what she encounters—for all her "ridling skill" and "commune wit" (3.11.54), she is "dismayd" when at the conclusion of book 3 the House of Busirane "vanisht vtterly" (3.12.42). Britomart's incomprehension is crucial to book 3's strategy: Her maidenly Chastity is defined in part through her ignorance of the threat from a weapon-wielding male.

Not only do the devices find in Britomart a naive audience, but they simultaneously separate the narrator—Spenser's most immediate voice— from full comprehension of Busirane's work. At the same time, however, the narrator possesses knowledge of the most intimate details of the horror. The narrator's ignorance bears examining because the closer Spenser's narrator comes to Spenser's bloody poet, the less explication we receive. As Paul Alpers describes him, Spenser's narrator is particularly unstable throughout *The Faerie Queene*: Although "we know this is a narration because we sense the presence of a narrator; nevertheless, we cannot assume that he is a dramatically consistent figure."[67] Consistent or not, the narrator usually provides the moral valence or actual explication of events in *The Faerie Queene,* although such explanations tend to complicate rather than clarify. In this way, Spenser's narrator fulfills a function identical to the role played by the explicator of a pageant.

As important as the comprehension of allegorical devices is to Elizabethan spectacle, it is the narrator (in pageantry, often called the poet) who determines the range of possible interpretations of any given allegory. The narrator supplements the device's own interpretive mechanisms—its correspondence among pictorial, verbal, and musical elements—with his own explication. His glosses form what an ethnographer would term "actor explications," explanations from within the ideology of the pageant's producers. The semi-omniscient, heterodiegetic narrator of canto 11, carefully reporting to us what the figures in the murals say, becomes the diegetic narrator of canto 12, standing so close to the masque that he can provide only a confused view of its conclusion without commenting on its confusing but unmistakably violent figures.

In the third room, we discover that the narrator's ignorance of Busirane's masque is part of the text's denial that the rape actually occurs, because he is suddenly privy to a great deal of detail. For example, once the spell on Amoret is reversed, he tells us that Amoret is now fully restored. The "cruell steele, which thrild her dying hart, / Fell softly forth" and

> . . . the wyde wound, which lately did dispart
> Her bleeding brest, and riuen bowels gor'd,
> Was closed vp, as it had not bene bor'd.

We are told that she is "as she were neuer hurt, was soone restor'd," although she is considerably weakened by the experience: "when she felt her selfe to be vnbound, / And perfect hole, prostrate she fell vnto the ground" (3.12.38).[68]

The happy ending suggests that the narrator is removed from the action he describes. But is this the case? The narrator's language continues Busirane's cruelties even as they supposedly end, by describing Amoret's violated body in terms that are less figuratively a rape, more like an actual penetration than any we have yet read. Her "riuen bowells" were "gor'd" and the opening to her heart was "bor'd." Thus the stanza describing the restoration of Amoret's body provides still another report of rape.

The narrator in fact provides three descriptions, each different enough from the others to constitute a separate rape. The instability created by these versions works to confuse the horror if not erase it. Not only do these descriptions make it difficult to establish what is happening to Amoret, but the second and third accounts point out that the real horror is located in the previous image instead of in the present. The first Amoret figure we see is the female in the masque, holding her pierced heart in a basin. We discover that she is a projection of the second Amoret, who is tied up. The second Amoret's heart is also pierced, but because of her loyalty to her future husband, at least it has not been removed. Once healed, this second Amoret becomes the third Amoret, who is made a "perfect hole" so that, we are told, the third and most brutal description of her violation no longer exists.

After Amoret's release to fall at the feet of Britomart, whom she assumes is a male, what the narrator includes and represses continues to suggest his complicity. Rather than excoriate Busirane, Spenser allows him to escape both retribution and the poem itself, because although Britomart chains him with the same chain he used to control Amoret, the poet-magician simply disappears from the poem. The way that Spenser's narrator tells the story with a mix of ignorance and lurid detail is part of a cultural and literary pattern in which rape is both obsessively inscribed and obsessively erased.[69] Despite the attempted disconnection between Spenser and his narrator, the narrator's ignorance originates in Spenser's need both to enforce the meaning of lawful chastity and to deny how closely it conspires in rape.[70]

Even beyond book 3, Spenser continues to display his affiliation with the rape through his narrator in terms revealing rape's centrality to his masculinist conceptions of chastity and love. The fragments of Amoret's history present in book 4 cannot be read as part of the narrative of book 3 of 1590 because they were written in response to that story. Yet book 4 repeatedly returns to Amoret's story in ways that illuminate Spenser's unease with it and reveal a conflicting wish to apologize for Amoret's rape and to recuperate it as part of the operations of love. In canto 1, stanza 1, the narrator observes that no story "more piteous euer was ytold, / Then that of *Amorets* hart-binding chaine" while he "oftentimes doe wish it neuer had bene writ" (4.1.1). In canto 2, he tells us that Busirane captured Amoret during the presentation of his "masque of love" at her wedding banquet. In canto 6, Britomart explains to Scudamour that she rescued Amoret "from enchaunters theft / Her freed, in which ye her all hopelesse left," lines that also recall the rape as a replay of the violence.

The retracing of the incident in canto 7, however, deletes the rapist from Amoret's suffering by conflating him with other agents of "love." In canto 7, Spenser's narrator links Amoret through the "Great God of love" to other female figures who have experienced "love" in different forms. Here love is pictured as necessarily violent for *all* females as the narrator explains that love's "cruell darts" have pierced the hearts of Florimell, Britomart, as well as

> . . . Amoret, whose gentle hart
> Thou [Love] martyrest with sorrow and with smart . . .
> That pittie is to heare the perils, which she tride. (4.7.1–2)

Although Amoret suffers the most, the cause of her suffering and that of Florimell and Britomart is the same: love.

By book 4's tenth canto, Amoret's rape becomes figuratively enmeshed in the story of her own courtship as Scudamour himself describes how he wrested Amoret from the Temple of Venus. The courtship story comes out as Scudamour and Britomart travel together for a time, in full armor as two knights. Scudamour explains to Britomart how he penetrated the perils of Venus's Temple, quieted the fears of its hermaphroditic goddess of generation by showing her his shield with "*Cupid* with his killing bow/And cruell shafts emblazond" (55), and forced Amoret to go with him in spite of her tears and entreaties (mixed with "witching smiles"). After all, as he tells Britomart, man to man,

> . . . sacrilege me seem'd the Church to rob,
> And folly seem'd to leaue the thing vndonne,
> Which with so strong attempt I had begonne. (4.10.53)

As Scudamour justifies the violence necessary to obtain Amoret in language that confuses the distinction between himself and Busirane, his telling of this story to Britomart makes it an analogue of Britomart's viewing of Busirane's rape of Amoret. On her quest to discover the meanings she embodies as Chastity, Britomart once again witnesses Chastity constructed through the association of love, forced courtship, and rape.[71]

Spenser and Busirane

Neither Spenser nor his narrator can openly acknowledge his kinship with Busirane because their own elusive identities as moralizers and definers depend on their maintaining this necessarily unstable distinction.[72] But the language of Busirane the magician is also the language of Spenser, and both rely on the figurative relations between eros and magic to bind their female audience.

The most significant connection between Busirane and Spenser is their similar use of language to "woo" that audience. As Spenser's creature, Busirane has complete access to Spenser's own discourse of love, especially as expressed later in his sonnet sequence, the *Amoretti*. After all, the name of his figure is Amoret, sometimes written Amoretta, a term that George Puttenham uses as synonymous with "court verses."[73] Through Busirane, Spenser literalizes his speaker's avowed task in the *Amoretti* to "lay incessant battery to her heart" (sonnet 14); he forces Amoret to behold him "that all the pageants play, / disguysing diversly [his] troubled wits" (54); and he plays out the desire located in the woman of sonnet 31 to "embrew" "her cruell hands" "in bloody bath."[74] Like the invocation to love that begins canto 3 and love in *An Hymne in Honour of Beautie,* the love in the *Amoretti* is connective, cosmic, and generative.

As in Scudamour's account of seizing Amoret from the Temple of Venus, the sonnets repeatedly suggest that love leads both lover and beloved to physical delight as well as to a higher moral plain. The fear and pain suffered by the woman lays the foundation for future joy. For instance, in sonnet 6, the speaker, in pursuit of the "chaste affects" of lawful female passion, emphasizes much of the same magical language as Busirane does, including "moving" the beloved, the fear and pain of the deep wound, and the pain of love. The speaker is situated in a position of mastery, comforting the male lover (a figure of himself) that in time his attempt to "kindle new desire" will find success.

> Be nought dismayd that her unmoved mind
>   doth still persist in her rebellious pride:
> such loue, not lyke to lusts of baser kynd,
>   the harder wonne, the firmer will abide.
> The durefull Oake, whose sap is not yet dride,
>   is long ere it conceive the kindling fyre:
> but when it once doth burne, it doth divide
>   great heat, and makes his flames to heauen aspire.
> So hard it is to kindle new desire
>   in gentle brest that shall endure for ever:
> deepe is the wound, that dints the parts entire
>   with chast affects, that naught but death can sever.
> Then thinke not long in taking litle paine,
>   to knit the knot, that ever shall remaine.

The masterful voice counsels is what Couliano calls "spiritual manipulation," which in Neoplatonism is "the definition of magic."[75] This kindling of desire is necessary because the female subject is distressingly resistant. By the end of the sonnet sequence, the woman addressed has "deignd so goodly to relent" (sonnet 82), but at this point in the sequence, like Amoret or Elizabeth, she is of "unmoved mind" and "in her rebellious pride" persists in not loving the speaker. How the connection is to be made remains unstated, but is implicit in the metaphoric ascent of the soul through love. The beloved's heart must be "moved," that is, manipulated, through the correspondence among all things that poetry can figure. The connection between the poem and its subject remains uncertain, however, even as the speaker counsels his male audience, ostensibly himself, with a decidedly phallic Neoplatonism: His love won "harder" will "abide" the "firmer"; as firm, presumably, as the "Oake, whose sap is not yet dride," which, conceiving "the kindling fyre," produces flames that aspire to heaven. He expounds the "chast affects" of the "deepe . . . wound" that with "litle paine" becomes the mutual commitment, and the "knit . . . knot" "that naught but death can sever" recalls the humanist assurance that in marriage "perfite love knitteth loving hearties, in an insoluble knot of amitie."[76]

This is the discourse that Spenser assigns to Busirane: the aspiring flames, the "sacred fire" of the cosmos surrounding his house; the deep wound inflicted in the written spell constructing his masque; and her "litle paine" suggesting the necessity of assailing her virginity in order to begin the ascent of love. Both Busirane's and the sonnet speaker's attitudes toward the feminine are founded on the same siege principle, the same doubt that despite their powers they will succeed in mastering the beloved, the same need to claim love as both their method and their rationale.

To a large extent, for both Spenser and Busirane, persuasion of the female is ultimately less important than her textualization. Busirane is a poet whose language amplifies, extends, and literalizes the conventional forms used to record male desires. His allegorical device, his house, is built not from inversions of the moral code, but from extensions of the strategies through which poets addressed and defined their subject. Through their shared language, Spenser is implicated in Busirane's project to literalize the male threat and thus to define chastity in masculinist terms. Conversely, Busirane is implicated in Spenser's translation of Chastity, the allegory created to represent the political power of Elizabeth's sexuality, into an allegory of possession and powerlessness.

The textualization of the female is one of the most effective means to belie the connection between poet and rapist, especially because the text so insistently asks us to separate Spenser and Busirane, to accept their relational instabilities as fixed. The text invites us to participate in the drama of the rape and rescue, to focus on the stage rather than on the man behind the curtain. But to accept the split between Spenser and Busirane—to see one simply as the writer and the other as his villain—is to accept the morality of the narrative of rape, restoration, and rescue instead of recognizing that the narrative exists to validate the morality that created the narrative in the first place. Because violence toward females creates a transparent account whose consequences we are accustomed to accept, it can be difficult to see that both the text's morality and its violence arise from the definition of chastity animated on its pages.

In *The Language of Allegory,* Maureen Quilligan suggests that the relation between Spenser and Busirane lies in Spenser's use of Busirane to call attention to poetic strategies, to parody Petrarchan convention. In her view, Spenser's awareness of the ways that Petrarchan poetics structure love is in part recuperative. When considering the "penning" of Amoret, Quilligan writes, "through a multifaceted pun on one word, 'pen,' which completes an extensive pattern of parodic criticism of Petrarchan conventions, Spenser demonstrates the imprisoning nature of this way of talking about love." In the process, Spenser rises above his imagery, creating an imprisoned Amoret to form part of a "process of redemption," whereby "Britomart learns" "how to speak of love."[77] Two other recent readings of the House of Busirane share the confidence that Spenser remains in control of his materials, that his poetry is something other than himself. Joseph Loewenstein describes both the *Amoretti* and cantos 11 and 12 as testing Spenser's "power to reform Petrarchism," while Lauren Silberman sees Busirane as a "master of Petrarchan sexual politics" whose "mere sadomasochism, the archetypal dualism, is rejected."[78]

Certainly Spenser parodies Petrarchan convention, and the abuse of Amoret seems to constitute such a parody. As Nancy Vickers observed, the fragmentation of the female body is endemic in Petrarchan forms.[79] Although Amoret's pierced heart is particularly extreme, the fragmentation of the female body is part of the larger cultural enterprise not only to control and to define the feminine, but also to define rape in terms of love, love as rape—the definitive threat to women that constructs the ideology of male supremacy.[80] But parodies do not necessarily challenge convention or suggest alternative conceptualizations, especially when situated in book 3's Neoplatonism that so carefully delineates the poet's power to manipulate a correspondent, procreative universe through language.

Like other educated Europeans in the sixteenth century, Spenser in part perceived love through Petrarchan structures, a way of seeing that, because it arrived in England so late, contained an awareness of its own limitations and an ironic sense of its clichés. Instead of standing outside Petrarchism and commenting on it, anti-Petrarchism exists within the tradition that it criticizes, providing the inversions, the paradigmatic "other," that establish the Petrarchan point of view. As Patricia Parker succinctly reminds us, "the vogue for Petrarchan lyric . . . was inseparable from the structure of a politics in which political and erotic codes interpenetrated to a remarkable degree." Because "Petrarchism was not just a lyric but also a dominant cultural form," it created "a politicized lyric structure inscribed within the complex sexual politics of the exceptional rule of a woman in an otherwise overwhelmingly patriarchal culture."[81]

As an Englishman in the late sixteenth century, Spenser was unable to step outside Petrarchan or Neoplatonic ways of figuring the feminine. He was just as likely to point out Petrarchism's defects as he was to use such codes in all seriousness, as when, for example, the narrator comments on Britomart as a "feeble vessell" piloted by Love upon the rocks (3.4.8–10). However much cantos 11 and 12 call attention to the problems of seeing love through Petrarchan forms, the text owes some of its representations of violence to them. Such violence arises in a hierarchy of difference that thwarted all of Elizabeth's courtly poets and Edmund Spenser in particular. This is why the concluding cantos of book 3, like the entire *Faerie Queene,* advocate Petrarch's great lesson, that poetry about women is really about the men who pen them.[82]

Captivity: Essex and the Queen

Spenser's text enforces its definition of lawful chastity through threat and rape and also through captivity. Threats are, after all, intermittent, however much they inspire a nearly continuous female fear, and rape is an action, however long lasting its psychological effects.

Captivity provides a paradigm of control at once temporal and physical for enforcing an entire matrix of approved female behavior, including passivity, silence, modesty, and consignment to a world hidden from the public eye. Recent critical attention has focused on the social marginalization of women during the Renaissance and the rhetorical fragmentation typifying their representation, and Patricia Parker and Peter Stallybrass have discussed women as rhetorical property and patriarchal territory.[83] We forget, though, that women lived within the confines of such masculinist codes as chivalry, poetry, and the law and that these codes were literalized whenever women were physically captured or their activity proscribed. The various forms of imprisonment invite discussion because, as Michel Foucault demonstrated, it is in the practice of confinement that operations of power are most visible; the real or fantasized captivity of women enacts a patriarchal culture's physical and mental proscriptions on even the most powerful female subject.

As I have already stated, captivity was a common structure in court entertainment. It was also a fact of life, as Elizabeth herself, imprisoned by her sister Mary, was frequently reminded. The wooing of Amoret through her captivity in Busirane's verse and her consequent definition as the feminine subject stand in inevitable relation to the discrepancy between the relation of Elizabeth's figuring of gender and those of her society at large. The allegory of Chastity presented in the House of Busirane through verse representations of picture, music, masque, and captivity narrative expose Spenser's attitude toward his female audience in Elizabeth I. Although as Elizabeth was reported to have stated, "no prince is able to fill the insatiable gulf of men's desires,"[84] Spenser's desire for a position of mastery was a projection of his response to the authority she posed as both a woman and his sovereign. He articulated that desire as a metaphoric assault on the queen herself through Amoret, as Belphoebe's twin, the most assailable Elizabeth figure in *The Faerie Queene*.[85] In making Busirane the master of his own privy chamber, a poet as well as a magician who escapes unpunished from the narrative, Spenser delegates the power to create devices addressed to Amoret and, through their relationship, exhibits the desires, frustrations, and fantasies that courtiers or would-be courtiers directed at Elizabeth.

Erase the mediation of figurative language and one result is Essex's rebellion, a direct attempt to seize the queen and bend her to the rebels' will confused with a desire to displace her entirely. Although Robert Devereux wrote poetry and letters and performed as an accomplished tournament knight, in the late 1590s he was increasingly unwilling to employ the queen's iconography of her isolate and unaging body. Elizabeth found it necessary to remind him that "kings have the honour to be titled earthly gods."[86] But as an unrepentant Essex wrote to Thomas Egerton after Elizabeth boxed his ears and he reached for his sword in response, "Cannot Princes err? Cannot subjects receive wrong? Is an earthly power or authority infinite?"[87]

Essex's attempts at literary address to Elizabeth culminated in his Accession Day entertainment of 1595, written with Francis Bacon. Just ten days before its presentation, Essex had been seen looking "wan and pale" after Elizabeth took him to task about a book that popularized him with its "dangerous praises." Even though Essex must in part have been seeking to reinstate himself in the queen's favor, the entertainment only glances at the queen's accepted iconography of power, mixing Essex's appearance as a foreign prince in search of Elizabeth's mythic court with a lengthy prose debate about those who would serve her best. Roland Whyte wrote to Robert Sidney about Elizabeth's lack of enthusiasm for his devices, "The Queen said that if she had thought their had bene so much said of her, she wold not have bene their that night, and soe went to bed."[88]

As the 1590s drew to a close, words continued to fail the Earl of Essex even as the proliferation of his engraved heroic image (Figure 24) challenged the static iconography of the aging queen. Once in Ireland, unlike Robert Sidney, Essex was not content to sue month after frustrating month through intermediaries and letters for his return to court, although both men were desperate to return to the presence of the queen. Nor could Essex patiently undertake negotiations with Tyrone. He opted instead for a speedy and thus suspicious truce, followed by a precipitate journey homeward. Without language and image to mediate between himself and his sovereign, at last in February 1600/1601 he again took refuge in action, imprisoning the Lord Keeper of the Great Seal, the Comptroller of Her Majesty's Household, and the Lord Chief Justice of England when they were sent to call him to the queen's accounting, and marched with

Figure 24. One of two engravings (ca. 1598) by Thomas Cockson of Robert Devereux, Second Earl of Essex, whose popularity in the late 1590s called attention to the threat to Elizabeth's throne. (British Library)

about two hundred men through the London streets in search of weaponry and followers.

But Essex could not escape language: The result of these ill-conceived activities was his trial's indictments, testimony, depositions, and confessions, whose language sheds light on the relation among threat, captivity, and the queen's body. Because Essex's conviction rested on the pretrial assumption that he had intended Elizabeth's death, the trial revolved around discussions of Essex's desire to have, in the words of Sir Charles Davers's confession, "access to the queen's presence without resistance." Davers confessed that the rebels hoped

> to take the Tower, for it would command London, then to surprize the court; and after, the court being taken and possessed, to have assembled

the rest of their friends, and to have presented themselves to the queen: and that being done, and the guards secured, sir Christ. Blunt should keep the outward gates of the court, sir John Davis the hall and water-gate, sir Charles Davers (this Deponent) should keep the presence and guard-chamber, and seize upon the halberts and pensioneres battle-axes.[89]

Sir Ferdinand Gorges independently confirmed that he had helped formulate a plan in which the "principal men" would "keep the gate, some the hall, some to be in the presence, lobby, and guard chamber, and others to come in with my Lord himself, so as to give him a passage to the privy chamber, when he presented himself to Her Majesty."[90]

Such descriptions of an assault on the queen's inner rooms could be regarded as a political or even a physical rape, as is evident in Robert Cecil's letter to William Barlow. Dr. Barlow was given the "thankless task," writes Paul Seaver, of preaching "to a hostile city the government's version of the Essex rebellion" at St. Paul's Cross.[91] Cecil dramatizes the atmosphere of captivity and attempted rape by suggesting to Barlow that in disseminating the story he "consider how perilous a thing it was to have put a lady, a Queen, in that fright she must have been in"—a picture at odds with the presence of mind that Elizabeth showed the impetuous Essex when he suddenly appeared in her chamber upon his return from Ireland, as well as with Cecil's own earlier reports to the Lord Lieutenant of Ireland, the English officers in the Low Countries, and Privy Councillor Sir George Carew that even when "a false alarm was brought to the Queen, that the city was revolted with them, she never was more amazed than she would have been to have heard of a fray in Fleet Street."[92]

Cecil's second strategy in describing the forced entry as a rape is to change a key verb in Davers's and Gorges's testimony. According to them, Essex's followers planned to "keep" various parts of the presence and privy chambers; Cecil preferred the verbs "seize," "possess," and "master." He also uses the passive voice so that it is unclear who the victim of this entry would be. Given their intentions, Cecil asks, "How can it be imagined but some resistance would be made?"—a question implying that he is discussing the "lady's" resistance as much as her guards'. He concludes with an image of the physical consequences of such a "passage to the privy chamber" that again leaves open whether he is describing the guards' bodies or the queen's body: "Blood once drawn, more would have followed, which would have been no small horror to the Queen's nature." Essex's defense, Cecil continued, went no further than to protest that he would "have all things done with as little blood as could be; and for the Queen's own person, would never have suffered it to receive any harm"— the bridegroom's version of his wedding night. But, insists Cecil, this was a case of force: These men could not have "cared much to commit any insolence rather than be frustrated in their designs."[93]

Essex's failed assault on the privy chamber and thus on Elizabeth's person was the end of neither the danger to Elizabeth nor the sexualization of the move toward the privy chamber. Captain Thomas Lee, arrested outside the privy chamber door, was indicted for treasonous intent to "go to the royal palace of our sovereign lady, . . . then and there to lay violent hands on her sacred person, and to take her prisoner." Lee's purpose was "by that means, to set at liberty the earls of Essex and Southampton." Specifically, Lee had "pressed in to the presence, even to the Privy-chamber door, with purpose to have taken the person of our said sovereign lady, and perform his other traitorous designs."[94] The deciding factors in Lee's conviction were the politics of the space in which he had been apprehended and his admission that he meant to "force" Elizabeth to sign for Essex's release. As the court's attorney put it in language ambiguous enough to suggest sexual meanings, "Mark . . . he said they might 'force' her majesty to do it: mark this word, 'force.' [quoting Lee's confession] 'Go in unto her, and never leave her till she had done it.'" In these texts, the imagined moment of a queen overcome, imprisoned, and forced to do a man's will is shared by Essex and Cecil, presumably by Barlow and his city audience at St. Paul's Cross, as well as by Lee and the court's attorney. As we have seen, it is among the most common narratives of Elizabeth's court, a narrative used to define Elizabeth's political self-sufficiency (that is, her chastity) and to redefine it.

Captivity: Sidney, Spenser, and the Queen

Rather than plot a direct assault on the queen's physical body, how much more prudent to address her in ways subtly undermining the representational basis of her authority, that self-sufficient, chaste, and unreachable body. To what extent could a writer entertain, convince, and even enthrall an audience at once royal and female through language? As in the case of Leicester's attempts to redefine Elizabeth, focusing on the intersection of court spectacle with the address, captivity, and assault of the female audience allows a specifically political discussion of this question. In book 3 of *The Faerie Queene,* Spenser chooses the genre of spectacle, the codes of masculinist poetics, and the instabilities of the queen's image through which to address the queen and her court on the subject of chastity. That the abuse of an imprisoned female audience occurs with a similarly obsessive urgency further suggests that in *The Faerie Queene* Spenser appropriates the connection between the court's focus on Elizabeth as the audience and the cultural currency of the captivity narrative.

Most of the differences between Spenser's texts and Sidney's devolve from the fact that Spenser uses a familiar allegorical narrative to address the queen in a book about her chief virtue in a volume named for herself as figured in the Faerie Queene. Sidney's own frustrations, more violently expressed in *The Arcadia* than in the immediately public *Four Foster Children of Desire,* are no less a result of court dynamics, but are nevertheless displaced because neither work was directly addressed to the queen or published while he lived. They also are more aristocratic. Sidney's concern is not to redefine chastity in terms of a definition increasingly dear to the middling sort or to create a place for himself at court, but to assert his own authority to an imagined female audience, the source of his frustrations and his hope. This is why Sidney's text answers the menacing question posed by Philisides in his song about his mistress—"What tongue can her perfections tell / In whose each part all pens may dwell?"[95]—by allowing his pen promiscuous play with his female subject.

Spenser shares this need to praise and penetrate his subject, addressing his work directly to the queen in a text that invokes and displaces her at every turn. In immediately publishing that courtly address, Spenser deliberately sought subsequent literary attention, and his redefinition of chastity in book 3 situates his text in the midst of a major cultural development: the growing acceptance of the concept of a Protestant marriage "bond," adapted from humanist texts like Erasmus's *Colloquies,* in which lawful chastity was a central legal and moral conception.[96]

Both Sidney and Spenser assert that the woman at the center is the creation of her writers, by making the definition of their audience the focus of their third, somewhat final, and certainly inconclusive books. At first free to entertain her—that is, to present their suits as praise—the writers produce elaborate literary versions of court pageantry. Even when abused and raped, however, their female figures remain frustratingly elusive, unmoved, and ultimately unsubjugated. Thus the violence of the females' fictional captivity sounds the depth of the authors' frustrations and measures the extent of Elizabeth's power over their lives.

In creating a captive audience as an allegory of courtier–monarch relations, both Sidney and Spenser represent courtly entertainment as a form of social intercourse that attempts to disempower and silence its female subject. The imprisonment of Amoret has its analogue in *The Four Foster Children of Desire,* in which Elizabeth actually participated as imprisoned Beauty, and in *The New Arcadia,* when Amphialus imprisons Philoclea and Pamela, his guilt not mitigated by the fact that his mother, Cecropia, engineered their capture. In both, the female figures find themselves besieged because they have inspired desire. In *The Four Foster Children,* a page dressed as Mercury explained "that desperate Desire with a wonderfull armie of affections hath laid his siege against the invincible Fortresse of Peerlesse Beautie." The rationale for the imprisonment of Beauty / Elizabeth is the rationale for the imprisonment of Philoclea, Pamela, and Amoret herself: "Desire vaunts to conquer Beawties Forte by force wherin the goddesse keepes continually watch and warde, so that Desire may dispaire to win one ynche of her against her will."[97] In the court entertainment, the assault with the four foster children's phallic lances is defeated by Elizabeth's magical self-protection in a demonstration of her unavailability to her French suitor. In the romance, the captivity of Philoclea and Pamela becomes the occasion for a lengthier examination of the need to imprison and entertain the female audience.

Although the folly of locating Amphialus's own intransigence in the woman is convincingly expressed by Philoclea and later by Pamela, their captivity forms the center of *The New Arcadia*'s book 3, which consists largely of battles and entertainments for the two women. Amphialus serenades Philoclea, in her presence fights Phalantus in allegorical armor painted with the flames of his desire, and stages a musical water entertainment for her, featuring cornets and a song expressing his own misery:

> Alas, alonely she no pity taketh
> To know my miseries, but chaste and cruel,
>   My fall her glory maketh;
> Yet still her eyes give to my flames their fuel.[98]

The Arcadia's entertainments culminate in the spectacle of the staged executions of Pamela in front of Philoclea, and Philoclea before Pamela. As in Busirane's masque of violence, the emphasis on theatricality asserts the figurative nature of the horror, thus distancing the author from the description of the mutilated female body. Philoclea even explains how she was "executed" by means of an old stage trick—her head was thrust into a bloody serving dish with a hole in the bottom (569) (Figure 25).

Read alongside Spenser, Sidney's own book 3 provides a prose gloss on how and why the female audience must be entertained, as the desire to persuade is realized as the desire to control. Philoclea protests her captivity to Amphialus in elegant anaphora:

> You call for pity and use cruelty; you say you love me, and yet do the effects of enmity. You affirm your death is in my hands, but you have brought me to so near a degree to death as when you will, you may lay death upon me; so that while you say I am mistress of your life, I am not mistress of mine own. . . . If then violence, injury, terror, and depriving of that which is more dear than life itself, liberty, be fit orators for affection, you may expect I will be easily persuaded.

In conclusion she pleads, "Let not my fortune be disgraced with the name of imprisonment: let not my heart waste itself by being vexed with feeling evil, and fearing worse" (449–50).[99] Amphialus's reply echoes the logic of Elizabeth's imprisonment in *The Four Foster Children of Desire*, a logic that overrides the female voice, imprisons Amoret, and locates the female's captivity in the definition of love: "I am not the stay of your freedom, but love, love, which ties you in your own knots. It is you yourself that imprisons yourself: it is your beauty which makes these castle-walls embrace you" (451).

Like Spenser's text, Sidney's suggests that imprisoning women in order to woo them is wrong, that when a male captor courts a captive female, he creates a relationship that is the antithesis of a connection based on mutual esteem and choice. Sidney uses the voices of his intelligent and outspoken female characters to make this point repeatedly. But in each writer's work, the attack on imprisoned women becomes deeply engaging in itself, allowing both writers to condemn such imaginary violence in order to explore it

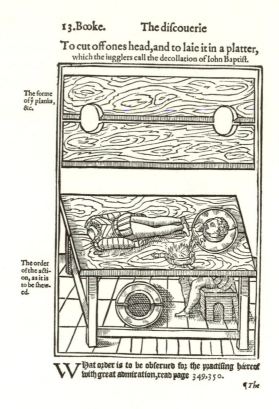

13.Booke.   The difcouerie

To cut off ones head, and to laie it in a platter,
which the iugglers call the decollation of Iohn Baptift.

The forme
of ỹ planks,
&c.

The order
of the acti-
on, as it is
to be fhew-
ed.

What order is to be obferued for the practifing heereof
with great admiration, read page 349, 350.
                                              ¶ The

Figure 25. "A juggler's trick" demonstrating the stage technique used for the staged beheading of Philoclea in Sir Philip Sidney's *Countess of Pembroke's Arcadia* (*The New Arcadia,* 1590). From Reginald Scot's *Discoverie of Witchcraft* (1584). (Huntington Library RB 69254)

freely. Although Sidney explains that Amphialus errs in locating the source of his desire and the potential for its fulfillment in the woman instead of in himself, Sidney's attitude toward the woman being "entertained" contaminates his moralization of the episode. Even as he emphasizes that it is wrong for a man to imprison a woman in the "embrace" of "castle-walls," Sidney describes Amphialus's actions as a pardonable form of cannibalism: "Amphialus was like the poor woman who, loving a tame doe she had above all earthly things, having long played withal and made it feed at her hand and lap, is constrained at length by famine (all her flock being spent and she fallen into extreme poverty) to kill the *dear* [*sic* Feuillerat][100] to sustain her life" (450, my emphasis).

Spenser likewise censures and surveys the violence he has created. In protesting that Amoret's heart was never actually removed, the narrator presents her ordeal as a test of chastity: A "thousand charmes could not her stedfast heart remoue" (12.31). However, the text that asserts that no damage is done is no more or less authoritative than the masque's description of her removed and bleeding heart. Whether her heart is removed or intact, Amoret is the defined subject, confirmed as "chaste" in the sense of possessed by the male, the definition appropriate to a figure who, whether Busirane's prisoner or Scudamour's bride, exists as desired object and the unstable feminine subject.

Even though the twentieth century is familiar enough with images of bound women and the test of female virtue as the occasion for descriptions of female suffering and the attempt to contain female sexuality,[101] what defines these literary structures as courtly is the captivity of females in order to define their sexuality and to present the courtiers' suits through elaborate and prolonged courtly entertainment. Busirane, Sidney, and Amphialus entertain and threaten their female victims through spectacles because they were among the most persuasive forms that court culture made available for presenting a male's suit for preferment not just to the queen, but also to an audience of divergent male interests. In presenting their suits to a female audience and in attempting to control their actual queen and her representations, Sidney and Spenser write like courtiers, regardless of the fact that Sidney was an aristocrat and Spenser was a product of Merchant Taylor's School, intent on acquiring the gentlemanly markers of land, a place at court, and royal favor.

The use of spectacle to persuade and the writers' frustration with their female audience (the queen) helps explain why, as David Norbrook observes, late in *The Arcadia* "the imagery of courtly ceremonial is associated with violence and imprisonment rather than delight." Norbrook reads in *The Arcadia*'s "claustrophobic atmosphere" Sidney's "frustration at enforced inactivity," an inactivity resulting from the queen's unwillingness to use Sidney as her military commander, explorer, or diplomat.[102] Steven May and David Starkey have noted that Elizabeth in fact treated Sidney well, making him a cupbearer in 1576, an escort to the Duke of Anjou in 1582 as he left the country, and the governor of Flushing in 1585.

Sidney nonetheless wrote to Leicester in 1580 that although he was "so full of the cold as one cannot hear me speak" he would not bother to come to court, "since my only service is speech and that is stopped."[103] Sidney was in constant despair that he received so little because, like everyone attendant on Elizabeth, he sought greater status and wealth. He also incurred a massive debt in pursuit of courtly self-representation, whose repayment after his death ruined his father-in-law, Walsingham. The favors that Sidney received were finally no more satisfying than Leicester's and Essex's were to them. As Francis Bacon stated in the remarks opening Essex's trial while attempting to sever his own ties with the traitor, "I much wonder that his heart could forget all the princely advancements given him by her majesty . . . but it seems . . . an aspiring mind to wished honour, is like the crocodile, which is ever growing as long as her liveth."[104]

Spenser's selection of the genre of spectacle and the cultural construct of violently imprisoning the female suggests his own frustration at not seeing the promise of *The Shepheardes Calender* fulfilled, although its popularity had led him to hope that he might take his place as a prominent court poet.[105] Instead of a rapid Hatton- or Ralegh-like rise to English lands, court appointments, governmental duties, and patent revenues, Spenser arrived in Ireland a year after the *Calender*'s publication as Lord Grey's secretary. Whatever unknown reason accounted for his exile, Spenser was not finally unemployed—the fate of the truly disgraced. He even prospered: The acquisition of his Irish estates in 1586/1587 made him an ostensible member of the gentry; he participated as an undertaker of Munster, renting three thousand acres in County Cork from the Crown;[106] and six years after having visited England and been presented at court by Ralegh on the publication of the first three books of *The Faerie Queene,* the Privy Council recommended Spenser for the position of Sheriff of Cork. Nevertheless, like Philip and Robert Sidney, Essex, Ralegh, and every other man of ambition, Spenser knew the value of personal attendance on the sovereign and formulated his own poetic requests for this honor through the humanist discourses that made them appropriate as well as morally necessary.

Epilogue: Reading Elizabeth Reading

In book 3 of *The Faerie Queene,* Spenser undertakes conflicting tasks that expose the paradoxes of his claim to power in the figurative realm. In the tradition of Mulcaster's *Queen's Majesty's Passage,* he attempts to figure the queen as a vulnerable wife and mother while granting her power; in the tradition of Leicester and Sidney, he uses the courtly discourses of patronage and place to reestablish more conventional gender relations with Elizabeth within an encomiastic display. Creating poetry that simultaneously disrupts and projects the queen's images generates instabilities that finally call attention to the constructed nature of both Elizabeth's and Spenser's figures of power: a Faerie Queene or a Gloriana who, although the most immediate figure of the queen, never appears in the poem bearing her name; a narrator whose moral vision dims as he approaches Busirane; a poet-magician who shares the author's language and talents, who tortures and rapes but escapes punishment at the hands of a morality he impersonates; Amoret, now Elizabeth, now a more passive Chastity, her outline shimmering, indeterminate, in the masque, but not in the masque, providing the blood in which it is written from a heart both removed and unremoved, pierced by a dart, "riven," and yet inviolate; and Britomart, now a figure of Elizabeth's androgynous power, now a female destined for marriage, her independence generated by her quest for her destined mate, her invulnerability to male attack while in the lists counteracted by her vulnerability in the bedroom and the torture cell.

The choice of a pageant structure itself creates contradictions that point to Spenser's attempt to construct his own power through his reconstructions of the queen's body: The text praises the queen while threatening her analogue, invites Elizabeth's interest but attempts to silence her response, and asserts that poets have a power in the land of Faery figuring their power in the real world, despite Spenser's frustrating experience to the contrary. Thus at the same time that his use of court spectacle announces Spenser's impotence and even feminization vis-à-vis the queen, through it he creates a world in which the poet-magician does as he pleases and even presses the queen to watch as he erodes her representations of autonomy and displaces her magical authority with the masterful magic of a Neoplatonic cosmos in the service of Protestant, middle-class codes.

Spenser's Book of Chastity sets up and exploits the instabilities of representation through which Elizabeth's Chastity is revised and through which this revision is screened, erased, and otherwise denied. Indeed, all of Faeryland, with its folkloric associations between nature and magic, functions as an indeterminate universe standing parallel to the court, a cosmos whose echoing correspondences Spenser the poet-magician devises in an attempt to assert and deny the power of his text. It is difficult to imagine any other realm through which Spenser could animate the volatile correspondences among politics, gender, morality, and representation; present them to his queen; and expect a reward.

Given *The Faerie Queene*'s demonstration of the ways in which revisions of Elizabeth's iconography might be inscribed in fairyland, Shakespeare's *Midsummer Night's Dream* (1595/1596) responds to Spenser with its own highly aesthetic and dramatically efficient associations among magic, the natural world, and the political plane. If Elizabeth saw the play, as is likely, she found herself in at least as problematic a relation to its fairy queen, Titania, and its Amazonian captive, Hippolyta, as she did to Spenser's Belphoebe, Britomart, Amoret, and Faerie Queene. As their audience, how might we expect her to respond? Earlier in her reign, possibly at the court revels in December 1558, certainly at a wedding masque in 1565, and at Kenilworth in 1575 and Whitehall in 1588, she responded angrily to performed challenges to her autonomy. By the 1590s, English writers who mixed encomia with subtle shifts of meaning, reproduced the discursive conflicts for the queen's representation visible at court and in society by aestheticizing and erasing the sexual violence at the base of their narratives. To the extent that these texts celebrate her sovereign authority as part of its appropriation, their strategic use of representational instability licensed both Shakespeare's dramatization of the problems endemic to love and Spenser's assertion of love as fundamental to the natural order.

We do not know whether the queen of England saw or responded to *A Midsummer Night's Dream*. Her response to *The Faerie Queene* was, however, recorded: She awarded Spenser an annuity of £50. Given the dynamics of her court in the 1590s, this £50 may be read as a complex but identifiable response to his poem. Because Spenser was Ralegh's client, the £50 formed one means by which Elizabeth could affirm Ralegh's influence with her in his perpetual competition with Essex. At the same time, the £50 also allowed her to exercise her own measure of figural control over Spenser. By providing Spenser with an annuity comparable to the salary of a councillor to the Council in Wales or a clerk of the Privy Council, and more than enough to qualify him to wear silk in his gown or "other uppermost apparel" or velvet "in his sleeveless coats, jackets, jerkins, coifs, caps, purses or partlets," according to the sumptuary statute of 1588,[107] Elizabeth resisted the poet's—and his sponsor, Ralegh's—desire to give him an actual position. Instead, she took him at his word that he was a professional poet. Through her payment, she defined him in much the same way that she would define Nicholas Hilliard as limner and goldsmith, when instead of granting him a post, she ordered him an annuity of £40 in 1601. Moreover, at court where such grants were frequently given and just as frequently blocked, she could probably count on Burghley's delaying payment to this client of a rival, and weaker faction, as indeed he did. It also seems clear that Elizabeth wanted Spenser back in Ireland. Her unwillingness to grant him a sinecure in England ensured his return there and his resentment toward her, the court, and Burghley.

One result was his taking refuge, in *Colin Clout's Come Home Again* and other later poems, in the role of poet that he had constructed for himself and that now remained to him. Spenser's return to Ireland could not, of course, exclude him from the politics of representation, since once again, published works gained a wider influence than Elizabeth could have imagined possible. But in reading her reign in terms of the conflict between her self-represented Chastity and the celebration of her image through codes that normalize violence and voyeurism, between the queen's attempts to represent an autonomous self and attempts to contain her in accepted definitions of the feminine, it is possible to imagine how our contemporary images of Elizabeth are the result of the competition for her representation that this book attempts to elucidate and in which it participates.

Two generations after Elizabeth's death, Anne Bradstreet began her catalog of the queen's accomplishments in her poem "In honour of that High and Mighty Princess, Queen ELIZABETH, of most happy memory" with the realization that no text could finally "compact" this queen, "No memories, nor volumes can containe" her, because her life was too complex and her performance of feminine power within and beyond masculine constructs was too unmistakable:

> No *Phoenix,* Pen, nor *Spencers* Poetry,
> No *Speeds,* nor *Chamdens* learned History; *Eliza's* works, war,
>   praise, can e're compact,
> The World's the Theater where she did act.

Elizabeth's success in performing herself beyond the "Pen"—the literature and history constructed about and through her image—demonstrated that "She hath wip'd off th'aspersion of her Sex, / That women wisdome lack to play the Rex."[108] To Bradstreet's seventeenth-century confidence that "Masculines, you have thus tax'd us long, / But she though dead, will vindicate our wrong," I add my own twentieth-century awareness that during her lifetime her power was constructed for herself rather than for other women, and that since her death Elizabeth has been very nearly compacted into a variety of biographical and historical images. Nevertheless, her struggle for self-definition created images that survive because they continue to engage those of the more dominant masculinist culture. In Bradstreet's poem as much as in any other text that attempts to make sense of her, Elizabeth I remains a figure of the complexity and power of the feminine ready to be made and remade familiar and unfamiliar.

Notes

Abbreviations

CSP   *Calendar of State Papers*
HMC   Royal Commission on Historical Manuscripts
PRO   Public Record Office
STC   *A Short-Title Catalogue of Books Printed in England, Scotland, & Ireland and of English Books Printed Abroad, 1475–1640.* Compiled by Alfred W. Pollard and G. R. Redgrave. Revised by W. A. Jackson, F. S. Ferguson, and Katharine F. Pantzer. 2nd ed. 3 vols. London: Bibliographical Society, 1976–1991.
Wing   *Short-Title Catalogue of Books Printed in England, Scotland, Ireland, Wales and British America . . . 1641–1700.* Compiled by Donald Wing. 2nd ed. 3 vols. New York: Modern Language Association, 1972.

Introduction

1. Alison Plowden, *Elizabeth Regina: The Age of Triumph, 1588–1603* (New York: Times Books, 1980), 11; Elizabeth Jenkins, *Elizabeth the Great* (1958; New York: Capricorn Books, 1967), 285; Carolly Erickson, *The First Elizabeth* (New York: Summit Books, 1983), 374–75. Compare Garrett Mattingly's similarly undocumented description in *The Armada* (Boston: Houghton Mifflin, 1959): "She was clad all in white velvet with a silver cuirass embossed with a mythological design, and bore in her right hand a silver truncheon chased in gold" (349).

2. In "The Myth of Elizabeth I at Tilbury," *Sixteenth Century Journal* 23 (1992): 95–114, I elaborate on how and why our picture of Elizabeth at Tilbury was constructed.

3. Leah Marcus, *Puzzling Shakespeare: Local Readings and Its Discontents* (Berkeley: University of California Press, 1988), 55.

4. Louis A. Montrose, "The Shaping Fantasies of Elizabethan Culture," in *Rewriting the Renaissance: The Discourses of Sexual Difference in Early Modern Europe,* ed. Margaret W. Ferguson, Maureen Quilligan, and Nancy J. Vickers (Chicago: University of Chicago Press, 1986), 80.

5. Isocrates, *To Nicocles* 21–23, trans. George Norlin (London: Heinemann, 1928), 1:53.

6. This is a difficult phrase to gloss, since in a chivalric twist on Isocrates, Elizabeth uses three words, "ensign," "badge," and "arms," each of which connects the prince's words to the heraldic images used to parade his supremacy. See Elizabeth I to James VI, 7 August 1583, *The Letters of Queen Elizabeth,* ed. G. B. Harrison (1935; New York: Funk & Wagnalls, 1968), 159.

7. PRO SP 11/4, no. 2.

8. Allison Heisch, ed., *Queen Elizabeth I: Political Speeches and Parliamentary Addresses, 1558–1601* (Madison: University of Wisconsin Press, 1994). The area in brackets is the simpler version (although probably not the speech as delivered), which George P. Rice prints in *The Public Speaking of Queen Elizabeth: Selections*

from Her Official Addresses (New York: Columbia University Press, 1951), 124. I include it under erasure because it is the one version of the speech that aptly summarizes the complex sentence that begins the actual speech.

9. Michel Foucault, *The Order of Things: An Archaeology of the Human Sciences* (New York: Vintage Books, 1973), xxiii, 17.

10. Michel Foucault's use of the term "discourse" relates social practice to conception within "power," that is, within the relational interplay among human beings. As a result, discourse inevitably forms a locus of conflict. "Discourse is not simply that which expresses struggles or systems of domination, but that for which, and by which, one struggles; it is the power which one is striving to seize," he wrote in *L'Ordre du discours* (quoted in Richard Terdiman, *Discourse/Counter Discourse: The Theory and Practice of Symbolic Resistance in Nineteenth-Century France* [Ithaca, N.Y.: Cornell University Press, 1985], 55). Moreover, as Foucault elaborated the problem of discourse during his inaugural lecture at the College de France, "discourse" exists in a number of "procedures": "I am supposing that in every society the production of discourse is at once controlled, selected, organized and redistributed according to a certain number of procedures." These "procedures" of discourse, including "exclusion" and "prohibition"—our sense of what we may or may not say and do—help constitute speech and other human relational activities. Taking speech as his example, Foucault notes the importance of our considering speech as part of discourse, that is, within the procedures shaping what is said. If we consider discursive procedure, then we can see that "in appearance, speech may well be of account, but the prohibitions surrounding it soon reveal its links with desire and power. This should not be very surprising, for psychoanalysis has already shown us that speech is not merely the medium which manifests—or dissembles—desire; it is also the object of desire. Similarly, historians have constantly impressed upon us that speech is no mere verbalisation of conflicts and systems of domination, but that it is the very object of man's conflicts." ("The Discourse on Language," in *The Archaeology of Knowledge and the Discourse of Language,* trans. A. M. Sheridan Smith [New York: Pantheon, 1972], 216).

11. Philippa Berry, *Of Chastity and Power: Elizabethan Literature and the Unmarried Queen* (London: Routledge, 1989), 7. Although I disagree with Leah Marcus on the question of agency and her discussion relies on Elizabeth's Tilbury myth, her analysis of Elizabeth and her examination of transmutations of the royal iconography in Shakespeare are illuminating. See especially the chapter on Elizabeth in Marcus, *Puzzling Shakespeare,* 51–105. (quotation from p. 57).

Lisa Jardine's trail-blazing discussion of Elizabeth as a woman whose representation is "of national concern" that "betrays . . . uneasiness about the instrumental power accorded to women in the period" (169), in *Still Harping on Daughters: Women and Drama in the Age of Shakespeare* (Totowa, N.J.: Barnes & Noble, 1983), reproduces both sides of the passive–active split. Although she sees the queen as passive—"On all public occasions Elizabeth I herself was metamorphosed into a *female personification,* an emblem" (173)—in discussing her chastity, Jardine also speculates on her agency: "It is likely that Elizabeth herself knowingly manipulated the emblems through which her court and counsellors perceived her" (178).

12. I am indebted to Judith Butler's entire discussion of agency but particularly to her conclusion in *Gender Trouble: Feminism and the Subversion of Identity* (New York: Routledge, 1990), 142–49 (quotation from p. 144), which I read as I prepared my manuscript for publication. Her relation of identity to agency helped me understand more precisely why I had first envisioned this book as a study of

Elizabeth's agency in her discursive construction. I again encountered this theoretical question in my discussion of Spenser's agency in constructing the text of *The Faerie Queene*; see my Chapter 3, notes. On the relation between discursive representation and the construction of gender, see Teresa de Lauretis, *Technologies of Gender: Essays on Theory, Film, and Fiction* (Bloomington: Indiana University Press, 1987), esp. chap. 1.

13. James Froude's entire sentence reads: "The great results of her reign were the fruits of policy which was not her own, and which she starved and mutilated when energy and completeness were most needed" (*The Reign of Elizabeth* [New York: Dutton, 1930], 5:476).

14. See, for example, John Neale, *Queen Elizabeth I: A Biography* (1934; Garden City, N.Y.: Doubleday, 1957), 401; Mattingly, *Armada;* Joel Hurstfield, *Elizabeth I and the Unity of England* (New York: Macmillan, 1960).

15. See John Foxe, *Acts and Monuments,* ed. George Townsend (New York: AMS Press, 1965), vol. 8. Among the first English editions of William Camden's histories of Elizabeth are *Annales: The True and Royall History of the famous Empresse Elizabeth queene of England,* trans. A. Darcie (London: B. Fisher, 1625), STC 4497; Camden, *The Historie of the most renowned and victorious princess Elizabeth,* trans. R. Norton (London: B. Fisher, 1630), STC 4500. For a careful overview of the influence of William Camden on accounts of Elizabeth through the 1960s, see Christopher Haigh's introduction to Christopher Haigh, ed., *The Reign of Elizabeth I* (Athens: University of Georgia Press, 1987), 1–25. John N. King, in "Queen Elizabeth I: Representations of the Virgin Queen," *Renaissance Quarterly* 43 (1990): 30–74, takes issue with a specific received notion of Camden's, that from the outset "the queen chose a life of perpetual virginity" (33).

16. Jenkins, *Elizabeth the Great,* 324. Paul Johnson's biography, *Elizabeth I* (New York: Holt, Rinehart and Winston, 1974), also finds comfort in circling back to Camden, in this case his observance that "though beset by divers nations her mortal enemies, she held the most stout warlike nation of the English four and forty years and upwards, not only in awe and duty, but even in peace also. Insomuch as, in all England, for so many years, never any mortal man heard the trumpet sound the charge to battle" (443).

More recently, Susan Bassnett's introduction to *Elizabeth I: A Feminist Perspective* (New York: St. Martin's Press, 1988) substitutes a feminist teleology based on an equal assurance that after reading all the materials available on the queen, she has arrived at "a reliable impression" of Elizabeth "and that impression is very close to the one I first had in my teens" (5–6). Bassnett's conclusion, that "Elizabeth should be seen as a woman who struggled against antifeminist prejudice and who has remained a symbol of active female assertiveness for future generations" (128), is worthwhile. Yet to this and similar feminist arguments I wish to add an examination of the issue of her agency, of the interplay and conflict between her representations of her body and those produced by others, as well as a sense of the ambiguities and instabilities attending the images of Elizabeth, including those that our own histories construct.

17. See, for example, Bassnett, *Elizabeth I: A Feminist Perspective;* Maria Perry, *The Word of a Prince: A Life of Elizabeth I from Contemporary Documents* (Woodbridge: Boydell Press, 1990).

18. Laurence Olivier, quoted in John Mortimer, *Olivier at Work: The National Years,* ed. Lyn Haill (New York: Routledge & Kegan Paul, 1990), 11.

19. "A Report of her Majestie's most gratious Answere, delivered by her selfe

verbally, to the first Petitions of the Lords and Commons . . . the xii Day of November 1586" (concerning the execution of Mary Queen of Scots), in *A Collection of Scarce and Valuable Tracts,* ed. Walter Scott (London: T. Cordell and W. Davies, 1809), 1:220. See also Frances Teague, "Elizabeth I: Queen of England," in *Women Writers of the Renaissance and Reformation,* ed. Katharina M. Wilson (Athens: University of Georgia Press, 1987), 541.

20. In the absence of a larger compendium of Elizabeth's letters, I am grateful for Harrison, ed., *Letters of Queen Elizabeth.* Also see Heisch, ed., *Queen Elizabeth I: Political Speeches;* Rice, ed., *Public Speaking of Queen Elizabeth;* Elizabeth I, *A Book of Devotions Composed by Her Majesty Elizabeth with translation by Rev. Adam Fox* (Gerards Cross: Colin Smythe, 1920); Elizabeth I, *The Sayings of Elizabeth,* ed. Frederick Chamberlin (London: John Lane, 1923); Alan Glover, comp., *Gloriana's Glass: Queen Elizabeth I reflected in verses and dedications addressed to her* (Barnet: Stellar Press, [1953]); and the particularly unreliable Frank A. Mumby, ed., *The Girlhood of Queen Elizabeth, a narrative in contemporary letters* (London: Constable & Col, 1909).

21. See Heisch, ed., *Queen Elizabeth I: Political Speeches;* and Teague's discussion of Elizabeth and editions of several key poems and speeches in "Elizabeth I: Queen of England," 522–47.

22. Lee Patterson, *Negotiating the Past: The Historical Understanding of Medieval Literature* (Madison: University of Wisconsin Press, 1987), 112.

23. Roy Strong, *The Cult of Elizabeth: Elizabethan Portraiture and Pageantry* (London: Thames and Hudson, 1977), 16.

24. Frances Yates, "Queen Elizabeth as Astraea," *Journal of the Warburg and Courtauld Institute* 10 (1947): 82. Yates does consider, however, the variations imposed on the royal image by Dutch supporters in their own interests (76). But to her, the cult of Elizabeth is a monolithic force, as can be seen in this typical sentence: "The lengths to which the cult of Elizabeth went are a measure of the sense of isolation which had at all costs to find a symbol strong enough to provide a feeling of spiritual security in face of the break with the rest of Christendom" (56).

25. Roy Strong, *Art and Power: Renaissance Festivals, 1450–1650* (Woodbridge: Boydell Press, 1984), 21.

26. Louis Montrose, "The Elizabethan Subject and the Spenserian Text," in *Literary Theory/Renaissance Texts,* ed. Patricia Parker and David Quint (Baltimore: Johns Hopkins University Press, 1986), 310. Montrose nevertheless finds that "Elizabeth was the createe of the Elizabethan image more than she was its creator" (310).

27. John Nichols, ed., *The Progresses and Public Processions of Queen Elizabeth* (London: John Nichols, 1823; New York: AMS Press, 1966), 1:315.

28. Philip Sidney, *The Four Foster Children of Desire,* in *Entertainments for Elizabeth,* ed. Jean Wilson (Totowa, N.J.: Rowman and Littlefield, 1980), 61–85; Elizabeth to Francis, Duke of Anjou, December–January, 1579/1580, in Harrison, ed., *Letters of Queen Elizabeth,* 135.

29. Guzman de Silva to Philip II, 12 March 1565, CSP Spanish, 1:405.

30. In *Mastering the Revels: The Regulation and Censorship of English Renaissance Drama* (Iowa City: University of Iowa Press, 1991), Robert Dutton considers the problem of why Elizabeth's Master of Revels often passed entertainments to be shown before the queen that proved offensive. He considers *Gorboduc's* pointed epilogue about the need for a king to secure the succession and Richard Edwards's *Palamon and Arcite,* in which Emilia's "prayer for a virgin life, received a divine

admonition to marry" (38–39) as examples of works that we might expect to have given offense, but that Elizabeth tolerated and even enjoyed. To his argument, I would add that *Gorboduc* may have been presented before the queen at the time when she was seriously considering marriage to Robert Dudley. Contextualizing each of the seemingly controversial performances may supply still other reasons for her accepting them.

Dutton concludes that "Tilney's job [Edmund Tilney, Master of Revels from 1579 to 1589] was not to superintend a narrow consensus view of the Elizabethan state and its policies, but to ensure that what was performed stayed within an acceptable band of loyal opinion" (72). It seems that this "band of loyal opinion" might be variously interpreted by the Master of Revels and Elizabeth on occasion. Dutton's interesting account also discusses the occasional conflicts that developed between the system of court censorship and the city's mechanisms, in which the court consistently argued for a broader view.

31. In Richard Johnson's *The most pleasant history of Tom a Lincolne* (London: A. Mathewes, 1631), STC 14684 [first entered to W. White, 24 December 1599], Celia kills herself when her lover fails to return, as did Dido, who also was the frequent parallel of Elizabeth in the queen's iconography.

32. "Mr. Edw: Dyer to Mr. Christopher Hatton," 9 October 1572, MS Harleian 787, fol. 88, in Ralph M. Sargent, *At the Court of Queen Elizabeth: The Life and Lyrics of Sir Edward Dyer* (New York: Oxford University Press, 1935), 24.

33. Joseph R. Tanner, ed., *Tudor Constitutional Documents, A.D. 1485–1603,* 2nd ed. (Cambridge: Cambridge University Press, 1930), 123–24, quoted in Mortimer Levine, "The Place of Women in Tudor Government," in *Tudor Rule and Revolution: Essays for G. R. Elton from His American Friends,* ed. Delloyd J. Guth and John W. McKenna (Cambridge: Cambridge University Press, 1982), 109. See also Constance Jordan, "Woman's Rule in Sixteenth-Century British Political Thought," *Renaissance Quarterly* 60 (1987): 421–51.

34. "Accession Speech," in Heisch, ed., *Queen Elizabeth I: Political Speeches,* lines 9, 12–13. On the idea of the sovereign's two bodies, see Ernst Kantorowicz, *The King's Two Bodies: A Study in Medieval Theology* (Princeton, N.J.: Princeton University Press, 1957); on the applicability of this idea to Elizabeth's iconography, see Montrose, "Elizabethan Subject and the Spenserian Text," 303–40. In his most recent essay, "The Work of Gender in the Discourse of Discovery," *Representations* 33 (1991), Montrose summarizes the complexity of the relation between the queen's two bodies when he writes that a discourse (here, that of discovery) "is inflected by the anomalous status of Queen Elizabeth—who is at once a *ruler* . . . and also a *woman,* whose political relationship to those subjects is itself frequently articulated in the discourses of gender and sexuality" (3).

For an insightful discussion of Elizabeth and her androgynous discourse, see Leah Marcus, "Shakespeare's Comic Heroines, Elizabeth I, and the Political Uses of Androgyny," in *Women in the Middle Ages and the Renaissance: Literary and Historical Perspectives,* ed. Mary Beth Rose (Syracuse, N.Y.: Syracuse University Press, 1986), 135–53.

35. "Golden Speech," Stow MS. 362, fol. 169–72, in Heisch, ed., *Queen Elizabeth I: Political Speeches,* lines 144–45, 128–29. See also Rice, ed., *Public Speaking of Queen Elizabeth,* 130, 109. I am using Teague's edition of the "Golden Speech," in "Elizabeth I: Queen of England," 545.

36. Aristotle, *Art of Rhetoric* I.ix, 1–7, trans. John Henry Freese (Cambridge, Mass.: Harvard University Press, 1982), 91. See also Desiderius Erasmus, *The*

Education of a Christian Prince, trans. Lester K. Born (New York: Norton, 1968), 151.

37. "The Quenes oration to the Polishe Ambassador at Greenwiche the 25. July. 1597," HMC Hatfield 53.63, in Heisch, ed., *Queen Elizabeth I: Political Speeches,* line 20. "And concerning your selfe," Elizabeth is said to have replied to the Polish ambassador in an impromptu display of her Latin, "you seeme vnto me to have red many bookes, but bookes of princes affairs you have not attayned vnto, and are further ignorant what is convenient betwene princes" (lines 19–22).

38. *The Quenes maiesties passsage through the citie of London to westminster the daye before her coronacion* (London: R. Tottel, 1559), STC 7591, B4–Cl.

39. "(1566) To a Joint Delegation from Parliament," in Heisch, ed., *Queen Elizabeth I: Political Speeches,* lines 156–60.

40. "The answere of the Quenes highnes to ye peticion proponed vnto hir by ye lower howse concerning hir mariage," in ibid., lines 21–23, 58–61. In "Queen Elizabeth I," King argues that Elizabeth did not lead her life according to some programmic sense of her own virginity. In pointing out that "Elizabethan iconography was closely tied to the life history of the monarch and to political events of her reign" (32), he demonstrates that Elizabeth herself remained open to the possibility of marriage. I agree with King that the speech carefully leaves open the question of marriage. But we disagree about the "face value" of this speech through which (I believe) Elizabeth searches and finds a preliminary icon of self-definition in the figure of the virgin queen. Moreover, I see her virginity, allegorized from the 1570s on as an increasingly potent chastity, as a system of self-signification whose interaction with material practice was too effective to abandon, even if she did rethink it frequently. For a more carefully contextualized discussion of this speech, see my Chapter 1, the section entitled, "Elizabeth's Early Self-Representation."

41. Susan Frye, "Allegories of Power in the England of Elizabeth" (Ph.D. diss., Stanford University, 1986). My dissertation constructs "a theory of how allegory worked in the visual, dramatic, courtly, and poetic forms" of the period, in contending that "the allegory of Elizabethan England was inherently political" (1, 5–6).

42. See Michel Foucault, "Two Lectures," in *Power/Knowledge: Selected Interviews and Other Writings, 1972–1977,* trans. Colin Gordon (New York: Pantheon, 1980), 78–108. As I use and develop Foucault's terminology, I extend his analyses to include gender, as he did not.

43. Ferdinand de Saussure, *Course in General Linguistics* (New York: McGraw-Hill, 1966), 67–69.

44. Carolynn Van Dyke, *The Fiction of Truth: Structures of Meaning in Narrative and Dramatic Allegory* (Ithaca, N.Y.: Cornell University Press, 1985), 27; George Puttenham, *The Arte of English Poesie,* ed. Edward Arber (1906; Kent, Ohio: Kent State University Press, 1970), 166; Paul de Man, *Allegories of Reading: Figural Language in Rousseau, Nietzsche, Rilke, and Proust* (New Haven, Conn.: Yale University Press, 1979), esp. 70–76 (quotation from p. 74). On allegory as writing, which calls attention to the gap between signifier and signified, see also Jonathan Culler, *Structuralist Poetics* (Ithaca, N.Y.: Cornell University Press, 1975), 229–30; Tzvetan Todorov, *The Poetics of Prose,* trans. Richard Howard (Ithaca, N.Y.: Cornell University Press, 1977), esp. 100–101.

45. I find helpful, however, other aspects of Abner Cohen's generalization about

spectacle: These performances do "objectify norms, values, and beliefs; interpret the private in terms of the collective, the abstract in terms of the concrete; confirm or modify relationships" ("Political Symbolism," *Annual Review of Anthropology* 8 [1979]: 106). But they do not do so in the same way for everyone in the spectacle, and they are just as likely to raise the specters of anxiety, dissent, and difference as much as function as a collective integration, as I discuss in Chapter 1.

Chapter 1

1. According to John Stow, the Exchange, begun in 1567, was not popular until 1570, when the queen visited it following dinner with Thomas Gresham, its builder. After a tour of "euery part therof aboue the ground, especially the Pawne, which was richly furnished with all sorts of the finest wares in the Citie: shee caused the same Bursse by an Herauld and a Trumpet, to be proclamed the *Royal Exchange,* and so to be called from thenceforth, and not otherwise" (*A Survey of London* [1603], ed. Charles Kingsford [Oxford: Clarendon Press, 1971], 1:193). The story's prevalence indicates how much the dynamic of named and namer had shifted ten years after the entry: In 1570 Elizabeth was the namer in the city precincts, and in 1559 (as I will be discussing) when she was less powerful, her citizens named *her.* For other accounts of the popular story, see Thomas Heywood, *If You Know Not Me, You Know Nobody Part II* (subtitled in part *The building of the Royall Exchange*), ed. Madeleine Doran (Oxford: Oxford University Press, Malone Society, 1934); M.P., *An Abstract of the Historie of the Renouned Maiden Queene Elizabeth* (London: Thomas Cotes, 1631), B8v–C3.

2. Stow's *Survey* notes a "picture of her Maiestie, Queene *Elizabeth* on the West side" of Ludgate put up in the twenty-eighth year (1586–1587) of her reign, when the entire gate was rebuilt "at the common charges of the citizens" (1:39). This "picture" must have been the statue that once stood at Ludgate (ca. 1586 by William Kirwan), and was moved in 1760 to St. Dunstan's on Fleet Street. See Ann Saunders, *The Art and Architecture of London* (Oxford: Phaidon Press, 1984), 25–26.

3. My reading of the youthful portraits of Elizabeth's declining years as attempting to revise the uncertainties of her early reign takes into account that their political function was also to assert the queen to be, in the words of her motto, *semper eadem.* Her aging was variously disguised and addressed in the drama, poetry, and portraiture at the end of her reign. To see the youthful portraits as attempts to rewrite the past as well as to demonstrate Elizabeth's youthfulness helps explain, for example, Nicholas Hilliard's miniature painted around 1570 and the other "coronation" portrait painted around 1600 of the queen in her coronation robes. Although Roy Strong finds it "puzzling" that two "coronation" portraits date from later in the reign, they clearly exist as a way of figuring (or refiguring) the past (*Gloriana: The Portraits of Queen Elizabeth I* [New York: Thames and Hudson, 1987], 163). On the construction of Elizabeth's youthfulness, see also Strong's chapter entitled "Hilliard and the Mask of Youth," 147–51. Even the earlier painting, *Allegory of the Tudor Succession* (70–77), commonly reproduced in the 1590s, directs us to read Elizabeth's succession in terms of her later stability and success. On the dating of the "coronation" portraits, see John Fletcher, "The Date of the Portrait of Elizabeth I in her Coronation Robes," and Janet Arnold, "The 'Coronation' Portrait of Queen Elizabeth I," both in *Burlington Magazine* 120 (1978). See also Richard McCoy, "'Thou Idol Ceremony': Elizabeth I, *The Henriad,* and the

Rites of the English Monarchy," in *Urban Life in the Renaissance,* ed. Susan Zimmerman and Ronald F. E. Weissman (Newark: University of Delaware Press, 1989), 260, 266n.

The image of Elizabeth as commander at Tilbury is largely the construction of the seventeenth century. See Susan Frye, "The Myth of Elizabeth I at Tilbury," *Sixteenth Century Journal* 23(1992): 95–114.

4. See Norman L. Jones, "Elizabeth's First Year: The Conception and Birth of the Elizabethan Political World," in *The Reign of Elizabeth I,* ed. Christopher Haigh (Athens: University of Georgia Press, 1987), 27–54, and Haigh's introduction, 1–25. See also Whitney R. D. Jones, *The Mid-Tudor Crisis, 1539–1563* (London: Macmillan, 1973), and a revision of its view, Jennifer Loach and Robert Tittler, eds., *The Mid-Tudor Polity, c. 1540–1560* (London: Macmillan, 1980). For a document illustrating an awareness of the crisis management necessary during the first months of Elizabeth's reign, see William Cecil's "Memorial," a careful list of twelve steps to be undertaken immediately upon Elizabeth's accession "in this change." See also Walter Scott, ed., *A Collection of Scarce and Valuable Tracts* (London: T. Cadell and W. Davies, 1809), 1:163–64.

5. "Accession Speech," in *Queen Elizabeth I: Political Speeches and Parliamentary Addresses, 1558–1601,* ed. Allison Heisch (Madison: University of Wisconsin Press, 1994), lines 12–13. See also Heisch, "Queen Elizabeth I: Parliamentary Rhetoric and the Exercise of Power," *Signs* 1 (1975): 33. For more on Elizabeth's two bodies, see the "Introduction" to this book, in which I discuss one of Elizabeth's representational problems—that on many occasions, as in the entry, the representations of herself sought to collapse the distinction between her natural and political bodies in order to emphasize her femininity.

6. Count of Feria to Philip II, 21 November 1558. Feria continues, "Really this country is more fit to be dealt with sword in hand than by cajolery, for there are neither funds, nor soldiers, nor heads, nor forces, and yet it is overflowing with every other necessary of life" (CSP Spanish, Elizabeth, 1:3).

7. Lucy Gent and Nigel Llewellyn, Introduction, to *Renaissance Bodies: The Human Figure in English Culture, c. 1540–1660* (London: Reaktion Books, 1990), 6.

8. Given the long, complex history of the term "ideology," I prefer Louis Althusser's definition: "Ideology represents the imaginary relationship of individuals to their real conditions of existence" ("Ideology and Ideological State Apparatuses [Notes Toward an Investigation]," in *Lenin and Philosophy and Other Essays,* trans. Ben Brewster [New York: Monthly Review Press, 1971], 162).

9. The full title of *The Queen's Majesty's Passage* is *The Quenes maiesties passsage through the citie of London to westminster the daye before her coronacion* (London: R. Tottel, 1559), STC 7591. The text I quote throughout is *The Quenes maiesties passsage through the cities of London to westminster the daye before her coronacion,* fascimile ed. (New Haven, Conn.: Yale Elizabethan Club, 1957). Page references for quotations appear in the text. On the textual history of the *Passage,* see Arthur Kinney's introduction to his edition in *Elizabethan Backgrounds* (Hamden, Conn.: Archon Books, 1975), 9–14.

10. Paul Rabinow observes in regard to such "central" symbols as the queen's body that they "are highly ambiguous, expressive, and inherently susceptible to many interpretations; this is what makes them central" (*Symbolic Domination: Cultural Form and Historical Change in Morocco* [Chicago: University of Chicago Press, 1975], 3). This ambiguity of meaning makes Elizabeth's image essentially political.

11. John N. King's analysis of Deborah as dependent on the city in the *Passage* is especially helpful in understanding the device's representation of the queen's relation to the city (*Tudor Royal Iconography: Literature and Art in an Age of Religious Crisis* [Princeton, N.J.: Princeton University Press], 227).

12. Clifford Geertz, "Kings, Centers, Charisma: Reflections on the Symbolics of Power," in *Local Knowledge: Further Essays in Interpretive Anthropology* (New York: Basic Books, 1983), 121–46; Steven Mullaney, *The Place of the Stage: License, Play, and Power in Renaissance England* (Chicago: University of Chicago Press, 1988), 1–25, esp. 9–15; Mark Breitenberg, "'. . . the hole matter opened': Iconic Representation and Interpretation in 'The Quenes Majesties Passage,'" *Criticism* 28 (1986): 1–25 (quotation from p. 2); McCoy, "'Thou Idol Ceremony,'" 243. McCoy is not explicit about who sought to control representation in the *Passage*, observing that "the government capitalized on the success of this performance by authorizing the prompt publication of the tract itself." But as he then states, "the published record reinforced the primacy of the civic progress by shifting the focus entirely from the sacred rite to the secular pageant" (245). See also Louis Adrian Montrose, "Gifts and Reasons: The Contexts of Peele's *Araygnement of Paris*," *ELH* 47(1980): 448–52; Jonathan Goldberg, *James I and the Politics of Literature* (Baltimore: Johns Hopkins University Press, 1983), 29–33.

Although these insightful discussions are sensitive to both the context and the tone of *The Queen's Majesty's Passage*, I believe they do not probe far enough. Mullaney, for instance, quotes Geertz's judicious statement that "the symbolism of the progress was . . . admonitory and covenantal: the subjects warned, and the Queen promised" (*Place of the Stage*, 11), but what did the queen promise, and why were her promises acted out in a form at once gendered and economic?

13. On the debate on the nature of women, see Linda Woodbridge, *Women and the English Renaissance: Literature and the Nature of Womankind, 1540–1620* (Urbana: University of Illinois Press, 1986); Constance Jordan, *Renaissance Feminism: Literary Texts and Political Models* (Ithaca, N.Y.: Cornell University Press, 1990).

14. Henry Machyn, *The Diary of Henry Machyn, Citizen and Merchant-Taylor of London from A.D. 1550 to A.D. 1563* (London: Camden Society, 1848), 182. Until Mary was actually entombed, Machyn continues to speak of her in the present tense, suggesting the sense of life-in-death that accompanies monarchs who have died but are not yet entombed in this period and that is likewise expressed in the life-sized representations of the monarch in the funeral procession itself. Mary's funeral image was "the pycture of emages lyke . . . , adorned with cremesun velvett and her crowne on her hed, her septer on her hand, and mony goodly rynges on her fyngers" (182).

15. On Mary Queen of Scots as a "reproducing monarch," see Karen Robertson, "The Body Natural of a Queen: Mary, James, *Horestes*," *Renaissance and Reformation* n.s. 14 (1990), 25–36.

16. Elizabeth responded to her sister's example throughout her life. In contrast with Mary, Elizabeth preferred to use the possibility of marriage to underpin the complexities of her position among the great European powers rather than as the means to structure domestic policy, although her marriage negotiations had profound domestic consequences.

It is interesting to note in this speech that Elizabeth anticipated something of the danger that the queen of Scots experienced on bearing her own heir: She told Parliament when speaking of her hypothetical offspring that even if she took great care with him, "yet may my issue grow out of kind and become perhaps ungracious." The text of Elizabeth's letter, read as a speech, "The answere of the Quenes highnes to ye peticion proponed vnto hir by ye lower howse concerning hir mariage," declaring her virginity, is in Heisch, ed., *Queen Elizabeth I: Political Speeches;* see also J. E. Neale, *Elizabeth I and Her Parliaments, 1559–1581* (London: Jonathan Cape, 1953), 48–49.

17. On Mary Tudor's existence while her father lived, see David Loades, *Mary Tudor: A Life* (Cambridge, Mass.: Basil Blackwell, 1989), 36–222.

18. R. M. Fisher ably summarizes the accounts of Mary's accession in the *Grey Friar Chronicle* and *Two London Chronicles*: "In July 1553, such was the excitement and relief at the accession of Queen Mary, that London went wild, with choirs singing, organs playing and bells ringing in the churches, night-time bonfires, food and wine on the streets. Almost immediately the Latin mass was resumed in various churches and quickly spread throughout the realm under encouragement of royal proclamation" ("The Reformation of Church and Chapel at the Inns of Court, 1530–1580," *Guildhall Studies* 3 [April 1979]: 237).

19. Thomas Gresham to Elizabeth I, autumn 1558, in *English Historical Documents,* ed. C. H. Williams (Oxford: Oxford University Press, 1967), 5:1021.

20. 'According to a document endorsed "Considerations delivered to the Parliament, 1559," there is an admonition to Elizabeth not to repeat the error of her sister in supporting the Hanse merchants in the Steelyard: "That the Queen's Highness in no wise restore to the Stillyard their liberties, for they not only intercepted much of the English merchants' trade, but by concealment of strangers' goods robbed the Queen of customs 10,000 marks a year at least, which was so sweet to them that, as some of them confess, they gained in Queen Mary's time amongst solicitors above 10,000 £. in bribes" (Salisbury: Historical Manuscripts Commission, 1: 263). Renard wrote to Charles V on 18 September 1554 that the "London merchants" had responded to Mary's request "to advance her the money" to make "an annual payment on account of a loan . . . with a flat refusal, which the merchants would not have ventured in the past" (CSP Spanish, Mary, 12:51). See also D. M. Loades, *The Reign of Mary Tudor: Politics, Government, and Religion in England, 1553–1558* (London: Ernst Benn, 1979), esp. 183–210, for an overview of Marian finance. A discussion of Mary's relation with the Hanse merchants and her subsequent lack of credit is on pp. 196–97. I am particularly indebted to G. D. Ramsay's discussion of the Merchant Adventurers' difficulties and recovery under Mary in *The City of London in International Politics at the Accession of Mary Tudor* (Manchester: University of Manchester Press, 1975), 33–80, esp. 69.

21. Simon Renard to Charles V, 8 November 1553, CSP Spanish, 11:347.

22. John Proctor, *The History of Wyat's Rebellion: With the order and manner of resisting the same* (London: Robert Caley, 1555), in *An English Garner: Tudor Tracts, 1532–1588,* ed. and introduction by A. F. Pollard (New York: Cooper Square, 1964), 199–257. Holinshed's *Chronicles* (London: T. Woodcocke, 1586–87) 3:1096, STC 13569, reproduces a longer, variant speech.

23. Proctor, *History of Wyat's Rebellion,* 208–9. As far as Proctor is concerned, religion forms a dubious pretext for Wyatt's actions.

24. William Camden quotes Elizabeth as answering Parliament's request that she marry, with the dramatic assertion that "to satisfie you, I have already joyned my self in Marriage to an Husband, namely, the Kingdom of England. And behold (said she, which I marvell ye have forgotten,) the Pledge of this my Wedlock and Marriage withe my Kingdom" (Wallace T. MacCaffrey, ed., *The History of the Most*

Renowned and Victorious Princess Elizabeth Late Queen of England [Chicago: University of Chicago Press, 1970], 29).

25. Raphael Holinshed, *Chronicles of England and Scotland* (London: J. Johnson, 1807–1808), 4:1096. See Richard Grafton, *Grafton's Chronicle; History of England* (London: G. Woodfall, 1809), 2:540.

26. As Paul de Man notes, "Metaphors are much more tenacious than facts" (*Allegories of Reading: Figural Language in Rousseau, Nietzsche, Rilke, and Proust* [New Haven, Conn.: Yale University Press, 1979], 5).

27. John Foxe, *Acts and Monuments,* ed. George Townsend (New York: AMS Press, 1965), 6:557–58. The evidence for censorship in the firsthand account of the entry is given in a crossed-out portion of the manuscript of J. G. Nichols, ed., *The Chronicle of Queen Jane and of Two Years of Queen Mary* (London: Camden Society, 1850): "Henry the eight . . . was paynted having in one hand a cepter and in the other hande a booke, whereon was wrytten *Verbum Dei* [but after the king was passed, the bushoppe of Winchester, noting the book in Henry the eightes hande, shortely afterwards called the paynter before him, and with ville wourdes calling him traytour. . . . And so he paynted him shortly after, in the sted of the booke of *Verbum Dei,* to have in his handes a newe payre of gloves]" (78–79).

28. Loades, *Reign of Mary Tudor,* 228. On Mary and Philip's entry, see Nichols, ed., *Chronicle of Queen Jane,* 11–30; and Sidney Anglo, *Spectacle Pageantry and Early Tudor Policy* (Oxford: Clarendon Press, 1969), 318–43.

29. This detail derives from the Venetian ambassador's account of 14 January: "Owing to the deep mud caused by the foul weather and by the multitude of people and of horses, everyone had made preparation, by placing sand and gravel in front of their houses" (CSP Venice, 1558–1580, 7:12). This is the kind of description omitted in the printed text. Its very existence serves as a reminder of what is missing in the published text—any sense of disorder, the tawdry, and the everyday that might taint the authority represented in the allegories.

30. Ian Archer, *The Pursuit of Stability: Social Relations in Elizabethan London* (Cambridge: Cambridge University Press, 1991), 33.

31. Frank Foster, *The Politics of Stability* (London: Royal Historical Society, 1977), 51. As careful and detailed as Foster's account of London government through the seventeenth century is, I have reservations about his argument for its stability. For example, his picture of a ruling elite—"So stable . . . and so dependent upon the crown to reinforce it, that gradually, imperceptively, the rulers became unable to change"—stands at odds not only with the complexity of individual and group interactions in London but also with the fact that the London elites supported Cromwell during the civil war.

32. Holinshed, *Chronicles,* 4:1172; Machyn, *Diary of Henry Machyn,* 186.

33. A succinct description of the habits and privileges of members of the Court of Aldermen appears in Frank Foster, "Merchants and Bureaucrats in Elizabethan London," *Guildhall Miscellany* 4 (1972): 155. See also Archer, *Pursuit of Stability,* 18–20; Ramsay, *City of London,* 34.

Richard Mulcaster was paid by the Court of Aldermen for "makyng of the boke conteynynge and declaryng the historyes set furth in and by the Cyties pageauntes at the tyme of the Quenes highnes commyng thurrough the Citye to her coronacion xls. which boke was geuyn vnto the Quenes grace" (4 April 1559, *Repertory Book* 14, fol. 143). This is also the source for the names of the entry's coauthors.

Charles Read Baskervill, in "Richard Mulcaster," *Times Literary Supplement* 15 (August 1935): 315, the source of this quotation, concluded from this account that Mulcaster followed tradition by presenting Queen Elizabeth with a manuscript version of the pageant, whose text served as the basis for Tottel's two editions. See also Richard Grafton, *Abridgement of the Chronicles of England* (London: J. Wolsey, 1576), fol. 167v, 195.

34. For additional background on Richard Mulcaster, see Richard L. DeMolen, "Richard Mulcaster and Elizabethan Pageantry," *Studies in English Literature* 14 (1974): 209–21. Albert Feuillerat's edition of the Revels Accounts lists a number of plays and provisions for "Munkester boyes" and the "Munkester Children" at Elizabeth's court (*Documents Relating to the Office of the Revels in the Reign of Elizabeth* [Louvain: A. Uystprupt, 1914], esp. 206, 213, 350).

35. See, for example, John Neale, *Queen Elizabeth I: A Biography* (Garden City, N.Y.: Doubleday, 1957), 59–63, which quotes and paraphrases the entry as an objective description of events. It is interesting to note that even though Holinshed's *Chronicles,* with its distinct city bias, prints the *Passage,* John Foxe finds its expression of religious sentiments inadequate. He chooses to "pass over" her triumphal entry and substitutes for it an oration by John Hales delivered to her majesty at the outset of her reign, which urges her in no uncertain terms to enforce Protestantism. Hales's (and through him, Foxe's) message is no less urgent than the London merchants', although it is more distinctly religious. Foxe thus was sensitive to the ideological content of the *Passage* in a way that few twentieth-century readers have been (*Acts and Monuments* 673–79). Even in the most recent treatments of the *Passage,* there is a tendency either to assume that the text is untroubled or to conflate the city's authority that the text represents with the Crown's authority. This is the point at which I disagree with Louis Montrose's reading of the entry as "an early example of the regime's cultivation of popular opinion" ("Gifts and Reasons: The Contexts of Peele's *Araygnement of Paris," ELH* 47 [1980]: 449). Because the city's citizens paid for the entry to a man and the aldermen paid for the text, this is an example not of the regime's cultivation of opinion but of the city's.

36. Arthur Bryant, *The Elizabethan Deliverance* (New York: St. Martin's Press, 1981), 25.

37. Gilbert Dugdale's account of a royalist citizen is addressed to a general audience and bears out Jonson's assertion that the devices did not exist for the average citizen to understand (*The Time Triumphant,* in *Progresses of King James I,* ed. J. G. Nichols [1828; London: B. Franklin, 1964], 409–19). Dugdale had difficulty seeing what was going on in the crowded streets and even more difficulty interpreting what he saw, at one point commenting, "There was cost both curious and comely, but the Devises of that afarre off I could not coniecture: but by report it was exceeding; . . . [it was] pompous both for glorie and matter, a stage standing by, on which were enacted strange things, after which an Oration delivered of great wisdome" (418). See also David M. Bergeron, "Gilbert Dugdale and the Royal Entry of James I (1604)," *Journal of Medieval and Renaissance Studies* 13 (1983): 111–25.

Stephen Harrison, a London joiner and architect, is the only writer whose text credits the city's government as his sponsor and directly addresses his fellow citizens. Harrison published his magnificent engravings with an abbreviated text in an effective attempt to preserve some of the glory of the temporary wooden arches that the city paid for and erected. Full of the details of city organization and finance, his text exists to "doe honour to this Citie, so long as the Citie shall beare a name" (*The Archs of Trivmph Erected in honor of the High and mighty prince James the first of that name King, of England, and the Sixt of Scotland, at his Maiesties Entrance and passage through His honorable Citty & Chamber of London opon the 15th day of march 1603* [London: William Kip, 1604], STC 12863, dedication to the Lord Mayor). See also David Bevington's discussion of the many discrepancies among these texts, in "Harrison, Jonson and Dekker: The Magnificent Entertainment for King James (1604)" *Journal of the Warburg and Cortauld Institute* 31(1968): 445–48.

38. See Thomas Dekker, *The Magnificent Entertainment: Giuen to King James . . .* , in *The Dramatic Works of Thomas Dekker*, ed. R. H. Shepherd (London: John Pearson, 1873), 162–339 (quotation from p. 302). Echoes of Mulcaster suggest that Dekker not only read *The Queen's Majesty's Passage,* but also saw his text as fulfilling a similar role.

39. Ben Jonson, *Part of the Kings Entertainment in Passing to his Coronation,* in *Ben Jonson,* ed. C. H. Herford, Percy Simpson, and Evelyn Simpson (Oxford: Oxford University Press, 1941), 7: 65–109. (This is the title that Jonson chose for the folio edition of his works, but it is not accurate, since the king was crowned long before the entertainment took place.)

40. Jonson, for example, scorned the use of the poet-presenter or "Truch-man," so crucial to explication in Elizabethan allegory: "Neither was it becomming, or could it stand with the dignitie of these shewes (after the most miserable and desperate shift of the Puppits) to require a Truch-man, or (with the ignorant Painter) one to write, *This is a Dog;* or, *This is a Hare*: but so to be presented, as vpon the view, they might, without cloud, or obscuritie, declare themselues to the sharpe and learned: And for the multitude, no doubt but their grounded iudgements did gaze, said it was fine, and were satisfied" (ibid., 91).

Jonson, who is at great pains to distinguish his entertainment from pageantry in his account (the Quarto adds, "neither are we ashamed to professe it [the device], being assured well of the difference betweene it and Pageantry"), prefers to leave behind his city roots and represent himself as the king's man (104n).

41. Ibid., 106–9. This portion of the entertainment took place in the Strand. In the Quarto's introduction to the final device in which Electra welcomes James as Augustus, Jonson's protest that he is no simple pageant-writer tells us how he imagined his audience as well as his role: "Thus hath both Court-Towne-and Countrey-Reader, our portion of deuise for the Cittie; neither are we ashamed to professe it, being assured well of the difference betweene it and Pageantry" (104n).

42. See David Riggs's discussion of James's entry and its success, as well as the success of the other text that Jonson wrote to mark the occasion, his *Panegyre,* in *Ben Jonson: A Life* (Cambridge, Mass.: Harvard University Press, 1989), 111–12.

43. Ben Jonson, *B. I. His Panegyre. On the happie entrance of Iames our Soueraigne to his first high Session of Parliament . . . March 1603,* in Herford, Simpson, and Simpson, eds., *Ben Jonson,* 7:114.

44. Mary Crane describes this aspect of Elizabeth's situation: "She knew that as a young woman, undertaking to rule England when the right of women to succeed to the throne was questioned and criticized on all sides, she should expect to be told what to do" ("'Video et Taceo': Elizabeth I and the Rhetoric of Counsel," *Studies in English Literature* 28 [1988]: 5). Crane's article provides an insightful analysis of Elizabeth's use of the symbolic system of political counsel. Her analysis of Elizabeth's coronation entry, however, suggests that "even her lowliest subjects be-

lieved that she needed advice," when it was London's chief citizens who addressed the queen.

45. Arthur Wilson, *The History of Great Britain, Being the Life and Reign of King James I* (London: R.W., 1653), 12; Dekker, *Magnificent Entertainment,* 168.

46. Dekker, *Magnificent Entertainment,* 304, 303, 323. Goldberg aptly summarizes the position of the monarch in the two entries: "Whereas Elizabeth played at being part of the pageants, James played at being apart, separate. The pageants presented for Elizabeth form a coherent, mutually reflective whole, and Elizabeth acted within the limits of its design (limits she may have helped design). James's pageants are not connected; each has its own symbolic center, its inherent design. The pageants do not build on each other or lead to each other, as Elizabeth's do. Yet they are connected: each exists only in and for the king. His presence gives them life; his absence robs them. Their existence depends upon him. In Elizabeth's entrance, she is an actor in a total script, given the part of the bride" (*James I and the Politics of Literature,* 31–46). In James's entrance, as Dekker notes, the city is the actor.

47. See Nicholas Udall, *The noble triumphant Coronation of Queen Anne, Wife unto the most noble King henry the viiith,* in Pollard, ed., *Tudor Tracts,* 9–28.

48. Henry VIII's Second Succession Act (1536) and Henry VIII's Will (selection) (1546), in Mortimer Levine, *Tudor Dynastic Problems, 1460–1571* (New York: Barnes & Noble, 1973), 155–56, 163–64.

49. Allegory in the genre of spectacle depends on explanation, but allegory in general includes "dark conceit" and enigma among its types. The meanings encoded in allegory are so slippery that one view of allegory has always been that its meanings remain difficult or impossible to discover. Renaissance writers frequently valued the concept of allegory as the signifier with no ascertainable signified because of the exclusivity and spirituality of "dark" conceits or enigma. Philip Sidney, for example, considers them to be an important force in poetry: There are "many mysteries contained in Poetry," he explains in the *Apology,* "which of purpose were written darkly, lest by profane wits it should be abused"—a view based at least as much on the intellectual complexity of interpreting classical texts according to the ideology of English classical humanism as on the writing of contemporary poetry. But at the same time that Sidney equates allegory with enigma, associating poetry's "darkness" with its divine sources of creativity, his entire ethical defense of poetry rests on poetry's ability to make clear through allegory a morality that philosophy teaches too abstractly and history, too particularly: "I say the philosopher teacheth, but he teacheth obscurely. . . . But the poet is the food for the tenderest stomachs . . . whose pretty allegories . . . make many . . . to hear the sound of virtue." Sidney commends poetry for its ability to enlighten, not darken: The "speaking picture of poesy" illuminates or figures forth "many infallible grounds of wisdom, which, notwithstanding, lie dark before the imaginative and judging power" (*An Apology for Poetry, or the Defence of Poesy,* ed. Geoffrey Shepherd [London: Thomas Nelson, 1965], 142, 109, 107).

In expressing the belief that dark poetic allegory shields truth from "abuse," the *Apology*'s discussion articulates allegory's central paradox, that it can be the most obscure and the most obvious of symbolic forms. This paradox of allegory's decipherability can be found in the differing perspectives offered by two of this century's great writers on allegory. Rosemund Tuve implies that although enigma was attractive to authors, the allegorist's delight lies in the ultimate comprehension of allegory: "There is much of the delight which traditional theory taught poets to achieve with *allegoria*: the tenuous but firm and pursuable connections between the multiplied terms of a continued metaphor, traceable like veins under the smooth surface of an ostensible concrete structure of meaning" (*Elizabethan and Metaphysical Imagery: Renaissance Poetic and Twentieth-Century Critics* [Chicago: University of Chicago Press, 1947], 134).

Angus Fletcher, however, takes issue with Tuve, insisting that "enigma, and not always decipherable enigma, appears to be allegory's most cherished function" (*Allegory: The Theory of a Symbolic Mode* [Ithaca, N.Y.: Cornell University Press, 1964], 72–73). For an overview of Elizabethan rhetorical discussions of enigma, see Michael Murrin, *The Veil of Allegory: Some Notes Toward a Theory of Allegorical Rhetoric in the English Renaissance* (Chicago: University of Chicago Press, 1969), 59–61. The split between those for whom allegory functions as mystery and those who see its value in multivalent interpretations results from the varied nature of allegory, the trope of tropes, itself the representation of the disconnection between a figure and its meaning.

50. In Elizabethan spectacle, the purpose of allegory was its interpretation, and the function of interpretation was to provide a crucial, if incomplete, unfolding of all that an allegory contained, of the ways that figures and iconography connected outward toward an ideologically constructed cosmology of "natural" associations. The task of explicating every conceivable authoritative meaning for each part of the device and for the device as a whole is too exhaustive for any narrator, even the intrepid Richard Mulcaster. But the open-endedness of allegorical interpretation made it serviceable to statesman, writer, and humanist alike. As John Harington noted in his preface to *Orlando Furioso,* the value of allegory lies in the encoded meanings of philosophy and divinity, as well as meanings of "politike gouerne-ment" that defy complete interpretation. Writes Harington of the figure Perseus, "Now let any man iudge if it be a matter of meane art or wit to containe in one historicall narration, either true or fained, so many, so diuerse, and so deepe conceits" (Preface to *Orlando Furioso,* in *Elizabethan Critical Essays,* ed. G. Gregory Smith [Oxford: Clarendon Press, 1904], 2:201–3). Or as Umberto Eco summarizes this attraction to allegory, "What is frequently appreciated in many so-called symbols is exactly their vagueness, their openness, their fruitful ineffectiveness to express a 'final' meaning, so that with symbols and by symbols one indicates what is always *beyond* one's reach" (*Semiotics and the Philosophy of Language* [Bloomington: Indiana University Press, 1984], 130).

51. Before Truth, the Daughter of Time, became associated with Elizabeth, it had enjoyed a long history of definition and appropriation. The biblical source of the humanist formula "Veritas filia temporis" is Psalm 85, which describes how peace will be restored when Truth springs from the ground and Righteousness looks down from the sky. D. J. Gordon traces the literary origins of this motto from John Knoblouch of Strasbourg in 1521, the Protestant publisher of Luther, Melanchthon, and Erasmus: "For Knoblouch the text and its illustration indicated the coming triumph of Protestantism" (*"Veritas Filia Temporis*: Hadrianus Junius and Geoffrey Whitney [1940]," in *The Renaissance Imagination: Essays and Letters of D. J. Gordon,* ed. Stephen Orgel [Berkeley: University of California Press, 1980], 220–32 [quotation from p. 222]). In England, the formula was appropriated in texts allegorizing Queen Mary. The play *Respublica,* published in 1553, uses the formula with reference to Mary, whereas Hadrianus Junius's dedication to Mary of *Philippeis,* a poem celebrating her marriage, reads: "Of Mary Truth the Daughter of Time. Nothing lies in darkness, for Truth brings all to light, and Time is the divider

of true from false." Because John Knox boldly reclaims the device for Protestantism by printing "Veritas Filia Temporis" on the 1559 title page of *First Blast Against the Monstrous Regiment of Women,* it is interesting to see that the *Passage* appropriates the emblem from both ends of the religious spectrum.

52. In *The Invention of Tradition* (Cambridge: Cambridge University Press, 1983), Eric Hobsbawm defines "invented tradition," such as that developed during the London entry, as "a set of practices, normally governed by overtly or tacitly accepted rules and of a ritual or symbolic nature, which seek to inculcate certain values and norms of behaviour by repetition, which automatically implies continuity with the past" (1)—a good description of allegory's legitimation practice.

53. Althusser elucidates the relation between ideas and the everyday in his statement that "where only a single subject . . . is concerned, the existence of the ideas of his belief is material in that *his ideas are his material actions inserted into material practices governed by material rituals which are themselves defined by the material ideological apparatus from which derive the ideas of that subject*" ("Ideology and Ideological State Apparatuses," 169).

54. See Katherine Parr, *Prayers stirrying the mynd unto heavenlye medytacions* (London: E. Whitchurche, 1547), STC 4827, which appeared in thirteen subsequent editions, and *The Lamentacion of a Sinner* (London: T. Berthelet, 1545), STC 4827, and in three subsequent editions, both of which are reprinted in *The Monument of Matrones: conteining seven severall Lamps of Virginitie, or distinct treatises . . . compiled . . . by Thomas Benley of Graies Inne Student* (London: H. Denhem, 1592), STC 1892, 221–46.

55. Machyn, *Diary of Henry Machyn,* 221.

56. Ibid.; CSP Spanish, Elizabeth, 1:404.

57. Robert Dutton describes this play in *Mastering the Revels: The Regulation and Censorship of English Renaissance Drama* (Iowa City: University of Iowa Press, 1991), 69. He points out that the new queen was also willing to extend the censorship that she personally imposed at court on England at large during the transition between reigns. From April 1559 to the following November, Elizabeth proclaimed that "the Quenes Majestie doth straightly forbyd all maner Interludes to be playde eyther openly or privately, except the same be notified before hande, and licenced within any Citie or towne corporate" (22).

58. Froude dates Elizabeth's reply to Parliament as 6 February 1559. I am relying on the edition and discussion of Elizabeth's letter "The answere of the Quenes . . . highnes to ye lower howse concerning hir mariage" in Heisch, ed., *Queen Elizabeth I: Political Speeches.* See also Neale, *Elizabeth I and Her Parliaments,* 48–49.

59. "The Lady Elizabeth hir Grace's Aunsweare, made at Hattfeilde, the 26th of April, 1558; to Sir Thomas Pope, Knight . . . ," in Scott, ed., *Collection of Scarce and Valuable Tracts,* 1:57.

60. That Elizabeth's circumspection grows from powerlessness and a resulting unwillingness to be open can be seen by contrasting Pope's report of her talk with a self-confident letter she wrote to her brother, Edward VI, about her image—her portrait, sent at his request and accompanied by this letter. In it, Elizabeth paraphrased Virgil in writing, "For the face, I grant, I might well blush to offer, but the mind I shall never be ashamed to present" (G. B. Harrison, ed., *The Letters of Queen Elizabeth* [1935; New York: Funk & Wagnalls, 1968], 15).

61. "The answere of the Quenes highnes to . . . ye lower howse concerning hir

mariage," in Heisch, ed., *Queen Elizabeth I: Political Speeches,* lines 7–19, 58–61. This does not mean, however, that the idea and iconography of Elizabeth's virginity remained static throughout her reign. Instead, shifts in the attitude toward her virginity—allegorized as Chastity—form an index of the shifting relation between iconography and policy throughout her reign. For discussion of the historical attitude that Elizabeth's virginity was an unchanging concept, see John N. King, "Queen Elizabeth I: Representations of the Virgin Queen," *Renaissance Quarterly* 43(1990): 30–74. See also Philippa Berry, *Of Chastity and Power: Elizabethan Literature and the Unmarried Queen* (London: Routledge, 1989).

62. "The answere of the Quenes hignes to . . . ye lower howse concerning hir mariage," in Heisch, ed., *Queen Elizabeth I: Political Speeches,* lines 19–23, 27–29; see also Neale, *Elizabeth I and Her Parliaments,* 48.

63. Eric Mallin, "Emulous Factions and the Collapse of Chivalry: *Troilus and Cressida,*" *Representations* 29 (1990): 145–79.

64. A. F. Pollard, "Local History," *Times Literary Supplement* 11 (March 1920): 1, 162.

65. See Adrian Prockter and Robert Taylor, *The A to Z of Elizabethan London,* with introduction by John Fisher, London Topographical Society Publication no. 122 (London: London Topographical Society, 1979), viii.

66. Thomas Gresham to Elizabeth I, autumn 1558, in Williams, ed., *English Historical Documents,* 5:1022; Ramsay, *City of London,* 50, 57. For an overview of Crown–city relations that supports this more detailed picture, see D. M. Palliser, *The Age of Elizabeth* (London: Longman Group, 1983), esp. 216.

67. Foster, "Merchants and Bureaucrats in Elizabethan London," 152. Foster also notes that the recorder worked to gain support for the city in its disputes with other jurisdictions, assignments that called for diplomacy and legal expertise.

68. In the Renaissance, the most obvious example of the association between the purse and sex lies in the language of Iago, who, like the morality vice figures from whom he derives, enters carrying a purse. The purse belongs to Roderigo, who provides the opening lines of *Othello*:

> [Tush,] never tell me! I take it much unkindly
> That thou, Iago, who hast had my purse
> As if the strings were thine, shouldst know of this. (I.i.1–3)

"This" is the knowledge of Desdemona and Othello's elopement, which dismays Roderigo because he has paid Iago to keep his hope for her alive. Although later counseled by Iago eight times in twenty-six lines to "put money in his purse," or, in brief, to "make money" at the thought of Desdemona's future infidelities, Roderigo's money is never realized as sex (I.iii.339–65), yet the association of Roderigo's money with Desdemona composes the first slander against her (*Riverside Shakespeare,* ed. G. Blakemore Evans [Boston: Houghton Mifflin, 1974]).

69. John Nichols, ed., *The Progresses and Public Processions of Queen Elizabeth* (London: John Nichols, 1823; New York: AMS Press, 1966), 3:231.

70. The device of Truth, the Daughter of Time, formed such a potent part of the seventeenth-century myth of Elizabeth as a militant Protestant that we must be particularly wary when reconstructing its significance in 1559. In addition to retelling the scene at the dramatic conclusion of *Englands Elizabeth,* Thomas Heywood adapted the device in *If You Know Not Me* (*Englands Elizabeth her life and troubles during her minoritie, from the cradle to the crowne* [London: John Beale, 1631], STC 13313; *If You Know Not Me, You Know Nobody,* pt. 1 [London: N. Butter, 1605],

STC 13328]). In *The Whore of Babylon,* Thomas Dekker staged a character named Titania receiving a book from Time and Truth in the opening dumbshow (*The Whore of Babylon* [London: N. Butter, 1607], STC 6532). David Bergeron discusses the two plays' scenes in *English Civic Pageantry, 1558–1642* (Columbia: University of South Carolina Press, 1971), 20–21; and Sheila Williams, "Two Seventeenth Century Semi-Dramatic Allegories of Truth the Daughter of Time," *Guildhall Miscellany* 5 (1963): 207–20, discusses the importance of the allegory in two Lord Mayors' pageants. For a discussion of other elements in *The Queen's Majesty's Passage* that appear in drama, see David Bergeron, "Middleton's *No Wit, No Help,*" in *Pageantry in the Shakespearian Theatre* (Athens: University of Georgia Press, 1985), 66.

71. "A Copy of the Devise for alteratione of Religione, at the first Year of Q. Eliz," in Scott, ed., *Collection of Scarce and Valuable Tracts,* 1: 61–64 (quotation from p. 64). For an alternative reading of this text, see Neale, *Elizabeth I and Her Parliaments,* 37.

72. Patrick Collinson, *Archbishop Grindal 1519–1583: The Struggle for a Reformed Church* (Berkeley: University of California Press, 1979), 117.

73. Observes Geertz: "Britain's political imagination . . . was allegorical, Protestant, didactic, and pictorial" ("Centers, Kings, Charisma," 129). Mullaney conceives of Protestantism as central to the entry: "While [the allegories] invited Elizabeth's response, making her both audience to and central actor in the ongoing dramaturgy of state, they also shaped and qualified that response, eliciting vows of a peaceful, harmonious, and above all Protestant rule from the incipient queen" (*Place of the Stage,* 11). And for Breitenberg, the device of Truth, the Daughter of Time, "declares in no uncertain terms the shift to Protestantism embraced by Elizabeth and her Parliament" ("' . . . the hole matter opened,'" 3).

74. Collinson, *Archbishop Grindal,* 114.

75. Il Schifanoya to the Castelan of Mantua, 23 January 1559, CSP Venice, 7:11.

76. In the following list of eighteen known members of the Court of Aldermen in 1558/1559, I have starred the names of those about whom some biographical information is known. The mayor in 1559 was *Thomas Leigh, a Mercer, and the sheriff was John Hawse. The other identifiable aldermen were John Lyon, Grocer; *William Garrarde, Haberdasher; *William Hewett, Clothworker; Thomas Curtes, Pewterer; *William Chester, Draper; *Thomas Lodge, Sr., Grocer; *William Harper, Merchant Taylor; Richard Foulkes, Clothworker; Thomas Rowe, Merchant Taylor; Alexander Avenon, Ironmonger; Humphrey Baskerfeld, Mercer; *Thomas Whyte, Merchant Taylor; and William Alleyn, Leatherseller. The Catholic members were *Thomas Offley, Merchant Taylor; *David Woodroffe, Haberdasher; and *John Cowper, Fishmonger. My sources are Alfred B. Beaven, *The Aldermen of the City of London* (London: Eden Fisher, 1913), 2:80–211; Foster, *Politics of Stability,* 127–28 (esp. on Catholic members); *Dictionary of National Biography;* Stow, *Survey;* M. B. Donald, *Elizabethan Copper* (London: Pergamon Press, 1955).

77. Patrick Collinson, "The Elizabethan Church and the New Religion," in Haigh, ed., *Reign of Elizabeth I,* 175. Wallace MacCaffrey concludes that "it is fair to guess that the queen was pushed farther and faster along the road from Rome than she would ideally have preferred" ("Parliament: The Elizabethan Experience," in *Tudor Rule and Revolution: Essays for G. R. Elton,* ed. Deloyd J. Guth and John W. McKenna [Cambridge: Cambridge University Press, 1982], 135).

78. For an analysis of Elizabeth's coronation ritual as pleasing neither Catholic nor Protestant, see McCoy, "'Thou Idol Ceremony,'" 240–43. The Count de Feria's description of the coronation appears in CSP Spanish, 31 January 1559.

79. Then Tiepolo procedes to tell how on St. George's Day, Elizabeth would allow no cross to be displayed in the procesion of the Knights of the Garter (4 May 1559, CSP Venice).

80. *A Diurnal of Remarkable Occurrents that Have Passed within the Country of Scotland since the Death of King James the Fourth* (Edinburgh, 1833), 68; Thomas Randolphe to Cecil, 7 September 1561, CSP Scottish, 1509–1589, 1017; John Knox, *History of the Reformation in Scotland* in *The Works of John Knox,* ed. David Laing (Edinburgh: James Thin, 1905), 2:288.

81. David Daiches, *Edinburgh* (London: Hamish Hamilton, 1978), 44–45; see esp. 26–46, for an excellent overview of the period.

82. *Extracts from the Records of the Burgh of Edinburgh,* A.D. *1557–1571* (Edinburgh: Scottish Burgh Records Society, 1875), 117; Daiches, *Edinburgh,* 35. These *Records* also document the council's decision to pay for Mary's entry through "ane generale taxt to be rasit of the hale toun" and the ensuing debate on that issue (119–20).

83. ". . . while it will be obvious that the Catholics were fighting for the past" (Herbert Butterfield, *The Whig Interpretation of History* [New York: Norton, 1965], 26).

84. The kind of Catholic–Protestant alliance evident in the religious makeup of the Court of Aldermen permeated London society and city–Crown relations. The evidence exists in the biographies of individual men, whether practicing or proto-Catholics, such as Edmund Plowden, the noted attorney and city gentleman, who, although an ardent Catholic, asked to be buried in the Protestant chapel of the Temple Chapel, where his fine tomb may be seen today. Two of the most thorough recorders of London life during the sixteenth century were proto-Catholic: Henry Machyn and John Stow, the latter nevertheless patronized by Robert Dudley of the militant Protestant faction. Henry Machyn's diary amply demonstrates that the return of Protestantism made little difference in the ritual of city life. Chiefly concerned with ritual and stability because of his business in funeral materials, he was slightly more enthusiastic about Elizabeth's accession than he had been at Mary's, in part because of his dismay at the increasing civil disorder under Mary. Foster notes that one of the Catholic aldermen at Elizabeth's entry, Thomas White, cooperated with Richard Hills, a Puritan, to found the Merchant Taylor's School—still another example of the potential for tolerance in the early years of Elizabeth's reign (*Politics of Stability,* 126).

85. "There was no inherent theological reason for the protestant emphasis on frugality, hard work, accumulation; but that emphasis was a natural consequence of the religion of the heart in a society where capitalist industry was developing. It was, if we like, a rationalization; but it flowed naturally from protestant theology, whose main significance, for our present purposes, is that in any given society it enabled religion to be moulded by those who dominated in that society" (Christopher Hill, "Protestantism and the Rise of Capitalism," in *Essays in the Economic and Social History of Tudor and Stuart England in Honour of R. H. Tawney,* ed. F. J. Fisher [Cambridge: Cambridge University Press, 1961], 36). On the relation between Protestantism and London, see also Whitney R. D. Jones, *The Tudor Commonwealth, 1529–1559: A Study of the Impact of the Social and Economic Developments of Mid-Tudor England upon Contemporary Concepts of the Nature and Duties of the*

Commonwealth (London: Athlone Press, 1970), 65–85. On the relation between London and the drama that considers religious questions as essentially civic, see Anne Barton, "London Comedy and the Ethos of the City," *London Journal* 4 (1978): 158–80. In her article, Barton relies heavily on Foster's *Politics of Stability,* quoting his view of the relation between city leaders and religion: "So great was their abiding loyalty to the City, and to each other, so deep and reverent their commitment to City politics, that their profoundest religious impulses seem understandable only if viewed as a blending of the civic and the spiritual" (5).

86. See Natalie Zemon Davis, "The Sacred and the Body Social in Lyon," *Past and Present* 90 (1981): 59. Davis's article examines the interplay of Catholicism and Calvinism in Lyon with a number of sociospecific conclusions, but her question, posed with Ernst Troelstch, Max Weber, and Bernd Moeller, "How can religion continuously shape a sense of urban community, of urban solidarity?" (41) is central to my analysis of London as well.

87. Foster, *Politics of Stability,* 145. D. M. Loades concludes, "The adventurers were the most important element in the economic structure of the city of London, and as such played a vital part in the maintenance of the government's credit, quite apart from the direct loans which they could occasionally be induced to grant. It was the resources of London which guaranteed to the bankers of Antwerp that the sums of ready money which they advanced to the English crown would eventually be repaid" (*Reign of Mary Tudor,* 197).

88. See Cyprian Blagden, *The Stationers Company: A History, 1403–1959* (Stanford, Calif.: Stanford University Press, 1960), 41; Erna Auerbach, "Portraits of Elizabeth I on Some City Companies' Charters," *Guildhall Miscellany* 1 (1956): 15–24.

89. Foster, *Politics of Stability,* 151.

90. David Bergeron, "Elizabeth's Coronation Entry (1559): New Manuscript Evidence," *English Literary Renaissance* 8 (1978): 4.

91. Albert Feuillerat, ed., *Documents Relating to the Revels at Court in the Time of King Edward VI and Queen Mary* (Loseley MSS.) (Louvain: A. Uystprust, 1914), 249. These items were noted as "Delyuerd vnto Stephyn Cobbe George Todlowe and Wylliam Mosyne the Xth daye of ffebruarye in Ano Regis Edwardi VI primo for thuse of the Cytie of London agaynste the coronacion."

92. Ferdinand Braudel, *The Structures of Everyday Life: The Limits of the Possible* (New York: Harper & Row, 1979), 481.

93. Palliser observes, "The numbers of cloths exported from London (the greater part of all exports) held steady between 1559 and 1603" (*Age of Elizabeth,* 251); on internal decay and recession, see 225–30.

94. Of the domestic traders, many "dabbled extensively in domestic concessions, such as customs farms, licenses and patents of monopoly" (Robert Ashton, *The City and the Court, 1603–1643* [Cambridge: Cambridge University Press, 1979], 28).

95. Ramsay, *City of London,* 42–43. It is important to note that "though the most influential Merchant Adventurers resided in London, there were many in other English towns" that frequently incorporated the Merchant Adventurers "as a separate fraternity" (Charles Gross, *The Gild Merchant: A Contribution to British Municipal History* [Oxford: Clarendon Press, 1890], 151). Like Ramsay, Ashton concludes that "the privileged overseas traders of London were among the chief beneficiaries of the commercial policies of the Elizabethan government." Ashton continues, "Correspondingly, the commercial fortunes of those rich merchants

whose main interests were in domestic rather than foreign trade, and who, as Lang's researchers have demonstrated, represent a highly significant sector of both the business and the aldermanic élites, were less intimately connected with the crown" (*City and the Court,* 15). At the same time, it is also true that the boundaries between these types of merchants were not entirely clear, since some merchants exported unfinished cloth and were involved with finished cloth as well.

96. Sybil M. Jack, *Trade and Industry in Tudor and Stuart England* (London: Allen & Unwin, 1977), 124.

97. Ramsay, *City of London,* 44.

98. Ibid., 39, 50, 151.

99. On the competition between the Clothworkers and the Merchant Taylors from the 1560s to 1614, the year that the Crown withdrew the Merchant Taylors' trading privileges, see G. D. Ramsay, "Clothworkers, Merchants Adventurers and Richard Hakluyt," *English Historical Review* 92 (1977): 504–21. I am grateful to Joan Linton for pointing out this article to me.

100. The evidence of the crucial relation between the Crown and London's merchants engaged in foreign trade helps explain one of the puzzling differences between Elizabeth's entry and that of her predecessor and successor. During the London entries of Queen Mary and King James, foreign interests were openly displayed alongside domestic allegories. For Mary's entry, the welcoming arches were in part sponsored by foreign interests: The Genoese sponsored a show at Fenchurch, and the Florentines, an arch at Grace Street. The entry of James I featured arches paid for and conceived by the Low Countries and the Italians. See Machyn, *Diary of Henry Machyn,* 43; Bergeron, "Gilbert Dugdale," 120. But it is a curious feature and one explained only by the aldermen's and Merchant Adventurers' distaste for foreign merchants, that a single device was sponsored by foreign interests. Not only was Elizabeth's entry apparently free of foreign support, but the narrator of *The Queen's Majesty's Passage* also is anxious to point out that the entry was prepared without foreign influence: "Thus the Queenes hyghnesse passed through the citie, whiche without anye forreyne persone, of it selfe beautifyed it selfe" (E2v). Throughout the pageant, "on eyther syde ther was nothing but gladnes, nothing but prayer, nothing but comfort" (A2–A2v). The city declares an end to imperial and Hanseatic interests by imagining itself in a politically advantageous match with a sovereign who guarantees independence from foreign powers.

101. Pierre Bourdieu, *Outline of a Theory of Practice,* trans. Richard Nice (Cambridge: Cambridge University Press, 1977), 170.

102. Thomas Norton, *To the queenes maiesties poore deceived subiectes of the northe contreye* (London: L. Harrison, 1569), STC 18679.5, Bv.

Chapter 2

1. Conyers Read, *Lord Burghley and Queen Elizabeth* (New York: Knopf, 1961), 70.

2. 18 July 1575, CSP Spanish, Elizabeth 2:497–99.

3. George Gascoigne, *The Princely Pleasures at the Courte at Kenelworth. That is to saye, The Copies of all such Verses, Proses, or poetical inventions, and other Devices of Pleasure, as were there deuised, and presented by sundry Gentlemen, before the Quene's Majestie . . . ,* in *The Progresses and Public Processions of Queen Elizabeth,* ed. John Nichols (London: John Nichols, 1823; New York: AMS Press, 1966), 1:485–523;

A Letter: Whearin, part of the Entertainment, untoo the Queenz Maiesty, at KILLINGWORTH CASTL, in Warwik Sheer, in this Soomerz Progress, 1575, iz signified: from a freend officer attendant in the Coourt, unto hiz freend a Citizen, and Merchaunt of London [known as *Laneham's Letter*], in Nichols, ed., *Progresses,* 1:420–84. Pages of subsequent citations from these works appear in the text.

Laneham's Letter—and, to a lesser extent, *The Princely Pleasures*—became the basis of two literary revisits to Kenilworth, Ben Jonson's *Masque of Owls,* whose several allusions to *Laneham's Letter* suggest that it had wide currency, and Walter Scott's *Kenilworth,* which creates Laneham as an Elizabethan eccentric and quotes *Laneham's Letter*'s descriptions of the fireworks. In providing Laneham with a complete fictive identity, the novel spawned two Victorian editions of *Laneham's Letter.* See Ben Jonson, *Masque of Owls,* in *Ben Jonson,* ed. C. H. Herford, Percy Simpson, and Evelyn Simpson (Oxford: Clarendon Press, 1952) 7:781–86; Walter Scott, *Kenilworth* (London: Macdonald, 1953).

4. 19 February 1566, CSP Venice, 7:374–75.

5. Paul L. Hughes and James F. Larkin, eds., *Tudor Royal Proclamations* (New Haven, Conn.: Yale University Press, 1969), 2:240–41.

6. *Laneham's Letter* describes the bride as a "thirtie-five yeer" old, "of colour broun-bay, not very beautifull indeed, but ugley, fooul ill favord, yet marveyloous fain of the offis . . . [to] dauns before the Queen, in which feat shee thought she woold foot it az finely az the best" (444). Could Elizabeth at thirty-nine have ignored the humor generated by the marriage of so old a bride? Although a woman at court aged far more slowly than a country woman of this period, the woman who says she dances "az finely az the best" herself suggests that she is a parallel figure of the queen.

7. I am grateful to Joan Linton for our discussions about George Gascoigne and many other subjects. Richard McCoy's discussions of Gascoigne's career in "Gascoigne's 'Poëmata castrata': The Wages of Courtly Success," *Criticism* 27 (1985): 29–54, and in *The Rites of Knighthood: The Literature and Politics of Elizabethan Chivalry* (Berkeley: University of California Press, 1989), esp. 42–45, are central to my conception of Gascoigne as well, although I differ from his analysis of Kenilworth on several points. For one thing, I examine *Laneham's Letter* as a more problematic text than McCoy does. For another, I question whether Gascoigne really had "secured" Leicester's patronage ("Gascoigne's 'Poëmata,'" 29), although he was clearly asked to organize and write much of the Kenilworth entertainments. I also question whether the problematic nature of those entertainments resulted so readily in the queen's support of Gascoigne. From my perspective, Elizabeth's next assigning Gascoigne to transcribe *The Tale of Hemetes the Heremyte,* which Sir Henry Lee presented for her at Woodstock that same summer, was in the nature of a courtly reproof. As McCoy points out, "Lee's show was as well thought of, as any thing ever done before her majestie," apparently because it more faithfully reproduced her preferred iconography of virginity. He finds this "a pointed snub to Leicester's entertainment, which immediately preceded it," but disassociates Gascoigne from that snub (*Rites of Knighthood,* 44–45). I believe that Gascoigne attempted to make the best of *Hemetes the Heremyte* by treating it as an unambiguous commission, paying for an elaborate frontispiece to illustrate his homage to the queen, displaying his learning by translating *Hemetes* into Latin, French, and Italian, and prefacing it with a lengthy self-advertisement, although the commission was a result of Elizabeth's displeasure. Thus I interpret Gascoigne's plea in the introduction, "Forgett, most excellent Lady, the poesies which I have scattered in

the world, and I vowe to wryte volumes of proffitable poems, wherwith your Majesty may be pleased. Only employ me, good Queene" (Nichols, ed., *Progresses,* 1:556–57), as a recognition both that his previous work had been censored and that the *Hemetes* constituted a royal lesson of the sort that Gascoigne felt gained him status.

8. In the sixteenth century, earls were not usually accustomed to think of themselves as princes in England. The *Oxford English Dictionary* records that the title of prince was not extended as a title of courtesy to dukes and earls until 1707.

9. David Scott, "William Patten and the Authorship of 'Robert Laneham's Letter' (1575)," *English Literary Renaissance* 7 (1977): 297–306; William Patten's letter appears on p. 301.

10. John Skelton, "The Bowge of Court," in *The Complete English Poems,* ed. John Scattergood (New Haven, Conn.: Yale University Press, 1983), 46–61.

11. The ideological sponsorship of *Laneham's Letter* is far more difficult to ascertain than is the aldermen-sponsored *Passage* or the Dudley-sponsored *Princely Pleasures.* Perhaps William Patten (if he is the author) produces hyperbolic praise of Kenilworth that makes Leicester's grandiosity look a bit silly in part because he was Burghley's man, and Burghley, who was conspicuously absent from Kenilworth, was the person generally opposed to Leicester's anti-Spanish views. In describing the illumination of the palace at night, for instance, the narrator compares the light with that of the lighthouse at Alexandria. Then the narrator draws attention to the way he is piling it on: "Or els (to talk merily with my mery freend) thus radiaunt, az thoogh *Phoebus* for hiz eaz woold rest him in the Castl, and not every night so to travel dooun untoo the *Antipodes*" (*Laneham's Letter,* 472).

12. For years, the queen had delayed elevating Dudley to the peerage, a hesitation that publicly emphasized how completely this was her gift to give.

13. Michael Pulman describes Leicester's especially close relation to Elizabeth as "largely based on the enduring hold he had on her affections" (*The Elizabethan Privy Council in the Fifteen-Seventies* [Berkeley: University of California Press, 1971], 28). Leicester claimed to have known Elizabeth since she was eight years old. See Alan Kendall, *Robert Dudley, Earl of Leicester* (London: Cassell, 1980), 5, 237n.

14. On the ivy impresa, see McCoy, *Rites of Knighthood,* 40–41. The Count of Feria, for example, wrote to Philip II that their marriage was generally expected (18 April 1559, CSP Spanish). Marie Axton argues that the representation of Dudley as Prince Pallaphilos described by Gerard Legh in his *Accedens of Armory* (London: R. Tottel, 1562) occurred at the Inner Temple Revels, which also featured a production of *Gorboduc,* with its pointed reminder to Elizabeth of the need to secure a succession ("Robert Dudley and the Inner Temple Revels," *Historical Journal* 13 [1970]: 365–78).

15. G. D. Ramsay, *The City of London in International Politics at the Accession of Elizabeth Tudor* (Manchester: University of Manchester Press, 1975), 56.

16. I am grateful to Christopher Highley for the information that Dudley's name is absent from the backers of such plantation schemes as that in Munster.

17. Richard Terdiman's discussion of ambition is, however, quite different from mine in that he is concerned with the French middle class in the nineteenth century: "We could understand ambition as the socialized form of desire specific to early capitalism. Through the plots it generates, ambition becomes a primary means of investigating structures of determination in social existence which had not yet been adequately conceptualized for bourgeois consciousness" (*Discourse/Counter-Dis-*

course: The Theory and Practice of Symbolic Resistance in Nineteenth-Century France
[Ithaca, N.Y.: Cornell University Press, 1985], 107).

18. Fulke Greville, *A Dedication to Philip Sidney* [otherwise known as *The Life of Sidney*], in *The Prose Works of Fulke Greville, Lord Brooke,* ed. John Gouws (Oxford: Clarendon Press, 1986), 105.

19. Quoted in Kendall, *Robert Dudley,* 87.

20. Simon Adams, "Eliza Enthroned? The Court and Its Politics," in *The Reign of Elizabeth I,* ed. Christopher Haigh (Athens: University of Georgia Press, 1987), 56.

21. Lawrence Stone, *The Crisis of the Aristocracy, 1558–1641* (New York: Oxford University Press, 1967), 16.

22. *Leicester's Commonwealth: The Copy of a Letter Written by a Master of Art of Cambridge* (1584), ed. D. C. Peck (Athens: Ohio University Press, 1985), 80.

Wallace MacCaffrey's description of Dudley's origins fills out the comment in *Leicester's Commonwealth:* "His grandfather, a parvenu of obscure origins—whatever the claims to a connection with the Lords Dudley—had gone to the block as the scapegoat for the shabbier political sins of Henry VII. John Dudley, his father, was a sinner on a far grander scale, and contemporaries were not likely to forget that he had committed the highest of all treasons in his attempt to displace the Tudors from the throne" (*The Shaping of the Elizabethan Regime* [Princeton, N.J.: Princeton University Press, 1968], 467).

23. What anthropologist Barbara Meyerhoff writes about ritual may be extended to the social function of the queen's welcome. She interprets "change . . . [as] being linked with the past and incorporated into a larger framework, where its variations are equated with grander, tidier totalities." Moreover, "inserting traditional elements into the present" asserts a coherent connection with both the past and the future. The result of mingling tradition with present concerns is that "the past is read as prefiguring what is happening in the here and now, and by implication the future is seen as foreshadowed in all that has gone before" ("A Death in Due Time: Construction of Self and Culture in Ritual Drama," in *Rite, Drama, Festival, Spectacle: Rehearsals Toward a Theory of Cultural Performance,* ed. John J. MacAloon [Philadelphia: Institute for the Study of Human Issues, 1984], 173).

24. It is possible that this Hercules represents loyalty, as he did during the Middle Ages because of his rescue of Pirotheus and Theseus from Hades, as Rosamond Tuve notes in *Allegorical Imagery: Some Mediaeval Books and Their Posterity* (1966; Princeton, N.J.: Princeton University Press, 1977), 295. Sydney Anglo notes that as Loyalty, Hercules appeared as a statue on the outer gateway at a theater during the Field of the Cloth of Gold, positioned to King Arthur's left with his club and *Fidelis amicus protectio fortis* at his feet (*Spectacle Pageantry and Early Tudor Policy* [Oxford: Clarendon Press, 1969], 191, 162). But if the pageant's devisers intended to encode Arthurian fealty in the comic Hercules at Kenilworth's gates and to associate that principle with Leicester's position in Elizabeth's court, his meaning was lost on the narrator of *Laneham's Letter,* who saw "a porter, tall of person, big of lim, and stearn of coountinauns . . . with a club and keiz of quantitee according" speaking impatiently and uncouthly when the queen's arrival disturbed him. Thus the *Letter* reduces Hercules to the stock giant porter—Ignaro at Orgoglio's castle in *The Faerie Queene* (1.8.31) or his worthy analogue, the Watchman and his sixteen "Tall yeomen . . . of great might" who guard Alma's castle in book 2, canto 9.

George Ferrers, who also collaborated on the most elaborate, queen-centered device—the rescue of the Lady of the Lake—was at one time Edward VI's Master of Revels. For his biography, see Lily Campbell, *The Mirror for Magistrates* (Cambridge: Cambridge University Press, 1938), 25–31.

25. E. K. Chambers, *The Elizabethan Stage* (Oxford: Clarendon Press, 1945), 1:118.

26. Considering the mixed message in the entertainments Dudley supplied, the masque's proposal seems entirely metaphoric. Gascoigne's text to the contrary, few of the entertainments were literary or allegorical. The hunting, bearbaiting, and fireworks that Leicester had arranged in advance were nicely calculated to please Elizabeth while reminding her to whom she was indebted for her pleasures—although the bride dael raised the issue of how ridiculous an unmarried middle-aged woman could look. For the extravagant plans for the fireworks and fountains that Leicester commissioned well before the entertainments, see Henry Killigrew to the Earl of Leicester, no fixed date in 1575, HMC Pepys, 70:178.

27. This masque of Juno and Diana took place under the sponsorship of Robert Dudley during the period when he was renewing his attentions to Elizabeth. Writes Guzman de Silva to Philip II, 12 March 1565, "I understood just so much as the Queen told me: The plot was founded on the question of marriage, discussed between Juno and Diana, Juno advocating marriage and Diana chastity. Jupiter gave a verdict in favour of matrimony after many things had passed on both sides in defence of the respective arguments. The Queen turned to me and said, 'This is all against me.' After the comedy there was a masquerade of satyrs, or wild gods, who danced with the ladies, and when this was finished there entered 10 parties of 12 gentlemen each, the same who had fought in the foot tourney [including the Earl of Leicester, the Earl of Sussex, and Hunsdon], and these, all armed as they were, danced with the ladies—a very novel ball, surely" (CSP Spanish, Elizabeth, 1:404–5).

28. "(1566) To a Joint Delegation from Parliament," in *Queen Elizabeth I: Political Speeches and Parliamentary Addresses, 1558–1601,* ed. Allison Heisch (Madison: University of Wisconsin Press, 1994), lines 66–69, 75–76. See also George P. Rice, ed., *The Public Speaking of Queen Elizabeth: Selections from Her Official Addresses* (New York: Columbia University Press, 1951), 79.

29. I have based my own account of Elizabeth's imprisonment on the following documents: CSP Domestic, Mary, 1547–1550, esp. item numbers 2:20; 3:21, 34; 8:52, 54; CSP Spanish, vols. 12 and 13, esp. 4, 5, 7, 8, 12, 17, 18, 19, 24 February; 1, 9, 14, 27 March; 3, 17, 22 April; 22–25 May; 4 June 1554; 21 April, 6 May 1555; CSP Venice, 1556–1557, vol. 6, pp. 1056–59, 1076; J. R. Dasent, ed., *Acts of the Privy Council of England, 1554–1556,* (London: HMSO, 1890–1907), 5:28, 29, 38, 79, 83, 109–10, 119; Henry Machyn, *The Diary of Henry Machyn, Citizen and Merchant-Taylor of London from A.D. 1550 to A.D. 1563* (London: Camden Society, 1848), 51–60; J. G. Nichols, ed., *The Chronicle of Queen Jane and of Two Years of Queen Mary Written by a Resident of the Tower of London* (London: Camden Society, 1850), 34–76; Charles Wriothesley, Windsor Herald, *A Chronicle of England During the Reigns of the Tudors, from A.D. 1485 to 1559,* ed. William Douglas Hamilton (London: Camden Society, 1877), 106–117. Secondary accounts include David Loades, *Mary Tudor: A Life* (Cambridge, Mass.: Basil Blackwell, 1989), 208–22, 283–93, and *The Reign of Mary Tudor: Politics, Government, and Religion in England, 1553–1558* (London: Ernst Benn, 1979), 70–82.

30. Paul Johnson, *Elizabeth I: A Study in Power and Intellect* (London: Weidenfeld and Nicolson, 1974), 46.

31. Simon Renard to the emperor, 1554, CSP Spanish, 12:339–40. The extent of Courtenay's and Elizabeth's perceived complicity can be seen in the carefully parallel treatment that each received. Courtenay was released from the Tower and placed under house arrest at Fatheringale within days of Elizabeth's proceeding to Woodstock. About the time Elizabeth returned to court, Courtenay agreed to travel to the Continent and died in Venice shortly thereafter.

32. Simon Renard to the emperor, 3 April 1555, CSP Spanish, 12:201.

33. "(1584) End of Parliamentary Session," in Heisch, ed., *Queen Elizabeth I: Political Speeches,* lines 30–31.

34. "(1566) To a Joint Delegation from Parliament," in ibid., lines 92–94.

35. Ibid., lines 94–95. See Carole Levin's discussion of the centrality of *Actes and Monuments,* a book "nearly as influential in Elizabethan England as the Bible itself," in *Propaganda in the English Reformation: Heroic and Villainous Images of King John* (Lewisten: Edwin Mellin, 1988), 110–21.

36. Michel Foucault, *The Order of Things: An Archaeology of the Human Sciences* (New York: Vintage Books, 1973), 16.

37. Foxe continues, "The thing is so manifest, that, what Englishman is he which knoweth not the afflictions of her grace, to have been far above the condition of a king's daughter: for there was no more behind, to make a very Iphigenia of her, but her offering up upon the altar of the scaffold" (*Acts and Monuments* ed. George Townsend [New York: AMS Press, 1965], 604–5). Pages of subsequent citations from this work appear in my text.

38. I have used the 1596 edition of John Foxe's *Acts and Monuments* (London: J. Day), STC 11226, 1895–98, because Townsend's edition tones down this section. Compare Townsend, ed., *Acts and Monuments,* 605.

39. The importance of her imprisonment also helps explain why in 1593 Elizabeth chose to translate Boethius's *Consolatio,* the classic of prison literature. See Elizabeth I, *Queen Elizabeth's Englishings of Boethius, De Consolatione Philosophiae A.D. 1593,* Early English Text Society no. 113 (London: Early English Text Society, 1899).

40. Compare Townsend, ed., *Acts and Monuments,* 624.

41. Elizabeth I, *A Book of Devotions Composed by Her Majesty Elizabeth,* trans. Rev. Adam Fox (Gerards Cross: Colin Smythe, 1920), 19.

42. Thomas Heywood, in *England's Elizabeth,* ed. Richard H. Perkinson (New York: Garland, 1982), recounts on pp. 50–111 the imprisonment, which culminates in Elizabeth's "Daniel" speech outside the Tower at the beginning of her coronation entry. The appeal of Elizabeth's imprisonment continued to increase in the seventeenth century and is evident both in Heywood's version and in the text of Christopher Lever, *Queene Elizabeths teares: or, her resolute bearing the Christian crosse, in the bloodie time of Queene Marie* (London: M. Lownes, 1607), STC 15540. During the seventeenth century, the image of the imprisoned Elizabeth became an element in the myth of her militant Protestantism that, like the related myth of Elizabeth's armor and speech at Tilbury, served the interests of those taking an anti-Catholic stance.

43. Dudley, of course, had more than the Netherlands on his mind while at Kenilworth. He wrote, for instance, on behalf of the queen from Kenilworth to John Selby in Scotland about the "late disorder" described in de Guaras's letter (Kenilworth, 12 July 1575, CSP Foreign).

44. R. B. Wernham, summarizing his article "English Policy and the Revolt of

the Netherlands," in *Britain and the Netherlands in Europe and Asia,* ed. J. S. Bromley and E. H. Kossman (New York: St. Martin's Press, 1968), 29–40, in R. B. Wernham, *The Making of Elizabethan Foreign Policy, 1558–1603* (Berkeley: University of California Press, 1980), 4.

45. "The commodity of England," states a paper endorsed by Burghley in 1585, "is that the Low Countries are the great vent for her trade" (CSP Spanish, Elizabeth, 3:258). As a result, the Merchant Adventurers actively sought markets for their cloth despite the disruptions of war, an interest often requiring the Protestant faction, including Leicester himself, to protest the rebels' barriers to trade, such as the sea beggars' piracy of English goods and the provinces' licensing system. See, for example, the correspondence of the Council of Zealand to the queen defending the necessity of licensing English goods (28 May 1575, CSP Foreign, Elizabeth, 1575–1577, 61–62).

46. Antonio de Guaras describes his private talk with Burghley in a letter to the Duke of Alba, 12 October 1572 (CSP Spanish, Elizabeth, 2:423).

47. In seeking to perpetuate the balance between France and Spain, William of Orange held that the queen "did suffer a Protestant party raised by God in that great kingdom of France to a balance or counterpoise to that dangerous heptarchy of Spain," reported Fulke Greville of their conversation in 1579. Greville himself, although allied with Sidney and Dudley at the time, was in retrospect able to recognize that the queen's earlier policy was based on the costs and uncertainties of war. As a result, "she showed herself more ambitious of balancing neighbour princes from invading one another than under any pretence of title or revenge apt to question or conquer upon foreign princes' possessions," Greville wrote in his *Life of Sidney,* 15, 47. Although Greville frequently became caught up in implied comparisons between the glories of Elizabeth and the corruption of James, at times he also shrewdly considered her motives.

The Venetian ambassador in France, Sigismondo de Cavalli, assessed Elizabeth's balancing act while it was occurring: "Though it is fortunate for the Queen of England that these two countries of France and Flanders should continue to be disturbed, yet other considerations openly prevent her taking any active part." She dreads a Spanish invasion, he suggests, and fearing "for her own security, she has no desire to deprive herself of her forces by sending them elsewhere. All that she can do is secretly to furnish money to the Germans in order to induce them the more speedily to invade France, where it is more to her advantage to maintain war than in Flanders" (Paris, 19 June 1574, CSP Venice, Elizabeth, 7:514).

Although Elizabeth's commitment to back neither France nor Spain prevented her more active support of the seventeen provinces, her support of the Protestant cause abroad in 1575 included approving covert aid in the form of a secret loan to Frederic, Elector Palatine of the Rhine, and her overlooking the semisecret shipment of English money, ships, armaments, and men to the Netherlands. She was careful that in lending 50,000 crowns to Frederic, "the Queen of England's name shall not appear in the transaction, and that the other conditions shall be observed" (23 July 1575, CSP Foreign, Elizabeth, 1575–1577, 95). On the elector's support of the revolt from 1572, see Geoffrey Parker, *Spain and the Netherlands, 1559–1659: Ten Studies* (Short Hills, N.J.: Enslow, 1979), 69. Elizabeth also tolerated personal contact and lengthy correspondence between the rebels and Walsingham, Dudley, the youthful Philip Sidney, and Fulke Greville.

48. Roger Williams, quoted in Geoffrey Parker, *The Dutch Revolt* (Ithaca, N.Y.: Cornell University Press, 1977), 50.

49. I have quoted the most judicious portion of the communication to Alba (7 August 1572, CSP Spanish, Elizabeth, 2:400).

50. As early as January 1573, the Low Countries began to bid for Elizabeth's wholehearted support by obliquely asking her "to take possession of the strong places" remaining in the northern provinces when the "States of Holland and the Prince of Orange sent four commissioners to the queen of England" (Antonio de Guaras to Zayas, 7 January 1573, CSP Spanish, Elizabeth, 2:455). The prince wrote to Leicester and Burghley that "they [the States General] are rather minded to make the Queen Lady and Countess of Holland and Zealand than to have any other dealing." During the summer of 1575, Elizabeth was offered sovereignty in the Lowlands. When she sent John Hastings to the Prince of Orange that October, it was with instructions that "as for the matter moved to her to receive him and the country of Holland into her protections, that cannot be." If she accepted Holland as her domain, "an open war must ensue betwixt her and the King of Spain, and perchance in respect of religion with the King of France. Considering also that she has no title to those countries, she requires the Prince not to think it is any lack of goodwill in her if she first tries all other means to do them good before she enters into a war with the King of Spain." Nor could the queen ignore economic motives for maintaining a peaceful stance: "Wisdom also would have her foresee that the great wealth of her subjects in that King's dominions should not be subject to seizure." Despite these instructions through Burghley, Walsingham continued to participate in forming a plan to divide the provinces and give Holland and Zeeland to England, a plan that took its first public form in the fall of 1575 when William of Orange addressed the States General about the possibility of offering the sovereignty of Holland to Elizabeth (Instructions for John Hastings, draft corrected by Burghley, 29 October 1575, CSP Foreign, Elizabeth, 1575–1577, 171; John Hastings, 26 December 1575, CSP Foreign, Elizabeth, 1575–1577, 211–12).

51. The idea of the family tree was that of Philip Marnix of St. Aldegonde, Prince William's "most trusted councillor." The plan came to nothing, although as Roy Strong and J. A. van Dorsten note, "for a brief period in 1585 and 1586 it did seem as if England and the United Provinces were to be joined under a single crown" (*Leicester's Triumph* [Leiden: Leiden University Press, 1964], 3–5). Strong and van Dorsten conclude that Elizabeth was first offered sovereignty in the Netherlands in October 1575, after William of Orange put the possibility before the States General. But as I pointed out earlier, Cobham's instructions ask him to tell Philip II that Elizabeth has been offered sovereignty already, if apparently through private negotiations (1 July 1575, CSP Foreign, Elizabeth, 1575–1577, 76–77).

52. In October 1573, the rebels won a decisive victory at Alkmaar, followed by the defeat of the Spanish fleet on the Zuider Zee. With his unpaid soldiers refusing orders, Alba left Brussels in December 1573. Then in January 1574, the Spanish fleet was again defeated on the Scheldt and Middleburg surrendered to the Gueux. The Spanish victory on Mookheath resulted in the deaths of William's brothers Henry and Louis and enabled a Spanish renewal of the siege at Leiden. In December 1574, Spanish troops mutinied, attacking the Spanish garrison at Utrecht.

53. Thomas Wilson to Lord Burghley, 1 February 1575, CSP Foreign, Elizabeth, 2:11.

54. See, for example, CSP Spanish, Elizabeth, 2:497–503, when de Guaras writes of the Protestant party's secret maneuvers to raise money and soldiers to aid the rebels, and to send small arms by ship to the Netherlands. Other forms of English support are reported: Inevitably, potential engagements of the rulers involved formed an important part of foreign policy because they sent inconclusive messages to allies and enemies alike. So it is that a dispatch of 11 July in discussing William of Orange's offer for the king of France's daughter also raises the question of whether Elizabeth will resume her marriage talks with Anjou (2:497).

55. Parker, *Dutch Revolt,* 167.

56. Antonio de Guaras to Zayas, 17 December 1575, CSP Spanish, Elizabeth, 2:515.

57. Heisch, ed., *Queen Elizabeth I: Political Speeches,* lines 33–34.

58. According to the news arriving at the Privy Council, France at this juncture appeared incapable of action. As the CSP Foreign, Elizabeth, 1575–1577, summarizes Edward Chester's report to Burghley from Paris, "The French King is very sick. M. Danville has surprised Narbonne. The University of Orleans is revolted from the King" (83).

In England the Protestant faction continued to agitate for action. A "Discourse on Flanders" among the state papers argued, for example, that England was at risk because a confederacy of Catholic princes existed to end the reign of "all those who profess the gospel." The Duke of Alba was present in the Netherlands to implement this resolve, not only to end the rebellion, but also to invade England. Further evidence includes the Spanish ambassador's strange behavior and the duke's "disdainful answers to the English merchants in the Low Countries." The "Discourse" mounts many of the same arguments that would work a decade later, but the fact that it is anonymous and unfinished suggests how far Elizabeth and Burghley were from acting on its argument for intervention (CSP Foreign, Elizabeth, 1575–1577, no. 542, 218–19).

59. McCoy, *Rites of Knighthood,* 28–54.

60. Sir Bruse is also a notorious coward, constantly fleeing Arthur's knights; he lies and tramples unconscious knights with his horse. See Thomas Malory, *Caxton's Malory: A New Edition of Sir Thomas Malory's La Morte Darthur,* ed. James W. Spisak (Berkeley: University of California Press, 1983), 10.53, 9.26, 9.41, 9.36, 10.2.

61. George Gascoigne, *The Spoyle of Antwerp* (London: R. Jones, 1576), STC 11644.

62. Quoted in Strong and van Dorsten, *Leicester's Triumph,* 60. During this period the Netherlands were commonly described as having been raped by the Spanish. For example, Thomas Dekker would later described the provinces as highborn ladies robbed of both virginity and status: "Thoas seuenteene Dutch Virgins of *Belgia,* (that had Kingdomes to theyr dowries, and were worthy to be courted by Nations) are now no more Virgins: the Souldier hath deflowred them, and robd them of theyr Mayden honor: Warre hath stil use of their noble bodyes, and discouereth theyr nakednes like prostituted Strumpets" (*The Seuen deadly Sinnes of London: Drawne in seuen seuerall Coaches, Through the seuen seuerall Gates fo [sic] the Citie Bringing the Plague with them* [London: Nathaniel Butler, 1606], in *The Non-Dramatic Works of Thomas Dekker,* ed. Alexander B. Grosart [New York: Russell and Russell, 1963], 9).

63. As Stone summarizes his activities during this period, "Much of Leicester's

wide-ranging patronage was inspired by a desire to encourage moderate puritanism at home and military aggression abroad" (*Crisis of the Aristocracy,* 321).

64. This letter, "Mr. Edw: Dyer to Mr. Christopher Hatton," dated "9th of October 1572," is largely reprinted in Ralph M. Sargent, *At the Court of Queen Elizabeth: The Life and Lyrics of Sir Edward Dyer* (New York: Oxford University Press, 1935), 24–26. In it, Dyer advises Hatton how to deal with the increasing favor that Elizabeth was showing to the young Earl of Oxford.

65. Joan Kelly, in her landmark essay "Did Women Have a Renaissance?" (*Becoming Visible: Women in European History,* ed. Renate Bridenthal, Claudia Koontz, and Susan Stuard [Boston: Houghlton Mifflin, 1987]), notes that according to Castiglione, the courtier's role is "to be attractive, accomplished, and seem not to care; to charm and do so coolly—how concerned with impression, how masked the true self. And how manipulative: petitioning his lord, the courtier knows to be 'discreet in choosing the occasion, and will ask things that are proper and reasonable; and he will so frame his request, omitting those parts that he knows can cause displeasure, and will skillfully make easy the difficult points so that his lord will always grant it.' . . . In short, how like a woman—or a dependent, for that is the root of the simile" (195).

66. Rogers' mission was primarily economic, as was usually the case of envoys sent to the Netherlands. Indeed, the Merchant Adventurers had elected Rogers as their secretary in Antwerp for the year. Elizabeth instructed Rogers to convey dissatisfaction at the seizure of English goods in Flushing, "a matter so touching her [Elizabeth] in honour as she neither may nor will suffer the said injuries unrevenged"; to insist on the Merchant Adventurers' right to continue trade in Spanish-controlled Flanders; and to warn Orange to halt the piracy of the sea beggars. Only two points toward the end of the instructions were diplomatic: Rogers was to warn Orange about consorting with the French and to exhort the governor of Flushing to continue refusing to help the French ("Instructions for Daniel Rogers Sent to the Prince of Orange," signed by Thomas Smith and Francis Walsingham, 8 June 1575, CSP Foreign).

Elizabeth's instructions to Henry Cobham for dealing with Philip II were similarly limited. The instructions began with the need to protest the treatment of English merchants in Flanders under the Inquisition, men whose plight prevented Elizabeth—or so she argued—from fully complying with Spanish requests to protect imperial goods and ships. Cobham's first diplomatic charge was to emphasize Elizabeth's noninvolvement in the Netherlands despite grave temptations: If the king "knew how often and earnestly she had been solicited to take possession of Holland and Zeeland, he might say he never had such a friend as she had been." His second charge was to warn Philip of her fear that "if some speedy remedy be not taken, those Countries will be at the devotion of the French King who, and his predecessor, have continually aided the Prince of Orange with money to maintain his wars and now continues the same with a monthly secret pay."

The queen's solution to the turmoil in the Netherlands is purposefully disingenuous. She suggests nothing less than Philip's compliance with the first of the rebels' demands of 1566, to allow "his subjects to enjoy their ancient privileges and suffering them to live freely from the extremities of the Inquisition"—a statement that makes clear the Crown's sympathy with the rebels' dissatisfactions. Furthermore, these instructions, signed by herself and Walsingham and drawn up immediately before Elizabeth became Dudley's guest at Kenilworth, also indicate an English willingness to enforce her point of view.

Although the convoluted prose of this portion of the instructions bespeaks its authors' hesitancy, in the final clause the key word "invade" does appear: Cobham "is to signify that, contrary to her disposition, she may be found for her own safety to be a dealer herein, whereunto if she shall be driven she desires him to interpret her doings in good and honorable part, and that the same proceeds of necessity to preserve her own realm rather than from desire to invade anything belonging to him" (1 July 1575, CSP Foreign, Elizabeth).

CSP Venetian, 11 September 1575, 2:77, provides an account of Cobham's reception in Apsin, suggesting that Cobham's task was also to continue playing off Spanish and French interests by reviving the suggestion that Elizabeth was about to marry Anjou—a suggestion that was a running joke of diplomatic correspondence throughout the 1570s and 1580s.

67. Elizabeth's reclaiming of the Lady of the Lake did not, however, end the question of what kind of chastity the Lady represented. E. K., the unknown commentator on Spenser's *Shepheardes Calender* whose notes were published as part of the text in 1579, also saw a relation between the queen and the Lady of the Lake. To his way of thinking, however, the Lady was a marriageable figure of the former. When glossing the lines,

> And whither rennes this bevie of Ladies bright,
>   raunged in a rowe?
> They bene all Ladyes of the Lake behight,
>   that unto her goe (118–21)

from the April Eclogue in *The Shepheardes Calender,* E. K. explains, "Ladyes of the Lake be Nymphes. For it was an olde opinion amongste the Auncient Heathen, that of euery spring and fountaine was a goddesse the Soueraigne . . . [;] the word Nymphe in Greeke signifieth Well water, or otherwise a Spouse or Bryde" (Edmund Spenser, *The Yale Edition of the Shorter Poems of Edmund Spenser,* ed. William A. Oram et al. [New Haven, Conn.: Yale University Press, 1989], 82).

Jean Wilson sees this connection between Elizabeth and the Lady of the Lake as "another example of the fusion of classical and romance so typical of Elizabethan court writing," but it should be added that the "romance" tradition associates the Lady's vulnerability with her availability as a spouse (*Entertainments for Elizabeth I* [Totowa, N.J.: Rowman and Littlefield, 1980], 26).

68. Stephen Orgel, *The Jonsonian Masque* (1965; New York: Columbia University Press, 1981), 42.

69. Clifford Geertz, "Centers, Kings, and Charisma: Symbolics of Power," in *Local Knowledge* (New York: Basic Books, 1983), 124. In making his transcultural case concerning power, however, Geertz is unable to consider many of the local difficulties complicating the equation of the display of power with its function.

70. Quoted in Carole Levin, "'Would I Could Give You Help and Succour': Elizabeth I and the Politics of Touch," *Albion* 21 (1989): 199. Richard McCoy informed me of this fascinating article on Elizabeth's healing.

71. See "Memoirs of the Lives and Actions of the Sidneys," in *Letters and Memorials of State* . . . *Memoirs of the Lives and Actions of the Sidneys,* ed. Arthur Collins (London: T. Osborne, 1746), 48. This unspecified account of the Kenilworth entertainments summarizes Gascoigne's text, but adds the detail about Elizabeth's reward of the players. This source also comments that "the Costs and Expences of these Entertainments may be guest at, by the Quantity of Beer then drunk, which amounted to 320 Hogsheads of the ordinary sort . . . and the next

ensuing year, this Earl obtained a Grant of the Queen, for a weekly Market at *Kenilworth,* on the *Wednesday,* with a Fair yearly on *Midsummerday*" (48).

72. These entertainments are in turn followed by the concluding device in which the woodman (Gascoigne) appears to run after Elizabeth as she leaves, delivering a lengthy oration as he goes.

73. Henri Kervyn de Lettenhove, ed., *Relations politiques des Pays-Bas et de l'Angleterre,* 11 vols. (Brussels: F. Have, 1882–1900), 9:159.

74. On the transition from England's pro-Spanish to anti-Spanish policy, see G. D. Ramsay, "The Foreign Policy of Elizabeth I," in Haigh, ed., *Reign of Elizabeth I,* esp. 158–60. See also Parker, *Dutch Revolt,* 169–224.

75. Quoted in Strong and van Dorsten, *Leicester's Triumph,* 36. They describe Leicester's entourage as "positively regal: ninety-nine gentlemen officers, yeomen and their servants and over seventy lords, knights and gentlemen. The household included chaplains and physicians, a steward, four secretaries, two engineers, pages, grooms, trumpeters, and footmen, and wherever they went forty-four beds were reserved for his kitchen personnel alone. There was even a troop of players to beguile the time in an alien land" (32). On the Treaty of Nonesuch, see Parker, *Dutch Revolt,* 216–218; the figure of eight thousand soldiers by December 1585 is Parker's (218).

76. On the attempt by the States General, Dudley, and her Privy Council to present Elizabeth with "the *fait accompli* of an Englishman's acceptance of supreme authority over foreign territory," see Strong and van Dorsten, *Leicester's Triumph,* 50–59.

77. The queen to the States General, 13 February 1585/1586, in *Correspondence of Robert Dudley, Earl of Leycester, During His Government of the Low Countries,* ed. John Bruce (London: Camden Society, 1844), 468.

78. Letter 39, the queen to the Earl of Leicester, 10 February 1585/1586, in ibid., 110.

79. Raphael Holinshed, *Chronicles of England, Scotland, and Ireland* (1808; New York: AMS Press, 1976), 4:645.

80. Strong and van Dorsten, *Leiceister's Triumph,* 48.

81. The queen to the Earl of Leicester, 1 April 1586, in Bruce, ed., *Correspondence of Robert Dudley,* 209. The queen continued that she was grieved "that a subject of ours, of that qualite that you ar, a creature of our own, and one that hath alwayes received an extraordinary portion of our favour" could "deale so carlesly, we will not saye contemptuously, as to geve the woorld just cause to think, that we are had in contempt by him."

82. I am grateful to Allison Heisch for pointing out the relevance of this speech to my material. See Heisch, ed., *Queen Elizabeth I: Political Speeches,* lines 33–35, 12–13.

83. T. D. (STC lists Robert Dudley as author), *A Briefe Report of the Militarie Services done in the Low Countries, by the Erle of Leicester* (London: Arnold Hatfield, 1587), STC 7285. It appeared at about the same time as Dudley's *Lawes and Ordinances, set down by Robert Earle of Leycester, the Queenes maiesties Lieutenant and Captaine GENERAL of her armie and forces in the Lowe Countries* (London: Christopher Barker, "Printer to the Queenes most excellent Maiestie," 1586), STC 7288, whose text also provides the straightforward, soldierly view of Leicester's service in the Netherlands, which he apparently thought was his best defense.

Chapter 3

1. The word "torture" is Spenser's, as when he describes how Busirane treats Amoret in book 3, canto 11, stanza 17, line 4:

> There he tormenteth her most terribly,
>> And day and night afflicts with mortall paine,
>> Because to yield him loue she doth deny,
>> Once to me yold, not to be yold againe:
>> But yet by torture he would her constraine
>> Loue to conceiue in her disdainfull brest,
>> Till so she do, she must in doole remaine,
>> Ne may by liuing meanes be thence relest:
> What boots it then to plaine, that cannot be redrest?

(Edmund Spenser, *Edmund Spenser: The Faerie Queene,* ed. Thomas P. Roche, Jr. [New Haven, Conn.: Yale University Press, 1978]). Pages of subsequent citations from this work appear in the text.

2. For an overview of the criticism of these cantos, see the section "The Topography of Threat and Rape" and notes 57, 58, and 59 in this chapter.

3. HMC Penshurst, 2:481. The manuscripts contained in this volume supplement and correct Arthur Collins's edition of the Sidney correspondence (*Letters and Memorials of State . . . Memoirs of the Lives and Actions of the Sidneys* [London: T. Osborne, 1746]). Unless stated otherwise, all HMC Penshurst quotations cited in this part are from Roland Whyte writing to Robert Sidney. Although admittedly Whyte was invested in the status quo, outsiders similarly evaluated Elizabeth's physical condition. The Venetian traveler Francesco Gradenigo reported home that "Her Majesty is about sixty-four years of age, short, and ruddy in complexion; very strongly built. This points to a long life" (CSP Venice, 9:239).

4. John Harington, *Nugae Antiquae* (1779; London: Hildesheim, 1968), 1:186; CSP Venice, 9:504; Elizabeth I to James VI, 21 August 1600, in *The Letters of Queen Elizabeth,* ed. G. B. Harrison (1935; New York: Funk & Wagnalls, 1968), 278–79.

5. Robert Sidney to John Harington, 1600, and John Harington to Mary Harington, 27 December 1602, in John Harington, *The Letters and Epigrams of Sir John Harington,* ed. Norman McClure (Philadelphia: University of Pennsylvania Press, 1930), 389–90, 97.

6. John Harington to Mary Harington, 27 December 1602, in ibid., 97.

7. Elizabeth's prayer is printed in *A Book of Devotions Composed by Her Majesty Elizabeth,* trans. Adam Fox (Gerrards Cross: Colin Smythe, 1920), 31.

8. Guzman da Silva to Philip II, 5 January 1567, CSP Spanish, 1:607.

9. HMC Penshurst, 2:386.

10. HMC Penshurst, 2:458, 227.

11. HMC Penshurst, 2:455.

12. Desiderius Erasmus, *The Colloquies of Erasmus,* trans. Craig R. Thompson (Chicago: University of Chicago Press, 1965), 95.

13. Robert Devereux, Earl of Essex, "The Passion of a Discontented Minde," in *The Elizabethan Courtier Poets: The Poems and Their Contexts,* ed. Steven W. May (Columbia: University of Missouri Press, 1991), 263. As May points out, this is Essex's "Tower" poem, written as he awaited execution for treason. A poem that repeatedly confesses Essex's many (largely unspecified) sins, it is curious in never

admitting treason as one of them. The quoted section occurs when the speaker (Essex) imagines himself as a woman who, having wronged her husband, returns to him for forgiveness, asking that her body

> . . . be withred with my verie cries,
> That when my wrinckles shall my sorrowes tell,
> The world may say, I joy'd not, though I fell

—a picture that simultaneously feminizes Essex and suggests a displaced picture of Elizabeth.

14. John Nichols, ed., *The Progresses and Public Processions of Queen Elizabeth* (London: John Nichols, 1823; New York: AMS Press, 1966), 3:495–96.

15. On the dating of the "coronation" portraits, see John Fletcher, "The Date of the Portrait of Elizabeth I in Her Coronation Robes," and Janet Arnold, "The 'Coronation' Portrait of Queen Elizabeth I," both in *Burlington Magazine* 120 (1978). See also Richard McCoy, "'Thou Idol Ceremony': Elizabeth I, *The Henriad,* and the Rites of the English Monarchy," in *Urban Life in the Renaissance,* ed. Susan Zimmerman and Ronald F. E. Weissman (Newark: University of Delaware Press, 1989), 260, 266.

16. "A Declaration of the favourable Dealing of her Majesties Commissioners, appointed for the Examination of certaine Traytours, and of Tortures unjustly reported to be done upon them for Matter of Religion, 1583. —By Lord Burghley," in *A Collection of Scarce and Valuable Tracts,* ed. Walter Scott (London: T. Cordell and W. Davies, 1809), 1:213.

17. Elizabeth I to James VI, 11 September 1592, in Harrison, ed., *Letters of Queen Elizabeth,* 22.

18. Giovanni Michiel to the doge and senate, 2 January 1559, CSP Venice, 7:6.

19. HMC Penshurst, 2:472, 390, 407, 409, 412.

20. See David Starkey, "Intimacy and Innovation: The Rise of the Privy Chamber 1485–1547," in *The English Court: From the Wars of the Roses to the Civil War,* ed. David Starkey et al. (New York: Longman, 1987), 71–118. In the same volume, Pam Wright has an essay specifically on Elizabeth's privy chamber, "A Change in Direction: The Ramifications of a Female Household, 1558–1603," pp. 147–72, although I disagree with her assumption that "as women, her Ladies could not be faction leaders; while as members of her *familia* they were not even faction followers either: their first loyalties were to the queen, not one of her great men" (159).

21. HMC Penshurst, 2:425–26; Nichols, ed., *Progresses,* 3:237–38.

22. HMC Penshurst, 2:395. The editor, C. L. Kingsford, noted that an attempt to erase the words "and her faire neck" from the manuscript had been made, apparently by the earlier editor, Arthur Collins, who omits these words from his edition of the letter.

23. *Cobbett's Complete Collection of State Trials* (London: T. C. Hansard, 1809), 1:1349.

24. Elizabeth's government took no chances that London dissidents would attempt to free Essex: The troops raised outside the city lay "in the suburbs adjoining the Court, which is guarded like a camp, and troops of armed men march up and down, as if the Spaniards were in the land" (18 February 1600/1601, CSP Domestic, 1598–1601, 584).

25. One popular discourse at the Elizabethan court that I do not discuss here is

the pastoral. But see Louis Adrian Montrose, "'Eliza, Queene of Shepheardes,' and the Pastoral of Power," *English Literary Renaissance* 10 (1980): 153–82.

26. Harington, *Letters and Epigrams,* 258.

27. Elizabeth I, "When I Was Fair and Young," in *The Norton Anthology of Poetry,* ed. Alexander W. Allison et al. (New York: Norton, 1970), 100. The remainder of the poem reads

> Then spake fair Venus' son, that proud victorious boy,
> And said, "Fine dame, since that you be so coy,
> I will so pluck your plumes that you shall say no more,
>> 'Go, go, go seek some otherwhere!
>> Importune me no more!'"

> When he had spake these words, such change grew in my breast
> That neither might nor day since that, I could take any rest
> Then lo! I did repent that I had said before,
>> "Go, go, go seek some otherwhere!
>> Importune me no more!"

28. HMC Penshurst, 2:317.

29. Ann Rosalind Jones, *The Currency of Eros: Women's Love Lyric in Europe, 1540–1620* (Bloomington: Indiana University Press, 1990), 34–35.

30. Note in addition that if the courtiers' verse to Elizabeth substantiated her distance and therefore her autonomous power, the address of outsiders did so even more. See, for example, the recorder for the city of London's speech in 1592 quoted in Chapter 1. Another contemporary example comes from Thomas Churchyard, *A Handefvl of Gladsome Verses, given to the Queenes Maiesty at Woodstocke this Prograce, 1592* (London: Ioseph Barnes, 1592), STC 5237, B3:

> Great princes haue made verse,
> And favred poetrie well:
> Verse hath a grace the clouds to pearce,
> and clime where Gods doe dwell.

Churchyard's dedication to Elizabeth and his final "Verse o[ ] variety to all those that honors the onely Phoenix of the worlde, which verses are but xx. lines and hath in them ten waies, finde out the same who pleaseth" also show the icon of the Phoenix representing Elizabeth's chastity as developed in a text aside from *The Phoenix Nest* and Shakespeare's *Henry VIII.*

31. Baldassare Castiglione, *The Book of the Courtier,* trans. Sir Thomas Hoby (New York: Dutton, 1928). *The Book of the Courtier*'s vision of the courtier's abilities also recognizes the frustrations of serving the prince. The primary reason that the courtier develops his learning, horsemanship, dancing, hunting, wrestling, and conversation is to "purchase the favour of a prince" (279) to whose needs he must remain flexible. He should "very seldom or (in manner) never shall he crave any thing of his Lorde for him selfe, least the Lorde having respect to deny it him for him selfe, should not graunte it him without displeasure, which is farre worse" (107). If invited into the lord's secret chamber, he ought "to deferr grave matters till an other time and place, and frame him selfe to pleasant communication . . . least hee hinder that good moode of his" (108). In short, the courtier should act like a woman. True, the "ende therefore of a perfect Courtier" is that

once having purchased his prince's favor with his accomplishments, "he may breake his minde to him, and alwaies enforme him franckly of the truth of every matter meeter for him to understand" (261).

32. Ibid., 1, 189. Hoby's translation appeared in 1561 and was reprinted in 1577, 1588, and 1603. Sackville's commendatory sonnet, which appears before Sir Thomas Hoby's dedication to the Lord Henry Hastings, reads

> These royall kinges, that reare up to the skye
> Their pallace tops, and deck the[m] all with gold:
> With rare and curious workes they feede the eye:
> And shew what riches here great Princes hold.
> A rarer worke and richer far in worth,
> Castilios hand presenteth here to thee.
> No proude, ne golden Court doth he set forth,
> But what in Court a Courtier ought to be.
> The prince he raiseth huge and mightie walles,
> Castilio frames a wight of noble fame:
> The king with gorgeous Tissue clads his halles,
> The Count with golden vertue deckes the same,
> Whose passing skill, to Hobbies pen displaies
> To Britaine folke, a worke of worthy praise. (1)

33. Lord Julian, for example, resolves first to "fashion" the perfect woman "after my mind" and then to "take her as mine owne, after the example of Pigmalion" (ibid., 189). *The Book of the Courtier* is very much engaged with the question of women's conduct and the degree of their equality with men. It actually ends with the question "whether women be not as meete for heavenlie love as men" (324) hanging in the air. In general, as Joan Kelly discusses this work in her essay, "Did Women Have a Renaissance?" (*Becoming Visible: Women in European History,* ed. Renate Bridenthal, Claudia Koontz, and Susan Stuard [Boston: Houghton Mifflin, 1987]), *The Book of the Courtier* participates in "the Renaissance reformulation of courtly manners and love" which makes "evident how the ways of the lady came to be determined by men in the context of the early modern state" (189).

34. See Kelly, "Did Women Have a Renaissance?" 194.

35. Marsilio Ficino, *Commentary on Plato's Symposium on Love,* trans. Sears Jayne (Dallas: Spring, 1985), 127. I am indebted to Ioan P. Couliano's discussion of the relation between Eros and magic. As he summarizes it, the relation lies in the belief that "love is the name given to the power that ensures the continuity of the uninterrupted chain of beings" (*Eros and Magic in the Renaissance,* trans. Margaret Cook [Chicago: University of Chicago Press, 1987], 87). See also Michel Foucault, *The Order of Things: An Archaeology of the Human Sciences* (New York: Vintage Books, 1973), esp. 17–45, for a discussion of the broader system of conceptualized resemblance of which Neoplatonism is a part.

36. Arthur Marotti, "'Love is not love': Elizabethan Sonnet Sequences and the Social Order," *ELH* 49 (1982): 398.

37. Harington, *Letters and Epigrams,* 125.

38. In the *Libelli de Lite* (ca. 1100), the Norman Anonymous—whom Ernst Kantorowitz cites as an important precedent for the sixteenth-century idea of the king's two bodies—stated that "the power of the king is the power of God. This power, namely, is God's by nature and the king's by grace. Hence, the king, too, is God and Christ, but by grace; and whatsoever he does, he does not simply as a

man, but as one who has become God and Christ by grace" (*The King's Two Bodies: A Study in Medieval Theology* [Princeton, N.J.: Princeton University Press, 1957], 48).

39. This caution helps explain the subordination of the rite that made her human body sacred—her coronation—to her coronation entry. Instead, the Crown sought to anchor its legitimacy in the more concrete aspects of the law, particularly in Parliament's Acts of Succession.

40. Walter Ralegh, *A Choice of Sir Walter Ralegh's Verse,* ed. Robert Nye (London: Faber & Faber, 1972), 26–27. As unguardedly as this poem seems to reproduce the most powerful elements of Elizabeth's self-representations, it still ends with a warning: "A knowledge pure it is hir worth to kno, / With Circes let them dwell that thinke not so." This warning records the possibility that not everyone accepts this iconography. It also recalls that another name for a woman who "moves the floods" through her power is a witch, a Circe who turns men to swine.

41. George P. Rice, ed. *The Public Speaking of Queen Elizabeth: Selections from Her Official Addresses* (1935; New York: Funk & Wagnalls, 1968), 98–99.

42. Text courtesy of Allison Heisch, ed., *Queen Elizabeth I: Political Speeches and Parliamentary Adresses, 1558–1601* (Madison: University of Wisconsin Press, 1994), lines 6–7, 17–29.

43. At an entertainment at Theobalds in 1592/1593, Robert Cecil presented Elizabeth with a bell of gold, a book of prayer, and a "candle of virgin's wax, meete for a Virgin Queene" with which to furnish his hermit's cell. See Nichols, ed., *Progresses,* 3:245.

44. I am mindful that as in my discussion of Elizabeth's agency in the Introduction, discussing Edmund Spenser as the agent of the text gives rise to various questions of intentionality. Since erasing the author carries the danger of naturalizing patriarchal values, I find useful Robert Weimann's analysis in *Structure and Society in Literary History: Studies in the History and Theory of Historical Criticism* (Baltimore: Johns Hopkins University Press, 1984) of the relation between social structures like court entertainments or the royal iconography and the individual author. For Weimann, "the social and the individual perspectives on experience are *within* the poet and the creative process itself, just as they are *in* the reader and form part of the receptive process. Structure is born out of this interaction by which the poet and his audience, also the self and the social within the poet, are all genetically connected. . . . Structure is 'historically given': it accommodates the traditional (or original) modes of rhetoric and mediation between the poet and his first audience, and it reflects or mirrors the form and pressure of the age in which the art work is created" (7–8, see also 46–56).

For Weimann's literary historian, the biography of the author and the reader are inseparable from the analysis of structure because "the issue of historicity must be discussed on more than one level: not only on the level of what is represented (which would reduce this project to some genealogy of the signified) but also on the level of who and what is representing. The point is to view these levels (the rupture between them as well as their independence) together and to attempt to interconnect the semiotic problematic of signification and the extratextual dimension of representativeness, as involving changeful relations of writing, reading, social reproduction, and political power" ("Text, Author-Function, and Appropriation in Modern Narrative: Toward a Sociology of Representation," in *Literature and Social Practice,* ed. Philippe Desan, Priscilla Parkhurst Ferguson, and Wendy Griswold [Chicago: University of Chicago Press, 1989], 30).

As Cheryl Walker pointed out, those who consider an author's biography must remain aware that in discussing the author, "we reveal our own epistemological assumptions and our own politics of interpretation by our insistence on a certain notion of subjectivity as speaking" ("Feminist Literary Criticism and the Author," *Critical Inquiry* 16 [1990]: 551–57).

45. The relation of the feminine to the law and of historical women to the law are subjects of increasing study. Julia Kristeva discusses the relation between biblical legal codes and the feminine in *Powers of Horror: An Essay on Abjection,* trans. Leon S. Roudiez (New York: Columbia University Press, 1982): The codification of "the cathexis of maternal function—mother, women, reproduction"—exists as the gesture of sacred text to control that cathexis. As a result, "the biblical text . . . performs the tremendous forcing that consists in subordinating maternal power (whether historical or phantasmatic, natural or reproductive) to symbolic order as pure logical order regulating social performance, as divine Law attended to in the Temple" (91).

On the relation between the heterosexual order and its enforcement through "its inquisitions, its courts, its tribunals, its body of laws, its terrors, its tortures, its mutilations, its executions, its police," see Monique Wittig, "On the Social Contract," *Feminist Issues* 9 (1989): 11. Wittig prefers the phrase "heterosexual law" to "male law," a terminology that emphasizes the participation of women in enforcing the code. I prefer "male law" because however much women participate in its existence, they were not its authors.

Maria L. Cioni, noting that "Lord Chancellor Christopher Hatton observed in 1587 that the law is 'the inheritance of all men,'" demonstrates that "the treatment of women in equity jurisdictions, and in particular in Chancery, became significant because relief was available there to both single and married women when, for numerous reasons, they could not go to the common law." Although this relief was gradually made available only to propertied women, Cioni's study is an insightful study of how this "male law" gradually worked to benefit some women ("The Elizabethan Chancery and Women's Rights," in *Tudor Rule and Revolution: Essays for G. R. Elton,* ed. Delloyd J. Guth and John W. McKenna [Cambridge: Cambridge University Press, 1982], 159).

46. For a discussion of the prevalent and conflicting views of the roles and virtues expected of sixteenth-century women, see Jones, *Currency of Eros,* 11–35.

47. Maureen Quilligan, *Milton's Spenser: The Politics of Reading* (Ithaca, N.Y.: Cornell University Press, 1983), 177. This discussion is indebted to the statement quoted and to "Book III and the Gender of the Reader," 185–208.

48. R. M., *The mothers counsell, or live within compasse* (London: Wright, 1636?), STC 20583, 3, 7. The author also shows familiarity with Spenser, quoting *The Faerie Queene.* For similar sentiments, see William Whately, *A care-cloth: or a treatise of the cumbers and troubles of marriage* (London: F. Kyngston, 1624), STC 25299.

49. See Margo Todd, *Christian Humanism and the Puritan Social Order* (Cambridge: Cambridge University Press, 1987). For Valerie Wayne's discussion of the dominance of "an ideology of marriage that is grounded in Erasmian humanism" in sixteenth-century England, see her Introduction to Edmund Tilney, *"The Flower of Friendshippe": A Renaissance Dialogue Contesting Marriage,* ed. Valerie Wayne (Ithaca, N.Y.: Cornell University Press, 1992), 37.

50. Erasmus, *Colloquies of Erasmus,* 86–87. *Courtship* appeared in foreign edi-

tions of 1523, 1526, and 1529; in English in 1568; and again in Thomas Heywood's verse adaptation of 1637. For Erasmus on marriage, see also *Encomium matriomonii* (1518), *Instituto Christiani matrimonii* (1526), and the *Vidua Christiana* (1526).

51. William Byrd, ed., *Psalms, Sonnets, and Songs of Sadness and Piety* (London, 1588), in *An English Garner,* ed. Edward Arber (Westminster: Archibald Constable, 1905), 85.

52. See *The Four Foster Children of Desire,* in Jean Wilson, ed., *Entertainments for Elizabeth* (Totowa, N.J.: Rowman and Littlefield, 1980), 61–85; George Gascoigne, *The Princely Pleasures at the Courte at Kenelworth,* in Nichols, ed., *Progresses,* 1: 485–523. In "Magic and Festivity at the Renaissance Court," *Renaissance Quarterly* 40 (1987): 636–59, Thomas Greene examines the *The Four Foster Children* in terms of its court antecedents in which women were successfully overcome, finding it a "dramatization of royal inviolability, sexual and political" (653).

53. Thomas Cain, in *Praise in The Faerie Queene* (Lincoln: University of Nebraska Press, 1978), examines the undermining of praise addressed to Elizabeth in the books first published in 1596 (130), an undermining that I see as beginning in the 1590 text of book 3, with Spenser's reworkings of encomiastic discourse and the exploration of the poet's relation to the royal audience.

54. By "masculinist poetics," I mean the prevalent codes, such as the topoi of rhetoric and poetry, and narratives, like the captivity narrative of romance, that serve to identify areas of life and language from which women were discouraged and through which women were defined. On the humanist attitudes toward women that helped disseminate these codes, see Constance Jordan, "Feminism and the Humanists: The Case of Sir Thomas Elyot's *Defence of Good Women,"* *Renaissance Quarterly* 36 (1983): 181–201. On the central question of the relation of women to male codes, especially language, see in particular Teresa de Lauretis, "The Violence of Rhetoric," in *Technologies of Gender: Essays on Theory, Film, and Fiction* (Bloomington: Indiana University Press, 1987), 31–50; Julia Kristeva, "About Chinese Women," in *The Kristeva Reader,* ed. Toril Moi (New York: Columbia University Press, 1986), 138–59; Gayatri Chakravorty Spivak, "Displacement and the Discourse of Woman," in *Displacement: Derrida and After,* ed. Mark Krupnick (Bloomington: Indiana University Press, 1983), 169–95; Luce Irigaray, "Women's Exile: Interview with Luce Irigaray," trans. Couze Venn, in *The Feminist Critique of Language: A Reader,* ed. Deborah Cameron (New York: Routledge & Kegan Paul, 1990), 80–96. On the conceptualization of male language as generating discourses, including that of psychoanalysis, whose "most consistent emphasis has been on localizing, defining, and confining the linguistic space of the Other," see Alice A. Jardine, *Gynesis: Configurations of Woman and Modernity* (Ithaca, N.Y.: Cornell University Press, 1985), esp. 88–102.

55. The text's general failure to name the queen outright is the source of the entire narrative of *The Faerie Queene,* according to Elizabeth Bellamy, "The Vocative and the Vocational: The Unreadability of Elizabeth in *The Faerie Queene,"* *ELH* 54 (1987): 1–30. The world of faerie, "far from standing in parallel relation [to the world of Briton], 'narrates the unreadability' of Elizabeth's name" (5), whereas "the proem to book 3 presents a particularly extreme example of the loss of Elizabeth's name to denominational aberration" (9). Bellamy regards the failure to name Elizabeth in *The Faerie Queene* as also resulting in Spenser's inability to name himself as the poet: "Spenser is still vocationally unfulfilled, and Elizabeth is still unreadable" (24).

56. For an account of Britomart's narrative as implying "a serious criticism of the Elizabethan cult," see Philippa Berry, *Of Chastity and Power: Elizabethan Literature and the Unmarried Queen* (London: Routledge, 1989), 163. Margaret Olofson Thickstun also notes in regard to Britomart's eventual marriage that "such an ending retrospectively redefines female independence by encoding it within the scripts of lawful heterosexual generation" (*Fictions of the Feminine: Puritan Doctrine and the Representation of Women* [Ithaca, N.Y.: Cornell University Press, 1988], 43).

57. Thomas Churchyard, *A Discovrse of the Queenes Maiesties entertainement in Suffolk and Norffolk . . .* (London, 1578), STC 5226. In this entertainment, there is a specific "Shew of Chastitie" in which Chastity "settes vpon Cupid, and spoyles hym of his Coatch, Bowe and all, and sets him afoote, and so rides in his Coatche to the Queene" (D2, D1). This vigorous, militant Chastity—a prototype of Britomart's most independent aspect—then addresses the queen in a long speech complimenting her on the choice of virginity. This would seem a reasonably orthodox representation of virginal Chastity, except that the queen may still have been of two minds about retaining her virginity, as her relationship with Anjou was to suggest. The orthodox meaning of Chastity thus was not so firmly established in the 1570s as it was in the 1590s and may in part have arisen from a desire to discourage the queen from making an unpopular marriage, at a time when no marriage would have been popular. That virginal Chastity had not yet become a firmly fixed concept is also seen in the entertainment's presentation of Chastity and the Faerie Queene as figures separate from Elizabeth herself.

58. See Louis Adrian Montrose, "The Elizabethan Subject and the Spenserian Text," in *Literary Theory/Renaissance Texts,* ed. Patricia Parker and David Quint (Baltimore: Johns Hopkins University Press, 1986), 326.

59. Christopher Highley, "Shakespeare, Spenser, and Elizabethan Ireland" (Ph.D. diss., Stanford University, 1991), 3.

60. Ficino, *Commentary,* 127.

61. James Nohrnberg, *The Analogy of The Faerie Queene* (Princeton, N.J.: Princeton University Press, 1976), 104–10. One crucial way in which Spenser deviates from the Italian Neoplatonists is that his magicians inevitably have a dark side. Darkness claims Archimago and Busirane, is dis-spelled at nightfall in the verses of *Epithalamion,* and is even hinted at in Merlin, who is glimpsed enslaving devils (3.14).

62. See Thomas P. Roche, Jr., "The Challenge to Chastity: Britomart in the House of Busirane," *PMLA* 76 (1961): 189–98, in *Essential Articles for the Study of Edmund Spenser,* ed. A. C. Hamilton (Hamden, Conn.: Archon Books, 1972), 195. Sean Kane accepts Roche's argument in *Spenser's Moral Allegory* (Toronto: University of Toronto Press, 1989), 100. See also Maurice Evans, *Spenser's Anatomy of Heroism: A Commentary on The Faerie Queene* (Cambridge: Cambridge University Press, 1970), 166; Harry Berger, "Busirane and the War Between the Sexes: An Interpretation of *The Faerie Queene* III.xi-xii," *English Literary Renaissance* 1 (1971): 99; Robin Wells, *Spenser's Faerie Queene and the Cult of Elizabeth* (Totowa, N.J.: Barnes & Noble, 1983), 82–83.

63. Judith Anderson, "'in liuing colours and right hew': The Queen of Spenser's Central Books," in *Poetic Traditions of the English Renaissance,* ed. Maynard Mack and George DeForest Lord (New Haven, Conn.: Yale University Press, 1982), 48.

64. Nichols, ed., *Progresses,* 3:232.

65. The use of "pen" creates a running pun that also functions as a reminder of

the relation between male creativity and procreativity. The "pen" momentarily preempts metaphors of female creativity, even those, like birth metaphors, often used by men. On the opposition of phallocentric and gynocentric metaphors of creativity, see Susan Stanford Friedman, "Creativity and the Childbirth Metaphor: Gender Difference in Literary Discourse," *Feminist Studies* 13 (1987): 49.

66. Lynn A. Higgins and Brenda R. Silver, "Introduction: Rereading Rape," in *Rape and Representation,* ed. Lynn A Higgins and Brenda R. Silver (New York: Columbia University Press, 1991), 1.

67. Paul Alpers, "Narration in *The Faerie Queene,*" *ELH* 44 (1977): 21.

68. Amoret's reaction to her release further incorporates her in the patriarchal definition of chastity: After falling prostrate at the feet of Britomart, whom she takes to be a knight, she is pulled up and told to take comfort, since "your louing Make [Mate], / Hath no lesse griefe endured for your gentle sake" (3.11.40).

69. Higgins and Silver introduce *Rape and Representation* by noting that "in this volume, analyses of specific texts, when read through and against each other, illustrate a number of profoundly disturbing patterns. Not the least of these is an obsessive inscription—and an obsessive erasure—of sexual violence against women (and against those placed by society in the position of 'woman')" (2).

70. It is a scene that places Busirane and Amoret, like any "torturer and victim . . . as close as lovers." What is the role of the author in such a scene? In *The Pornography of Representation* (Minneapolis: University of Minnesota Press, 1986), Susanne Kappeler describes the modern relation among victim, torturer, and photographer in a way that suggests points of comparison with the relation among Amoret, Busirane, and Spenser: "Hardly any less close (than the victim and the torturer) is the man who offers this view, the white man behind the Instamatic who frames a picture of the proximity of two humans, eye to eye, breath on breath, a view so naturalized, so disinterested, so aesthetically accomplished as to obliterate any distinction between the torturer–victim pair and the pair of lovers. . . . From the male viewing perspective with its focus through the active subject, there is no difference between the hero-torturer and the hero-lover: each has his own object from whom he derives his pleasure" (213). A photograph is not a poem; Amoret and Busirane are allegorical figures rather than real people, but both photographer and poet select their materials and, in the process of creating the picture, stand within it: The scene juxtaposing Amoret and Busirane necessarily includes its author. On the relation of torturer and lover, Kappeler quotes Michael Ignatieff, "Torture's Dead Simplicity," *New Statesman,* 20 September 1985, 24.

71. Compare Stephanie Jed, *Chaste Thinking: The Rape of Lucretia and the Birth of Humanism* (Bloomington: Indiana University Press, 1989). Jed observes that "Every encounter with a representation of the rape of Lucretia is an encounter with a literary *topos* of Western civilization. And, as a *topos,* the meaning of this rape is constructed as universal, transcending historical conditions: in every age and place, Lucretia had to be raped so that Rome could be liberated from tyranny" (51). In the same way that rape stands at the heart of the mythic narrative of humanism and republicanism, because it is the necessary prelude to the overthrow of Tarquin, it also stands at the center of the companionate marriage as a form of possession when all other forms fail.

72. The distinction, however, results in a fundamental instability making it difficult to construct either Busirane or Spenser from the text. Moreover, in creating Busirane, Spenser may have also increased his sense of his own instability. As Elizabeth Gross comments in her discussion of Julia Kristeva's *Powers of Horror,*

because "the subject must disavow part of itself in order to gain a stable self," this distancing "marks whatever identity it acquires as provisional, and open to break-down and instability" ("The Body of Signification," in *Abjection, Melancholia and Love,* ed. John Fletcher and Andrew Benjamin [New York: Routledge & Kegan Paul, 1990], 86).

73. George Puttenham, *The Arte of English Poesie,* ed. Edward Arber (1906; Kent, Ohio: Kent State University Press, 1970), 104.

74. I quote portions of the *Amoretti* from Edmund Spenser, *The Yale Edition of the Shorter Poems of Edmund Spenser,* ed. William A. Oram et al. (New Haven, Conn.: Yale University Press, 1989). Pages of subsequent citations from this work appear in the text.

75. Couliano, *Eros and Magic,* 103.

76. Tilney, *"Flower of Friendshippe,"* 405–6.

77. See Maureen Quilligan, *The Language of Allegory: Defining the Genre* (Ithaca, N.Y.: Cornell University Press, 1979), 84–85.

78. Loewenstein and Silberman make their observations in the midst of very different, although equally provocative, arguments. They do, however, share Quilligan's sense that the House of Busirane's violence should finally be con-structed as redemptive or transcendent of its cultural milieu. See Joseph Loewen-stein, "Echo's Ring: Orpheus and Spenser's Career," *English Literary Renaissance* 16 (1986): 294, in which he comments on how the *Epithalamion* "celebrates the social and psychological redemptions that enable us to leave Busyrane's erotic culture behind" (295). See also Lauren Silberman, "Unsung Heroines: Androgynous Dis-course in Book 3 of *The Faerie Queene,"* in *Rewriting the Renaissance: The Discourses of Sexual Difference in Early Modern Europe,* ed. Margaret W. Ferguson, Maureen Quilligan, and Nancy J. Vickers (Chicago: University of Chicago Press, 1986). She emphatically rejects the idea that Amoret is the source of her own situation, con-cluding that "the text itself creates a reader who . . . transcends the partiality Spenser attributes to men, who, when they write and when they read, praise only themselves" (271).

79. "Specifically Petrarchan . . . is the obsessive insistence on the particular, an insistence that would in turn generate multiple texts on individual fragments of the body or on the beauties of women" (Nancy J. Vickers, "Diana Described: Scattered Woman and Scattered Rhyme," in *Writing and Sexual Difference,* ed. Elizabeth Abel [Chicago: University of Chicago Press, 1982], 96). See also Ann Rosalind Jones and Peter Stallybrass, "The Politics of *Astrophil and Stella,"* *Studies in English Literature* 24 (1984): 53–68.

80. On the operation of rape to assert and enforce patriarchy at all levels of society, Susan Brownmiller's *Against Our Will: Men, Women, and Rape* (New York: Simon and Schuster, 1975) was germinal. Jonathan Crewe discusses Shake-speare's *Rape of Lucrece* with reference to Brownmiller in *Trials of Authorship: Anterior Forms and Poetic Reconstruction from Wyatt to Shakespeare* (Berkeley: Uni-versity of California Press, 1990), 140–63. See also Terry Castle's discussion of Lovelace's rape of Clarissa for its discussion of rape as patriarchal: "The quintessen-tial act of violence against women, it is that hidden physical threat held over the woman who tries, wittingly or unwittingly, to overstep any of the fundamental restrictions on her power—in any area" (*Clarissa's Ciphers: Meaning and Disruption in Richardson's "Clarissa"* [Ithaca, N.Y.: Cornell University Press, 1982], 117 and, on Clarissa's rape, 108–35). The most recent sociological studies on the subject of rape acknowledge this feminist argument. In particular, see Linda Brookover

Bourque, *Defining Rape* (Durham, N.C.: Duke University Press, 1989), 14–58; Larry Baron and Murray A. Straus, *Four Theories of Rape in American Society: A State-Level Analysis* (New Haven, Conn.: Yale University Press, 1989), 61–94.

81. See Patricia Parker, *Literary Fat Ladies: Rhetoric, Gender, Property* (New York: Methuen, 1987), 61.

82. Additional evidence that Petrarchism and anti-Petrachism are mutually constitutive discourses in male poetics lies in the responses of contemporary women writers to its forms. Such different authors as Mary Sidney Herbert, Countess of Pembroke, and Isabella Whitney offer particularly female responses to Petrarchism from the margins of discourse. Working in a culture that so often equated silence with lawful chastity, women who wrote had first to select materials and tropes through which to speak. Their rejoinders may be read through the selection of materials examining, appropriating, and circumventing the exclusionary male tropes of Petrarchism in particular and humanism in general. Mary Sidney found the voice, however muted, of selector and translator in Petrarch's *Trionfo della morte,* by choosing to rewrite the moment in Petrarch's corpus when the physical becomes the spiritual (*"The Triumphe of Death" Translated out of Italian by the Countess of Pembroke,* ed. Frances B. Young, *PMLA* 27 [1912]: 47–75). Isabella Whitney, a London poet of the middle class, frequently avoids Petrarchism by grounding her imagery in the everyday sights of London—its streets, bookstalls, and serving women (*A sweet Nosegay or pleasant posye. Contayning a hundred and ten Phylosophicall flowers* (1573), in *The Floures of Philosophy* (1572) *by Hugh Plat and A Sweet Nosegay* (1573) *and The Copy of a Letter* (1567) *by Isabella Whitney,* facsimile ed. [New York: Richard J. Panofsky, 1982]; Betty Travitsky, "The 'Wyll and Testament' of Isabella Whitney," *English Literary Renaissance* 10 [1980]: 76–95).

83. See Parker, *Literary Fat Ladies,* 126–54; Peter Stallybrass, "Patriarchal Territories: The Body Enclosed," in Ferguson, Quilligan, and Vickers, eds., *Rewriting the Renaissance,* 123–42.

84. "An Interview with Maitland Concerning Mary Queen of Scots" (1561), in Rice, ed., *Public Speaking of Queen Elizabeth,* 69.

85. Cain also pointed out the relation between Amoret and Elizabeth, although he prefers to see a specific historical incident in the allegory by suggesting that Busirane is the Duke of Anjou or someone closely associated with him (*Praise in the Faerie Queene,* 104). Alastair Fowler notes Amoret's "central place of sovereignty" in the masque of Cupid (*Triumphal Forms: Structural Patterns in Elizabethan Poetry* [Cambridge: Cambridge University Press, 1970], 52).

86. Elizabeth I to Robert Devereux, Earl of Essex, 8 July 1597, in Harrison, ed., *Letters of Queen Elizabeth,* 248.

87. Quoted in John E. Neale, *Queen Elizabeth I: A Biography* (1934; Garden City, N.Y.: Doubleday, 1957), 349.

88. HMC Penshurst, 2:182; Roland Whyte, quoted in HMC Penshurst, 2:187. "Device exhibited by the Earl of Essex before Queen Elizabeth, on the Anniversary of her Accession to the Throne, November 17, 1595," in Nichols, ed., *Progresses,* 3:371–79. CSP Domestic, 1598–1601, prints a different version of the entertainment. At this time, because Sidney and Essex were politically aligned, Whyte's description seems especially believable.

89. *Cobbett's Complete Collection of State Trials,* 1345–46.

90. 18 February 1600[1], CSP Domestic, 1598–1601, 577.

91. Paul Seaver, *The Puritan Lectureships* (Stanford, Calif.: Stanford University Press, 1970), 58.

92. Robert Cecil to Dr. Barlow, 26 February (?) 1601, CSP Domestic, 1598–1601, 598–99; Robert Cecil to the Lord Lieutenant of Ireland and to the English officers in the Low Countries, 10 February 1601, CSP Domestic, 1598–1601, 546–47; Robert Cecil to George Carew, 10 February 1600[1], CSP Carew, 1601–1602.

93. CSP Domestic, 1598–1601, 598–99.

94. Although at his brief trial Lee protested his service in Ireland, this served as a reminder to the court's attorney that he had served as Essex's messenger to Tyrone: "and Tyrone made him his bedfellow, and Capt. Lee brought a message back to the Earl of Essex" (*Cobbett's Complete Collection of State Trials,* 1:1403, 1407). Neither Essex's nor Lee's treachery on that occasion could be proved, but the rebellion provided Elizabeth's government with the opportunity to displace the nebulous issue of the Irish truce with material crimes against the queen's person.

95. These are the first lines of "a song the shepherd Philisides had in [Pyrocles'] hearing sung of the beauties of his unkind mistress, which in Pyrocles' judgement was fully accomplished in Philoclea" (Philip Sidney, *The Countess of Pembroke's Arcadia (The Old Arcadia),* ed. Jean Robertson [Oxford: Clarendon Press, 1973], 238).

96. The emergent idea of a companionate marriage did have its advantages over the Calvinistic idea of marriage, which condemned nonprocreative sex. The bond also subordinated the female while sanctifying her subordination. On the evolution of the relation between marital partners in the English Renaissance, see Lawrence Stone, *The Family, Sex, and Marriage in England, 1500–1800* (New York: Harper & Row, 1977), esp. 135–38, 499, 530. See also Mary Beth Rose, *The Expense of Spirit: Love and Sexuality in English Renaissance Drama* (Ithaca, N.Y.: Cornell University Press, 1988), esp. 15–18, 93–131; Theodore de Welles, "Sex and Sexual Attitudes in Seventeenth-Century England: The Evidence from Puritan Diaries," *Renaissance and Reformation* 24 (1988): 45–64.

97. Wilson, ed., *Four Foster Children of Desire,* 79.

98. Philip Sidney, *The Countess of Pembroke's Arcadia,* ed. Maurice Evans (Harmondsworth: Penguin Books, 1982), 523. Pages of subsequent citations from this work appear in the text.

99. For a reading of Amphialus as himself a captive of a cultural paradigm, see Michael McCanles's sensitive analysis of a character whose "emotions and thoughts, motivations and actions, indeed his very words, are imprisoned within the rhetorical figuration that consititutes the Renaissance understanding of human love" (*The Text of Sidney's Arcadian World* [Durham, N.C.: Duke University Press, 1989], 65).

100. I have adopted McCanles's correction of Feuillerat's text for the spelling of "dear" (ibid., 69).

101. For images of the caged and fragmented female in the twentieth century, see, for example, the illustrations for Mary Ann Caws, "Ladies Shot and Painted: Female Embodiment in Surrealist Art," in *The Female Body in Western Culture: Contemporary Perspectives,* ed. Susan Rubin Suleiman (Cambridge, Mass.: Harvard University Press, 1986), 262–87.

102. David Norbrook, *Poetry and Politics in the English Renaissance* (New York: Routledge & Kegan Paul, 1984), 106. For a view of Sidney as more empowered than frustrated by the language he directed at Elizabeth, see Maureen Quilligan, "Sidney and His Queen," in *The Historical Renaissance: New Essays on Tudor and Stuart Literature and Culture,* ed. Heather Dubrow and Richard Strier (Chicago: University of Chicago Press, 1988), 171–96.

103. Philip Sidney to the Earl of Leicester, 2 August 1580, in David Starkey, *Rivals in Power: Lives and Letters of the Great Tudor Dynasties* (New York: Grove Weidenfeld, 1990), 221. Compare Steven May, "Sir Philip Sidney and Queen Elizabeth," in *English Manuscript Studies, 1100–1700,* ed. Peter Beal and Jeremy Griffiths (London: Basil Blackwell, 1990), 257–67.

104. *Cobbett's Complete Collection of State Trials,* 1:1337.

105. "Edmond Spenser" is listed among the Undertakers of Munster, and his Cork holdings are specified in a note in CSP Carew, 1589–1600, 61. On Spenser in Ireland, see Highley, "Shakespeare, Spenser," chap. 1. See also Ciaran Brady, "Spenser's Irish Crisis: Humanism and Experience in the 1590s," *Past and Present* 111 (1986): 17–49, and the subsequent reply: Nicholas Canny, "Debate: Spenser's Irish Crisis: Humanism and Experience in the 1950s," *Past and Present* 120 (1988): 201–15.

Although disappointed and, because of his location in Ireland, a marginal court figure at best, Spenser continued to function in the court's system of patronage and praise. Jonathan Goldberg noted the paradox of Spenser's position in *Endlesse Worke: Spenser and the Structures of Discourse* (Baltimore: Johns Hopkins University Press, 1981). Despite Spenser's many complaints in verse about the court, "his fortunes grew; a pension was awarded; over the years there was the patronage of royal favorites, Leicester, Ralegh, Essex" (173). Spenser's bitterness seems to have been based on his inability to realize the upwardly mobile, humanist conception of the poet centered at court and advising his sovereign, a place and function he nevertheless attempted to appropriate in devising *The Faerie Queene* in order to "fashion a gentleman or noble person in vertuous and gentle discipline."

106. CSP Carew, 1589–1600, no. 128.

107. Sums from "Queen Elizabeth's Annual Expense, Civil and Military, c. 1578," in *Tudor Constitutional Documents, A.D. 1485–1603,* ed. J. R. Tanner (Cambridge: Cambridge University Press, 1922), 209–10; Paul L. Hughes and James F. Larkin, eds., *Tudor Royal Proclamations* (New Haven, Conn.: Yale University Press, 1969), 3:5; R. K. R. Thornton and T. G. S. Cain, Introduction to Nicholas Hillard, *A Treatise Concerning the Arte of Limning* (Hatfield: Stellar Press, 1981), 32.

108. Anne Bradstreet, *Complete Works of Anne Bradstreet,* ed. Joseph R. McElrath, Jr., and Allan P. Robb (Boston: Twayne, 1981), 155–56. *Phoenix*: the anthology containing many poems written in the queen's iconographic discourse, *The Phoenix Nest* (1593), facsimile ed. (London: Scolar Press, 1973). *Speeds*: John Speed, *The history of Great Britain* (London: J. Sudbury and G. Humble, 1611), STC 23045. *Chamdens*: William Camden, *Annales: The True and Royall History of the famous Empresse Elizabeth queene of England,* trans. A. Darcie (London: B. Fisher, 1625), STC 4497, and *The Historie of the most renowned and victorious princess Elizabeth,* trans. R. Norton (London: B. Fisher, 1630), STC 4500.

Selected Bibliography

Primary Sources

Acts of the Privy Council of England. 32 vols. Ed. J. R. Dasent. London: HMSO, 1890–1907.

Ariosto, Iodovico. *Orlando Furioso.* Trans. Barbara Reynolds. Harmondsworth: Penguin Books, 1977.

Aristotle. *Art of Rhetoric.* Trans. John Henry Freese. Cambridge, Mass.: Harvard University Press, 1932.

Bacon, Francis. *A declaration of the practices & treasons committed by Robert late Earle of Essex.* London: R. Barker, 1601. STC 1133.

———. *The Works of Francis Bacon.* 6 vols. Ed. James Spedding, Robert Ellis, and Douglas Heath. London, 1857–1874.

Bradstreet, Anne. *Complete Works of Anne Bradstreet.* Ed. Joseph R. McElrath, Jr., and Allan P. Robb. Boston: Twayne, 1981.

Byrd, William, ed. *Psalms, Sonnets, and Songs of Sadness and Piety.* London, 1588. Reprint in *An English Garner.* Ed. Edward Arber. Westminster: Archibald Constable, 1905.

Calendar of the Carew Manuscripts preserved in the Archepiscopal Library at Lambeth. 7 vols. Ed. J. S. Brewer and William Bullen. London: Longman, 1867–1873.

Calendar of Letters and Papers relating to English affairs preserved in the archives of Simancas. 4 vols. Ed. Martin A. S. Hume. London: HMSO, 1892–1899.

Calendar of the State Papers, Domestic Series of the Reigns of Edward VI, Mary, Elizabeth, and James I, preserved in the Public Record Office. 12 vols. Ed. Robert Lemon and Mary Anne Everett Green. London: Longman, 1856–1872.

Calendar of State Papers, Foreign. Edward VI and Mary. 23 vols. Ed. Joseph Stephenson et al. London: Longman, 1863–1950.

Calendar of State Papers and Manuscripts Relating to English affairs existing in the archives and collections of Venice, and in other libraries of northern Italy. 38 vols. Ed. Rawdon Brown et al. London: HMSO, 1864–1947.

Calendar of State Papers Relating to Mary, Queen of Scots. 1547–1603. Edinburgh: H. M. General Register Office, 1898–1952.

Camden, William. *Annales: The True and Royall History of the famous Empresse Elizabeth queene of England.* Trans. A. Darcie. London: B. Fisher, 1625. STC 4497.

——. *The Historie of the most renowned and victorious princess Elizabeth.* Trans. R. Norton. London: B. Fisher, 1630. STC 4500.

——. *The History of the Most Renowned and Victorious Princess Elizabeth Late Queen of England.* Ed. Wallace T. MacCaffrey. Chicago: University of Chicago Press, 1970.

Cary, Elizabeth Tanfield. *The Tragedie of Mariam, the Faire Queene of Iewry* (1613). Ed. W. W. Greg. London: Early English Text Society, 1914.

Castiglione, Baldassare. *The Book of the Courtier.* Trans. Sir Thomas Hoby. New York: Dutton, 1928.

——. *The Book of the Courtier.* Trans. Charles S. Singleton. Garden City, N.Y.: Doubleday, 1959.

The Chronicle of Queen Jane and of Two Years of Queen Mary written by a Resident of the Tower of London. Ed. J. G. Nichols. London: Camden Society, 1850.

Churchyard, Thomas. *A Discovrse of the Queenes Maiesties entertainement in Suffolk and Norffolk.* . . . London, 1578. STC 5226.

——. *A Handefvl of Gladsome Verses, given to the Queenes Maiesty at Woostocke this Prograce, 1592.* London: Ioseph Barnes, 1592. STC 5237.

Clifford, Anne. *The Diary of the Lady Anne Clifford.* Ed. Vita Sackville-West. London: Heinemann, 1924.

Cobbett's Complete Collection of State Trials and Proceedings for High Treason and Other Crimes and Misdemeanors. Vol. 1. London: T. C. Hansard, 1809.

Collection of State Papers . . . *Left by William Cecil, Lord Burghley.* Ed. Samuel Haynes. London, 1740.

Collection of State Papers relating to the Affairs in the Reign of Queen Elizabeth from the Year 1571 to 1596. Transcribed from Original Papers . . . *at Hatfield House.* Ed. William Murdin. London, 1759.

Collins, Arthur, ed. *Letters and Memorials of State* . . . *Memoirs of the Lives and Actions of the Sidneys.* London: T. Osborne, 1746.

Corporation of London Records Offices. *Repertories.*

Cumberland Westmorland Gloucestershire. Records of Early English Drama. Ed. Audrey Douglas and Peter Greenfield. Toronto: University of Toronto Press, 1986.

Dekker, Thomas. *The Dramatic Works of Thomas Dekker.* Ed. Fredson Bowers. London: John Pearson, 1873.

——. *The Non-Dramatic Works of Thomas Dekker.* Ed. Alexander B. Grosart. New York: Russell and Russell, 1963.

——. *The Whore of Babylon.* London: N. Butter, 1607. STC 6532.

D'Ewes, Simonds. *The Journals of all the Parliaments during the reign of Queen Elizabeth.* London: John Starkey, 1682.

Dudley, Robert. *Correspondence of Robert Dudley.* Camden Society No. 27. Ed. J. Bruce. London: Camden Society, 1844.

——. *Lawes and Ordinances, set down by Robert Earle of Leycester, the Queenes maiesties Lieutenant and Captaine General of her armie and forces in the Lowe Countries.* London: Christopher Barker, 1586. STC 7288.

Elizabeth I. *A Book of Devotions Composed by Her Majesty Elizabeth with translation by Rev. Adam Fox.* Gerards Cross: Colin Smythe, 1920.

——. *A declaration of the causes moving the Queene of England to giue aide to the defence of the people afflicted & oppressed in the Lowe Countries*. London: Christopher Barker, 1585. STC 9189.

———. *A godly medytacyon of the christen sowle concerninge a love towarde God and hys Christe . . . Translated by Elyzabeth doughter to our late soverayne kynge Henry the viii*. London: John Bale, 1548. Reprint. 1590.

———. *Her maiesties most princelie answere, deliuered by her selfe at White-hall, on the last day of Nouember 1601*. London: R. Barker, 1601.

———. *The Letters of Queen Elizabeth*. Ed. G. B. Harrison. 1935. Reprint. New York: Funk & Wagnalls, 1968.

———. "A most excellent and remarkable speech delivered by that mirrour and miracle of princes, Queen Elizabeth of famous memory. . . ." London: Humphrey Richardson, 1643. Wing E531.

———. *The Public Speaking of Queen Elizabeth*. Ed. George P. Rice. New York: Columbia University Press, 1951.

———. *Queen Elizabeth I: Political Speeches and Parliamentary Addresses, 1558–1601*. Ed. Allison Heisch. Madison: University of Wisconsin Press, 1994.

———. *Queen Elizabeth's Englishings of Boethius, De Consolatione Philosophiae* A.D. *1593*. Early English Text Society No. 113. Ed. Caroline Pemberton. London: Early English Text Society, 1899.

———. *The Sayings of Elizabeth*. Ed. Frederick Chamberlin. London: John Lane, 1923.

———. *Supplications of saints: a book of prayers and praises . . . wherein are three most excellent prayers, made by the late famous Queen Elizabeth*. London: Peter Parker, 1678. Wing S4706.

———. *The true copie of a letter from the queenes maiestie, to the lord maior of London*, [*concerning*] *the ioy her subiectes took vpon the apprehension of diuers* [*traitors*]. London: C. Barker, 1586. STC 7577.

Erasmus, Desiderius. *The Colloquies of Erasmus*. Trans. Craig R. Thompson. Chicago: University of Chicago Press, 1965.

———. *The Education of a Christian Prince*. Trans. Lester K. Born. 1936. Reprint. New York: Norton, 1964.

———. *A modest meane to mariage, pleasantly set forth. . . .* Trans. N. Leigh. London: H. Denham, 1568.

———. *A ryght frutefull Epystle by the moste excellent clerke Erasmus in laude and prayse of matrymony*. Trans. Rychard Tauernour. London, 1532. STC 10492.

Extracts from the Records of the Burgh of Edinburgh, 1557–1571. Edinburgh: Scottish Burgh Records Society, 1875.

Feuillerat, Albert, ed. *Documents Relating to the Office of the Revels in the Reign of Elizabeth*. Louvain: A. Uystprust, 1908.

———. *Documents Relating to the Revels at Court in the Time of King Edward VI and Queen Mary*. Louvain: A. Uystprust, 1914.

Ficino, Marsilio. *Commentary on Plato's Symposium on Love*. Trans. Sears Jayne. Dallas: Spring, 1985.

Foxe, John. *Actes and Monuments of these latter and perillous dayes. . . .* London: J. Day, 1596. STC 11226.

———. *Acts and Monuments*. 8 vols. Ed. George Townsend. New York: AMS Press, 1965.

Gascoigne, George. *The Complete Works*. 2 vols. Ed. John W. Cunliffe. Cambridge: Cambridge University Press, 1907, 1910.

———. *The Spoyle of Antwerpe*. London: R. Jones, 1576. STC 11644.

Glover, Alan, ed. *Gloriana's Glass: Queen Elizabeth I reflected in verses and dedications addressed to her*. Barnet: Stellar Press, [1953].

Grafton, Richard. *Abridgement of the Chronicles of England*. London: J. Waley, 1576. STC 12156.

———. *The Chronicle of Iohn Harding . . . Together with the Continuation by Richard Grafton*. London: F. C. and J. Rivington, 1812.

———. *Grafton's Chronicle; History of England*. 2 vols. London: J. Johnson, 1809.

Greville, Fulke. *The Prose Works of Fulke Greville, Lord Brooke*. Ed. John Gouws. Oxford: Clarendon Press, 1986.

Greyfriars Chronicle. Ed. J. G. Nichols. London: Camden Society, 1852.

Hardwicke, Philip York. *Miscellaneous State Papers from 1501 to 1726*. London: W. Strahan and T. Cadell, 1778.

Harington, John. *Letters and Epigrams of Sir John Harington*. Ed. Norman McClure. Philadelphia: University of Pennsylvania Press, 1930.

———. *Nugae Antiquae*. London: T. Caddell, 1779. Reprint. Hildesheim, 1968.

Harrison, Stephen. *The Archs of Trivmph Erected in honor of the High and mighty prince James the first of that name King, of England, and the Sixt of Scotland, at his Maiesties Entrance and passage through His honorable Citty & Chamber of London opon the 15th day of march 1603*. London: William Kip, 1604. STC 12863.

Heywood, Thomas. *England's Elizabeth*. New York: Garland, 1982.

———. *Englands Elizabeth her life and troubles during her minoritie, from the cradle to the crowne*. London: John Beale, 1631. STC 13313.

———. *Gynaikeion or nine bookes of various history, concerninge women*. London: A. Islip, 1624. STC 13326.

———. *If You Know Not Me, You Know Nobody Part I*. London: N. Butter, 1605. STC 13328.

———. *If You Know Not Me, You Know Nobody Part II* [subtitled in part *The building of the Royall Exchange*]. Ed. Madeleine Doran. London: Malone Society, Oxford University Press, 1934.

Hilliard, Nicholas. *A Treatise Concerning the Arte of Limning*. Ed. R. K. R. Thornton and T. G. S. Cain. Hatfield: Stellar Press, 1981.

Historical Manuscripts Commission. *Calendar of the Manuscripts of the Most Honorable the Marquesss of Salisbury*. 14 vols. Ed. Edward Salisbury. London: HMSO, 1883–1923.

———. *The Manuscripts of His Grace the Duke of Rutland, G.C.B., Preserved at Belvoir Castle*. 4 vols. London: HMSO, 1888–1905.

———. *Report on the Manuscripts of Lord De L'Isle and Dudley Preserved at Penshurst Place*. 6 vols. London: HMSO, 1888–1905.

———. *Report on the Pepys Manuscripts, preserved at Magdalen College, Cambridge*. Ed. Edward K. Purnell. London: HMSO, 1911.

Holinshed, Raphael et al. *Chronicles of England and Scotland*. London: J. Johnson, 1807–1808.

———. *The Third Volume of Chronicles . . . Now newlie recognised, augmented, and continued . . . to the year 1586*. London: T. Woodcocke, 1586–1587. STC 13569.

Jane by the grace of God quene. London: Richard Grafton, 1553.

Isocrates. *To Nicocles*. Trans. George Norlin. London: Heinemann, 1928.

Johnson, Richard. *The most pleasant history of Tom a Lincolne. The Sixth Impression*. London: A. Mathewes, 1631. STC 14684.

Jonson, Ben. *Ben Jonson*. 11 vols. Ed. C. H. Herford, Percy Simpson, and Evelyn Simpson. Oxford: Oxford University Press, 1925–1952.

Kinney, Arthur, ed. *Elizabethan Backgrounds*. Hamden, Conn.: Archon Books, 1975.

Knox, John. *The Works of John Knox*. 6 vols. Ed. David Laing. Edinburgh, 1895.

Langham, Robert [pseud.]. *A Letter*. Ed. Roger J. P. Kuin. Leiden: Brill, 1983.

Layamon's Brut: A History of the Britains. Trans. Donald G. Bzdyl. Binghamton, N. Y.: Medieval and Renaissance Texts and Studies, 1989.

Layamon's Brut, or Chronicle of Britain. Ed. Frederic Madden. London: Society of Antiquaries, 1847.

Legh, Gerard. *Accedens of Armory*. London: R. Tottel, 1562.

Leicester's Commonwealth: The Copy of a Letter Written by a Master of Art of Cambridge (1584). Ed. D. C. Peck. Athens: Ohio University Press, 1985.

Lever, Christopher. *Queene Elizabeth's Teares: or, her resolute bearing the Christian crosse, in the bloodie time of Queene Marie*. London: M. Lownes, 1607. STC 15540.

Machyn, Henry. *The Diary of Henry Machyn, Citizen and Merchant-Taylor of London from A.D. 1550 to A.D. 1563*. London: Camden Society, 1848.

Mahl, Mary R., and Helene Koon, eds. *The Female Spectator: English Women Writers before 1800*. Bloomington: Indiana University Press, 1977.

Malory, Thomas. *Caxton's Malory: A New Edition of Sir Thomas Malory's La Morte Darthur*. Ed. James W. Spisak. Berkeley: University of California Press, 1983.

M. P. *An Abstract of the Historie of the Renouned Maiden Queene Elizabeth*. London: Thomas Cotes, 1631.

Mulcaster, Richard. *In Mortem Serenis simae Reginae Elizabethae* and *The Translation of certain latine verses vppon her maiesties death, called A Comforting Complaint*. London: Edward Aggas, 1603. STC 18252.

———. *Positions . . . for the training vp of children*. London: Thomas Vautrollier, 1581. STC 18253.

———. *The Quenes maiesties passsage through the citie of London to westminster the daye before her coronacion*. London: R. Tottel, 1559. STC 7589.5.

———. *The Quenes maiesties passsage through the citie of London to westminster the daye before her coronacion*. Facsimile ed. New Haven, Conn.: Yale Elizabethan Club, 1957.

Naunton, Robert. *Fragmenta Regalia*. Ed. John S. Cerovski. Washington, D.C.: Folger Shakespeare Library, 1985.

Nichols, John, ed. *Progresses, Processions, and Magnificent Festivities of King James the First*. 4 vols. London: J. B. Nichols, 1828.

———. *The Progresses and Public Processions of Queen Elizabeth*. 3 vols. London: John Nichols, 1823. Reprint. New York: AMS Press, 1966.

Norton, Thomas. *To the queenes maiesties poore deceived subiectes of the northe contreye*. London: H. Bynneman, 1569. STC 18679.5.

Petrarch. *Petrarch's Lyric Poems: The Rime sparse and Other Lyrics*. Trans. and ed. Robert M. Durling. Cambridge, Mass.: Harvard University Press, 1976.

———. *The Triumphs of Petrarch*. Trans. Ernest H. Wilkins. Chicago: University of Chicago Press, 1962.

The Phoenix Nest (1593). Facsimile ed. London: Scolar Press, 1973.

Pollard, A. F., ed. *An English Garner: Tudor Tracts, 1532–1588*. New York: Cooper Square, 1964.

Proctor, John. *The History of Wyat's Rebellion: With the order and manner of resisting the same*. London: Robert Caley, 1555.

Public Record Office. *Tudor Royal Letters: Elizabeth I and the Succession*. London: HMSO, 1972.

Puttenham, George. *The Arte of English Poesie*. Ed. Edward Arber. Westminster: Archibald Constable, 1906. Reprint. Kent, Ohio: Kent State University Press, 1970.

Ralegh, Walter. *A Choice of Sir Walter Ralegh's Verse*. Ed. Robert Nye. London: Faber & Faber, 1972.

———. *The Historie of the World*. London: W. Burre, 1614. STC 20637.

———. *The Works of Sir Walter Raleigh, Kt., now first collected*. 8 vols. Oxford: Oxford University Press, 1829.

Respublica, A.D. 1553: A Play on the social condition of England at the accession of Queen Mary. Early English Text Society No. 226. Ed. W. W. Greg. London: Early English Text Society, 1952.

Reynolds, John. *Vox Coeli of a consultation there held by King Hen. 8 King Edw. 6. . . .* London: W. Jones, 1624. STC 20946.4 (formerly 22094).

R. M. *The mothers counsell, or live within compasse*. London: Wright, 1636?, entered 1623. STC 20583.

Sackville, Thomas, and Thomas Norton. *Gorboduc; or, Ferrex and Porrex*. Ed. Irby B. Cauthen, Jr. Lincoln: University of Nebraska Press, 1970.

Scott, Thomas. *The wicked Plots, and perfidious Practices of the Spaniards, against the 17. Provinces of the Netherlands, before they tooke up Arms*. London, 1642. STC 22105a.

Scott, Walter. *Kenilworth*. London: Macdonald, 1953.

———, ed. *A Collection of Scarce and Valuable Tracts . . . Selected from an Infinite Number in Print & Manuscript in the Royal Cotton, Sion . . . Libraries . . . Particularly that of the late Lord Somers*. Vols. 1 and 2. London: T. Cordell and W. Davies, 1809.

Shakespeare, William. *The Riverside Shakespeare*. Ed. G. Blakemore Evans. Boston: Houghton Mifflin, 1974.

Sidney, Mary. *The Triumph of Death and Other Unpublished and Uncollected Poems*. Ed. Gary F. Waller. Salzburg: Institut für Englische Sprache und Literatur, 1977.

———. *"The Triumphe of Death" Translated out of Italian by the Countess of Pembroke*. Ed. Frances B. Young. *PMLA* 27(1912): 47–75.

Sidney, Philip. *An Apology for Poetry, or the Defence of Poesy*. Ed. Geoffrey Shepherd. London: Thomas Nelson, 1965.

———. *The Countess of Pembroke's Arcadia (The Old Arcadia)*. Ed. Jean Robertson. Oxford: Clarendon Press, 1973.

———. *The Countess of Pembroke's Arcadia* [New or 1621 version]. Ed. Maurice Evans. Harmondsworth: Penguin Books, 1982.

Skelton, John. *The Complete English Poems*. Ed. John Scattergood. New Haven, Conn.: Yale University Press, 1983.

Smith, G. Gregory, ed. *Elizabethan Critical Essays*. Oxford: Clarendon Press, 1904.

Speeches Delivered to Her Maiestie This Last Progresse, at the Right Honorable the Lady Russells, at Bissam. . . . Oxford: Joseph Barnes, 1592.

Speed, John. *The history of Great Britain.* London: J. Sudbury and G. Humble, 1611. STC 23045.

Spenser, Edmund. *The Faerie Queene.* Ed. Thomas P. Roche. New Haven, Conn.: Yale University Press, 1978.

———. *Spenser's Minor Poems.* Ed. Ernest de Selincourt. Oxford: Clarendon Press, 1910.

———. *The Works of Edmund Spenser: A Variorum Edition.* 9 vols. Ed. E. Greenlaw, C. G. Osgood, F. M. Padelford et al. Baltimore: Johns Hopkins University Press, 1932–1949.

———. *The Yale Edition of the Shorter Poems of Edmund Spenser.* Ed. William A. Oram et al. New Haven, Conn.: Yale University Press, 1989.

Stow, John. *A Survey of London* (1603). 2 vols. Ed. Charles Kingsford. Oxford: Clarendon Press, 1971.

Tanner, Joseph R., ed. *Tudor Constitutional Documents, A.D. 1485–1603.* 2nd ed. Cambridge: Cambridge University Press, 1930.

Taylor, John. *A brief remembrance of all the English monarchs from the Normans Conquest.* London: G. Eld, 1618. STC 23736.

T. D. *A Briefe Report of the Militarie Services done in the Low Countries, by the Erle of Leicester.* London: Arnold Hatfield, 1587. STC 7285.

Tilney, Edmund. *"The Flower of Friendshippe": A Renaissance Dialogue Contesting Marriage* (1568). Ed. Valerie Wayne. Ithaca, N.Y.: Cornell University Press, 1992.

Tudor Royal Proclamations. 3 vols. Ed. Paul L. Hughes and James F. Larkin. New Haven, Conn.: Yale University Press, 1969.

Whately, William. *A care-cloth: or a treatise of the cumbers and troubles of marriage.* London: F. Kyngston, 1624. STC 25299.

Whitney, Geoffrey. *A Choice of Emblemes.* Ed. Henry Green. New York: Benjamin Blom, 1967.

Whitney, Isabella. *The Floures of Philosophy* (1572) *by Hugh Plat and A Sweet Nosegay* (1573) *and The Copy of a Letter* (1567) *by Isabella Whitney.* Facsimile ed. New York: Richard J. Panofsky, 1982.

———. *A sweet nosegay, or pleasant posye: contayning a hundred and ten phylosophicall flowers.* London: R. Jones, 1573. STC 25440.

Williams, C. H., ed. *English Historical Documents.* Vol. 5. Oxford: Oxford University Press, 1967.

Wilson, Arthur. *The History of Great Britain, Being the Life and Reign of King James I.* London: R. W., 1653.

Wilson, Jean, ed. *Entertainments for Elizabeth I.* Totowa, N.J.: Rowman and Littlefield, 1980.

Wriothesley, Charles. *A Chronicle of England During the Reigns of the Tudors, from A.D. 1485 to 1559.* Ed. William Douglas Hamilton. London: Camden Society, 1877.

Secondary Sources

Adams, Simon. "Eliza Enthroned? The Court and Its Politics." In *The Reign of Elizabeth I.* Ed. Christopher Haigh, 55–77. Athens: University of Georgia Press, 1987.

Alpers, Paul. "Narration in *The Faerie Queene.*" *ELH* 44 (1977): 19–39.

Althusser, Louis. *Lenin and Philosophy and Other Essays.* Trans. Ben Brewster. New York: Monthly Review Press, 1971.

Anderson, Judith H. "'In liuing colours and right hew': The Queen of Spenser's Central Books." In *Poetic Traditions of the English Renaissance.* Ed. Maynard Mack and George DeForest Lord, 47–66. New Haven, Conn.: Yale University Press, 1982.

Anglo, Sidney. *Spectacle Pageantry and Early Tudor Policy.* Oxford: Clarendon Press, 1969.

Appleby, Joyce Oldham. *Economic Thought and Ideology in Seventeenth-Century England.* Princeton, N.J.: Princeton University Press, 1978.

Archer, Ian. *The Pursuit of Stability: Social Relations in Elizabethan London.* Cambridge: Cambridge University Press, 1991.

Arnold, Janet. *Patterns of Fashion: The Cut and Construction of Clothes for Men and Women, c. 1560–1620.* London: Macmillan, 1985.

———. *Queen Elizabeth's Wardrobe Unlock'd.* Leeds: W. S. Maney and Son, 1985.

Ashton, Robert. *The City and the Court.* Cambridge: Cambridge University Press, 1979.

Attridge, Derek. *Peculiar Language: Literature as Difference from the Renaissance to James Joyce.* Ithaca, N.Y.: Cornell University Press, 1988.

Auerbach, Erna. "Portraits of Elizabeth I on Some City Companies' Charters." *Guildhall Miscellany* 6 (1956): 15–24.

Auerbach, Nina. *Romantic Imprisonment: Women and Other Glorified Outcasts.* New York: Columbia University Press, 1985.

Axton, Marie. "Robert Dudley and the Inner Temple Revels." *Historical Journal* 13 (1970): 365–78.

Baron, Larry, and Murray A. Straus. *Four Theories of Rape in American Society: A State-Level Analysis.* New Haven, Conn.: Yale University Press, 1989.

Barton, Anne. "London Comedy and the Ethos of the City." *London Journal* 4 (1978): 158–80.

Baskervill, Charles Read. "The Genesis of Spenser's Queen of Faerie." *Modern Philology* 18 (1920): 49–54.

———. "Richard Mulcaster." *Times Literary Supplement* 15 (August 1935): 315.

Bassnett, Susan. *Elizabeth I: A Feminist Perspective.* New York: St. Martin's Press, 1988.

Beaven, Alfred B. *The Aldermen of the City of London.* 2 vols. London: E. Fisher, 1908, 1913.

Beilin, Elaine V., ed. *Redeeming Eve: Women Writers of the English Renaissance.* Princeton, N.J.: Princeton University Press, 1987.

Bellamy, Elizabeth. "The Vocative and the Vocational: The Unreadability of Elizabeth in *The Faerie Queene.*" *ELH* 54 (1987): 1–30.

Belsey, Andrew, and Catherine Belsey. "Icons of Divinity: Portraits of Elizabeth I." In *Renaissance Bodies: The Human Figure in English Culture, c. 1540–1660.* Ed. Lucy Gent and Nigel Llewellyn, 9–35. London: Reaktion Books, 1990.

Belsey, Catherine. "Disrupting Sexual Difference: Meaning and Gender in the Comedies." In *Alternative Shakespeares.* Ed. J. Drakakis, 166–90. New York: Methuen, 1985.

Bennett, Josephine Waters. *The Evolution of "The Faerie Queene."* New York: Burt Franklin, 1960.

Benson, Pamela Joseph. "Rule, Virginia: Protestant Theories of Female Regiment in *The Faerie Queene.*" *English Literary Renaissance* 15 (1985): 277–92.

Berger, Harry. "Busirane and the War Between the Sexes: An Interpretation of *The Faerie Queene* III.xi–xii." *English Literary Renaissance* 1 (1971): 99–121.

Bergeron, David M. "Elizabeth's Coronation Entry (1559): New Manuscript Evidence." *English Literary Renaissance* 8 (1978): 3–12.

———. *English Civic Pageantry*. Columbia: University of South Carolina Press, 1971.

———. "Gilbert Dugdale and the Royal Entry of James I (1604)." *Journal of Medieval and Renaissance Studies* 13 (1983): 111–25.

———. "Middleton's *No Wit, No Help*." In *Pageantry in the Shakespearian Theatre*. Ed. David Bergeron, 65–82. Athens: University of Georgia Press, 1985.

Berry, Philippa. *Of Chastity and Power: Elizabethan Literature and the Unmarried Queen*. London: Routledge, 1989.

Bevington, David. "Harrison, Jonson and Dekker: The Magnificent Entertainment for King James (1604)." *Journal of the Warburg and Cortauld Institute* 31 (1968): 445–48.

Blagden, Cyprian. *The Stationers Company: A History, 1403–1959*. Stanford, Calif.: Stanford University Press, 1960.

Bloomfield, Morton W. "Allegory as Interpretation." *New Literary History* 3 (1972): 301–17.

Bourdieu, Pierre. *Outline of a Theory of Practice*. Trans. Richard Nice. Cambridge: Cambridge University Press, 1977.

Bourque, Linda Brookover. *Defining Rape*. Durham, N.C.: Duke University Press, 1989.

Brady, Ciaran. "Spenser's Irish Crisis: Humanism and Experience in the 1590s." *Past and Present* 111 (1986): 17–49.

Braudel, Ferdinand. *The Structures of Everyday Life: The Limits of the Possible*. New York: Harper & Row, 1979.

Breitenberg, Mark. "' . . . the hole matter opened': Iconic Representation and Interpretation in 'The Quenes Majesties Passage.'" *Criticism* 28 (1986): 1–25.

Brooke, Tucker. "Queen Elizabeth's Prayers." *Huntington Library Quarterly* 2 (1938): 69–77.

Brownmiller, Susan. *Against Our Will: Men, Women, and Rape*. New York: Simon and Schuster, 1975.

Bryant, Arthur. *The Elizabethan Deliverance*. New York: St. Martin's Press, 1981.

Burke, Kenneth. *Language as Symbolic Action: Essays on Life, Literature, and Method*. Berkeley: University of California Press, 1966.

Butler, Judith. *Gender Trouble: Feminism and the Subversion of Identity*. New York: Routledge, 1990.

Butterfield, Herbert. *The Whig Interpretation of History*. New York: Norton, 1965.

Cain, Thomas. *Praise in The Faerie Queene*. Lincoln: University of Nebraska Press, 1978.

Campbell, Lily. *The Mirror for Magistrates*. Cambridge: Cambridge University Press, 1938.

Canny, Nicholas. "Debate: Spenser's Irish Crisis: Humanism and Experience in the 1590s." *Past and Present* 120 (1988): 210–15.

Castle, Terry. *Clarissa's Ciphers: Meaning and Disruption in Richardson's "Clarissa."* Ithaca, N.Y.: Cornell University Press, 1982.

Chalfant, Fran C. *Ben Jonson's London: A Jacobean Placename Dictionary*. Athens: University of Georgia Press, 1978.

Chambers, E. K. *The Elizabethan Stage*. 4 vols. 1935. Reprint. Oxford: Clarendon Press, 1945.

———. *Notes on the History of the Revels Office Under the Tudors*. London: A. H. Bullen, 1906.

Cioni, Maria L. "The Elizabethan Chancery and Women's Rights." In *Tudor Rule and Revolution: Essays for G. R. Elton from His American Friends*. Ed. Delloyd J. Guth and John W. McKenna, 159–82. Cambridge: Cambridge University Press, 1982.

Cohen, Abner. "Political Symbolism." *Annual Review of Anthropology* 8 (1979): 87–113.

———. *The Politics of Elite Culture: Explorations in the Dramaturgy of Power in a Modern African Society*. Berkeley: University of California Press, 1981.

Coleman, D. C. "The 'Gentry' Controversy and the Aristocracy in Crisis, 1558–1641." *History* 51 (1966): 165–78.

Collinson, Patrick. *Archbishop Grindal, 1519–1583: The Struggle for a Reformed Church*. Berkeley: University of California Press, 1979.

———. "The Elizabethan Church and the New Religion." In *The Reign of Elizabeth I*. Ed. Christopher Haigh, 169–94. Athens: University of Georgia Press, 1987.

Condon, M. M. "Ruling Elites in the Reign of Henry VII." In *Patronage, Pedigree and Power in Later Medieval England*. Ed. Charles Ross, 109–42. Totowa, N.J.: Rowman and Littlefield, 1979.

Cook, Ann Jennalie. *The Privileged Playgoers of Shakespeare's London, 1576–1642*. Princeton, N.J.: Princeton University Press, 1981.

Couliano, Ioan P. *Eros and Magic in the Renaissance*. Trans. Margaret Cook. Chicago: University of Chicago Press, 1987.

Crane, Mary. "'Video et Taceo': Elizabeth I and the Rhetoric of Counsel." *Studies in English Literature* 28 (1988): 1–15.

Cressy, David. *Literacy and the Social Order: Reading and Writing in Tudor and Stuart England*. Cambridge: Cambridge University Press, 1980.

Crewe, Jonathan. *Trials of Authorship: Anterior Forms and Poetic Reconstruction from Wyatt to Shakespeare*. Berkeley: University of California Press, 1990.

Culler, Jonathan. *Structuralist Poetics*. Ithaca, N.Y.: Cornell University Press, 1975.

Daiches, David. *Edinburgh*. London: Hamish Hamilton, 1978.

Davis, Natalie Zemon. "The Sacred and the Body Social in Lyon." *Past and Present* 90 (1981): 40–70.

de Lauretis, Teresa. *Technologies of Gender: Essays on Theory, Film, and Fiction*. Bloomington: Indiana University Press, 1987.

de Man, Paul. *Allegories of Reading: Figural Language in Rousseau, Nietzsche, Rilke, and Proust*. New Haven, Conn.: Yale University Press, 1979.

———. "The Rhetoric of Temporality." In *Interpretation: Theory and Practice*. Ed. Charles S. Singleton, 173–209. Baltimore: Johns Hopkins University Press, 1969.

DeMolen, Richard L. "Richard Mulcaster and Elizabethan Pageantry." *Studies in English Literature* 14 (1974): 209–21.

Derrida, Jacques. *Of Grammatology*. Trans. Gayatri Chakravorty Spivak. Baltimore: Johns Hopkins University Press, 1976.

———. *Writing and Difference*. Trans. Alan Bass. Chicago: University of Chicago Press, 1978.

de Saussure, Ferdinand. *Course in General Linguistics*. New York: McGraw-Hill, 1966.

de Welles, Theodore. "Sex and Sexual Attitudes in Seventeenth-Century England: The Evidence from Puritan Diaries." *Renaissance and Reformation* 24 (1988): 45–64.

Dollimore, Jonathan, and Alan Sinfield, eds. *Political Shakespeare: New Essays in Cultural Materialism*. Manchester: University of Manchester Press, 1985.

Donald, M. B. *Elizabethan Copper: The History of the Company of Miners Royal, 1568–1605*. London: Pergamon Press, 1955.

Dop, Jan Albert. *Eliza's Knights: Soldiers, Poets and Puritans in the Netherlands, 1572–1586*. Alblasserdam: Remak, 1981.

Douglas, Mary. *Purity and Danger: An Analysis of the Concept of Pollution and Taboo*. London: Routledge & Kegan Paul, 1966.

Durling, Nancy Vine. "La Bielle Jeane and the Body of the Text." *Romance Language Annual II* (1991): 93–99.

Dutton, Robert. *Mastering the Revels: The Regulation and Censorship of English Renaissance Drama*. Iowa City: University of Iowa Press, 1991.

Eco, Umberto. *Semiotics and the Philosophy of Language*. Bloomington: Indiana University Press, 1984.

Elton, G. R. *England Under the Tudors*. London: Methuen, 1955.

Emerson, Kathy Lynn. *Wives and Daughters: The Women of Sixteenth Century England*. Troy, N.Y.: Whitston, 1984.

Emmison, F. G. *Elizabethan Life: Disorder*. Chelmsford: Essex County Council, 1970.

Evans, Maurice. *Spenser's Anatomy of Heroism: A Commentary on The Faerie Queene*. Cambridge: Cambridge University Press, 1970.

Everitt, Alan. "Social Mobility in Early Modern England." *Past and Present* 33 (1966): 56–73.

Farrell, Kirby, Elizabeth Hageman, and Arthur Kinney, eds. *Women in the Renaissance: Selections from English Literary Renaissance*. Amherst: University of Massachusetts Press, 1990.

Ferguson, Margaret W. "A Room Not Their Own: Renaissance Women as Readers and Writers." In *The Comparative Perspective on Literature: Approaches to Theory and Practice*. Ed. Clayton Koelb and Susan Noakes, 93–116. Ithaca, N.Y.: Cornell University Press, 1988.

Ferguson, Margaret W., Maureen Quilligan, and Nancy J. Vickers, eds. *Rewriting the Renaissance: The Discourses of Sexual Difference in Early Modern Europe*. Chicago: University of Chicago Press, 1986.

Fish, Stanley. *Self-consuming Artifacts: The Experience of Seventeenth-Century Literature*. Berkeley: University of California Press, 1972.

Fisher, F. J. *Essays in the Economic and Social History of Tudor and Stuart England in Honour of R. H. Tawney*. Cambridge: Cambridge University Press, 1961.

Fisher, R. M. "The Reformation of Church and Chapel at the Inns of Court, 1530–1580." *Guildhall Studies in London History* 3 (1979): 223–47.

Fisher, Sheila, and Janet E. Hailey. *Seeking the Woman in Late Medieval and Renaissance Writings: Essays in Feminist Contextual Criticism*. Knoxville: University of Tennessee Press, 1989.

Fletcher, Angus. *Allegory: The Theory of a Symbolic Mode*. Ithaca, N.Y.: Cornell University Press, 1964.

Foster, Frank. "Merchants and Bureaucrats in Elizabethan London." *Guildhall Miscellany* 4 (1972): 149–60.

———. *The Politics of Stability: A Portrait of the Rulers in Elizabethan London*. London: Royal Historical Society, 1977.

Foucault, Michel. *The Archaeology of Knowledge and the Discourse of Language*. Trans. A. M. Sheridan Smith. New York: Pantheon, 1972.

———. *Discipline and Punish: The Birth of the Prison*. Trans. Alan Sheridan. New York: Vintage Books, 1979.

———. *The History of Sexuality*. Vol. 1: *An Introduction*. Trans. Robert Hurley. New York: Vintage Books, 1980.

———. *The Order of Things: An Archaeology of the Human Sciences*. New York: Vintage Books, 1973.

———. *Power/Knowledge: Selected Interviews and Other Writings, 1972–1977*. Trans. Colin Gordon. New York: Pantheon, 1980.

Fowler, Alastair. *Triumphal Forms: Structural Patterns in Elizabethan Poetry*. Cambridge: Cambridge University Press, 1970.

Freedman, Barbara. *Staging the Gaze: Postmodernism, Psychoanalysis, and Shakespearian Comedy*. Ithaca, N.Y.: Cornell University Press, 1991.

Friedman, Susan Stanford. "Creativity and the Childbirth Metaphor: Gender Difference in Literary Discourse." *Feminist Studies* 13 (1987): 49–82.

Froude, James. *The Reign of Elizabeth*. 5 vols. Reprint. New York: Dutton, 1930.

Frye, Susan. "The Myth of Elizabeth I at Tilbury." *Sixteenth Century Journal* 23 (1992): 95–114.

Gallagher, Lowell. *Medusa's Gaze: Casuistry and Conscience in the Renaissance*. Stanford, Calif.: Stanford University Press, 1991.

Garber, Marjorie. *Vested Interests: Cross-dressing and Cultural Anxiety*. New York: Routledge & Kegan Paul, 1992.

Gates, Henry Louis, Jr., ed. *"Race," Writing, and Difference*. Chicago: University of Chicago Press, 1985.

Geertz, Clifford. *The Interpretation of Cultures*. New York: Basic Books, 1973.

———. *Local Knowledge: Further Essays in Interpretive Anthropology*. New York: Basic Books, 1983.

Gent, Lucy, and Nigel Llewellyn, eds. *Renaissance Bodies: The Human Figure in English Culture, c. 1540–1660*. London: Reaktion Books, 1990.

Giamatti, A. Bartlett. *Play of Double Senses: Spenser's Faerie Queene*. Englewood Cliffs, N.J.: Prentice-Hall, 1975.

Gies, Joseph, and Frances Gies. *Marriage and the Family in the Middle Ages*. New York: Harper & Row, 1987.

Goldberg, Jonathan. *Endlesse Worke: Spenser and the Structures of Discourse*. Baltimore: Johns Hopkins University Press, 1981.

———. *James I and the Politics of Literature: Jonson, Shakespeare, Donne, and Their Contemporaries*. Baltimore: Johns Hopkins University Press, 1983.

Gordon, D. J. *The Renaissance Imagination: Essays and Letters of D. J. Gordon*. Ed. Stephen Orgel. Berkeley: University of California Press, 1980.

———. *"Veritas Filia Temporis*: Hadrianus Junius and Geoffrey Whitney (1940)." In *The Renaissance Imagination: Essays and Letters by D. J. Gordon*. Ed. Stephen Orgel, 220–32. Berkeley: University of California Press, 1980.

Greenblatt, Stephen, ed. *Allegory and Representation: Selected Papers from the English Institute, 1979–1980*. Baltimore: Johns Hopkins University Press, 1981.

————, ed. *The Power of Forms in the English Renaissance*. Norman, Okla.: Pilgrim Books, 1982.

————. *Renaissance Self-fashioning: From More to Shakespeare*. Chicago: University of Chicago Press, 1980.

Greene, Thomas M. "Magic and Festivity at the Renaissance Court." *Renaissance Quarterly* 40 (1987): 636–59.

Gross, Charles. *The Gild Merchant: A Contribution to British Municipal History*. Oxford: Clarendon Press, 1890.

Gross, Elizabeth. "The Body of Signification." In *Abjection, Melancholia and Love: The Works of Julia Kristeva*. Ed. John Fletcher and Andrew Benjamin, 80–103. New York: Routledge & Kegan Paul, 1990.

Guth, Delloyd J., and John W. McKenna, eds. *Tudor Rule and Revolution: Essays for G. R. Elton from His American Friends*. Cambridge: Cambridge University Press, 1982.

Guy, John. *Tudor England*. New York: Oxford University Press, 1988.

Hageman, Elizabeth. "Recent Studies in Women Writers of Tudor England: Women Writers, 1485–1603." *English Literary Renaissance* 34 (1984): 409–25.

Haigh, Christopher, ed. *The Reign of Elizabeth I*. Athens: University of Georgia Press, 1987.

Hannay, Margaret P. *Philip's Phoenix: Mary Sidney, Countess of Pembroke*. New York: Oxford University Press, 1990.

————, ed. *Silent But for the Word: Tudor Women as Patrons, Translators and Writers of Religious Works*. Kent, Ohio: Kent State University Press, 1985.

Haselkorn, Anne M., and Betty S. Travitsky. *The Renaissance Englishwoman in Print: Counterbalancing the Canon*. Amherst: University of Massachusetts Press, 1990.

Heisch, Allison. "Queen Elizabeth I: Parliamentary Rhetoric and the Exercise of Power." *Signs* 1 (1975): 31–55.

————, ed. *Queen Elizabeth I: Political Speeches and Parliamentary Addresses, 1558–1601*. Madison: University of Wisconsin Press, forthcoming.

Helgerson, Richard. *The Elizabethan Prodigals*. Berkeley: University of California Press, 1976.

————. *Self-crowned Laureates: Spenser, Jonson, Milton and the Literary System*. Berkeley: University of California Press, 1983.

Higgins, Lynn A., and Brenda R. Silver, eds. *Rape and Representation*. New York: Columbia University Press, 1991.

Highley, Christopher. "Shakespeare, Spenser, and Elizabethan Ireland." Ph.D. diss., Stanford University, 1991.

Hill, Christopher. "Protestantism and the Rise of Capitalism." In *Essays in the Economic and Social History of Tudor and Stuart England in Honour of R. H. Tawney*. Ed. F. J. Fisher, 15–39. Cambridge: Cambridge University Press, 1961.

Hoak, Dale E. "The King's Privy Chamber, 1547–1553." In *Tudor Rule and Revolution: Essays for G. R. Elton from His American Friends*. Ed. Delloyd J. Guth and John W. McKenna, 87–108. Cambridge: Cambridge University Press, 1982.

Hobsbawm, Eric. *The Invention of Tradition*. Cambridge: Cambridge University Press, 1983.

Hodges, C. Walter. *The Globe Restored: A Study of the Elizabethan Theatre*. New York: Coward-McGann, 1954.

Hofgrefe, Pearl. "Legal Rights of Tudor Women and the Circumvention by Men and Women." *Sixteenth Century Journal* 3 (1972): 97–105.

———. *Tudor Women: Commoners and Queens*. Ames: Iowa State University Press, 1975.

Howard, Jean. "The New Historicism in Renaissance Studies." *English Literary Renaissance* 16 (1986): 13–43.

Hull, Suzanne W. *Chaste, Silent and Obedient: English Books for Women, 1475–1640*. San Marino, Calif.: Huntington Library, 1982.

Hurstfield, Joel. *Elizabeth I and the Unity of England*. New York: Macmillan, 1960.

———. *The Queen's Wards: Wardship and Marriage Under Elizabeth I*. Cambridge, Mass.: Harvard University Press, 1958.

Irigaray, Luce. "Women's Exile: Interview with Luce Irigaray." Trans. Couze Venn. In *The Feminist Critique of Language: A Reader*. Ed. Deborah Cameron, 80–98. New York: Routledge & Kegan Paul, 1990.

Ives, Eric. *Anne Boleyn*. New York: Basil Blackwell, 1986.

Jack, Sybil M. *Trade and Industry in Tudor and Stuart England*. London: Allen & Unwin, 1977.

James, Mervyn. *Society, Politics and Culture: Studies in Early Modern England*. Cambridge: Cambridge University Press, 1986.

Jameson, Frederic. *The Political Unconscious: Narrative as a Socially Symbolic Act*. Ithaca, N.Y.: Cornell University Press, 1981.

Janeway, Elizabeth. "On the Power of the Weak." *Signs* 1 (1975): 103–9.

Jardine, Alice A. *Gynesis: Configurations of Woman and Modernity*. Ithaca, N.Y.: Cornell University Press, 1985.

Jardine, Lisa. *Still Harping on Daughters: Women and Drama in the Age of Shakespeare*. Totowa, N.J.: Barnes & Noble, 1983.

Javitch, Daniel. "The Impure Motives of Elizabethan Poetry." *Genre* 15 (1982): 225–38.

———. *Poetry and Courtliness in Renaissance England*. Princeton, N.J.: Princeton University Press, 1978.

Jed, Stephanie. *Chaste Thinking: The Rape of Lucretia and the Birth of Humanism*. Bloomington: Indiana University Press, 1989.

Jenkins, Elizabeth. *Elizabeth the Great*. New York: Capricorn Books, 1967.

Johnson, Paul. *Elizabeth I: A Study in Power and Intellect*. London: Weidenfeld & Nicholson, 1974.

Jones, Emrys. "London in the Early Seventeenth Century: An Ecological Approach." *London Journal* 6 (1980): 123–33.

Jones, Ann Rosalind. *The Currency of Eros: Women's Love Lyric in Europe, 1540–1620*. Bloomington: Indiana University Press, 1990.

———. "Writing the Body: Toward an Understanding of *L'Ecriture Feminine*." *Feminist Studies* 7 (1981): 247–63.

Jones, Ann Rosalind, and Peter Stallybrass. "The Politics of *Astrophil and Stella*." *Studies in English Literature* 24 (1984): 53–68.

Jones, Norman L. "Elizabeth's First Year: The Conception and Birth of the Elizabethan Political World." In *The Reign of Elizabeth I*. Ed. Christopher Haigh, 27–54. Athens: University of Georgia Press, 1987.

Jones, Whitney, R. D. *The Mid-Tudor Crisis, 1539–1563*. New York: Barnes & Noble, 1973.

————. *The Tudor Commonwealth, 1529–1559*. London: Athlone Press, 1970.

Jordan, Constance. *Renaissance Feminism: Literary Texts and Political Models.* Ithaca, N.Y.: Cornell University Press, 1990.

————. "Representing Political Androgyny: More on the Siena Portrait of Queen Elizabeth I." In *The Renaissance Englishwoman in Print: Counterbalancing the Canon.* Ed. Anne M. Haselkorn and Betty S. Travitsy, 157–76. Amherst: University of Massachusetts Press, 1990.

————. "Woman's Rule in Sixteenth-Century British Political Thought." *Renaissance Quarterly* 60 (1987): 421–51.

Judson, A. C. *The Life of Edmund Spenser*. Baltimore: Johns Hopkins University Press, 1945.

Kane, Sean. *Spenser's Moral Allegory*. Toronto: University of Toronto Press, 1989.

Kantorowicz, Ernst. *The King's Two Bodies: A Study in Medieval Theology*. Princeton, N.J.: Princeton University Press, 1957.

Kappeler, Susanne. *The Pornography of Representation*. Minneapolis: University of Minnesota Press, 1986.

Kelly, Joan. "Did Women Have a Renaissance?" In *Becoming Visible: Women in European History.* Ed. Renate Bridenthal, Claudia Koontz, and Susan Stuard, 175–201. Boston: Houghton Mifflin, 1987.

Kelso, Ruth. *Doctrine for the Lady of the Renaissance*. Urbana: University of Illinois Press, 1956.

Kendall, Alan. *Robert Dudley, Earl of Leicester*. London: Cassell, 1980.

Kervyn de Lettenhove, Henri, ed. *Relations politiques des Pays-Bas et de l'Angleterre.* 11 vols. Brussels: F. Haye, 1882–1900.

King, John N. "The Godly Woman in Elizabethan Iconography." *Renaissance Quarterly* 38 (1985): 41–84.

————. "Queen Elizabeth I: Representations of the Virgin Queen." *Renaissance Quarterly* 43 (1990): 30–74.

————. *Tudor Royal Iconography*. Princeton, N.J.: Princeton University Press, 1989.

Kristeva, Julia. *The Kristeva Reader*. Ed. Toril Moi. New York: Columbia University Press, 1986.

————. *Powers of Horror: An Essay on Abjection*. Trans. Leon S. Roudiez. New York: Columbia University Press, 1982.

Lamb, Mary Ellen. *Gender and Authorship in the Sidney Circle*. Madison: University of Wisconsin Press, 1990.

Levin, Carole. *Propaganda in the English Reformation: Heroic and Villainous Images of King John*. Lewisten: Edwin Mellin, 1988.

————. "'Would I Could Give You Help and Succour': Elizabeth I and the Politics of Touch." *Albion* 21 (1989): 191–205.

Levine, Mortimer. "The Place of Women in Tudor Government." In *Tudor Rule and Revolution: Essays for G. R. Elton from His American Friends.* Ed. Delloyd J. Guth and John W. McKenna, 109–23. Cambridge: Cambridge University Press, 1982.

————. *Tudor Dynastic Problems, 1460–1571*. New York: Barnes & Noble, 1973.

Lewalski, Barbara Kiefer. *Renaissance Genres: Essays on Theory, History, and Interpretation.* Cambridge, Mass.: Harvard University Press, 1986.

Lewis, C. S. *The Allegory of Love: A Study in Medieval Tradition*. 1936. Reprint. New York: Oxford University Press, 1981.

Loach, Jennifer, and Robert Tittler, eds. *The Mid-Tudor Polity, c. 1540–1560*. London: Macmillan, 1980.

Loades, David. *Mary Tudor: A Life*. Cambridge, Mass.: Basil Blackwell, 1989.

———. *The Reign of Mary Tudor: Politics, Government, and Religion in England, 1553–1558*. London: Ernst Benn, 1979.

Loewenstein, Joseph. "Echo's Ring: Orpheus and Spenser's Career." *English Literary Renaissance* 16 (1986): 287–302.

Lotman, Yu. M., and B. A. Uspensky. "On the Semiotic Mechanism of Culture." *New Literary History* 9 (1978): 211–32.

Lytle, Guy, and Stephen Orgel, eds. *Patronage in the Renaissance*. Princeton, N.J.: Princeton University Press, 1981.

MacAloon, John J. *Rite, Drama, Festival, Spectacle: Rehearsals Toward a Theory of Cultural Performance*. Philadelphia: Institute for the Study of Human Issues, 1984.

MacCaffrey, Wallace. "Parliament: The Elizabethan Experience." In *Tudor Rule and Revolution: Essays for G. R. Elton from His American Friends*. Ed. Delloyd J. Guth and John W. McKenna. Cambridge: Cambridge University Press, 1982.

———. *The Shaping of the Elizabethan Regime*. Princeton, N.J.: Princeton University Press, 1968.

Mallin, Eric. "Emulous Factions and the Collapse of Chivalry: *Troilus and Cressida*." *Representations* 29 (1990): 145–79.

Marcus, Leah. *Puzzling Shakespeare: Local Readings and Its Discontents*. Berkeley: University of California Press, 1988.

———. "Shakespeare's Comic Heroines, Elizabeth I, and the Political Uses of Androgyny." In *Women in the Middle Ages and the Renaissance*. Ed. Mary Beth Rose, 135–54. Syracuse, N.Y.: Syracuse University Press, 1986.

Marotti, Arthur. "'Love is not Love': Elizabethan Sonnet Sequences and the Social Order." *ELH* 49 (1982): 396–428.

Mattingly, Garrett. *The Defeat of the Spanish Armada*. Boston: Houghton Mifflin, 1959.

May, Steven W. *The Elizabethan Courtier Poets: The Poems and Their Contexts*. Columbia: University of Missouri Press, 1991.

———. "Sir Philip Sidney and Queen Elizabeth." In *English Manuscript Studies, 1100–1700*. Ed. Peter Beal and Jeremy Griffiths, 257–67. London: Basil Blackwell, 1990.

McCanles, Michael. *The Text of Sidney's Arcadian World*. Durham, N.C.: Duke University Press, 1989.

McCoy, Richard. "Gascoigne's 'Poëmata castrata'": The Wages of Courtly Success." *Criticism* 27 (1985): 29–54.

———. *The Rites of Knighthood: The Literature and Politics of Elizabethan Chivalry*. Berkeley: University of California Press, 1989.

———. *Sir Philip Sidney: Rebellion in Arcadia*. New Brunswick, N.J.: Rutgers University Press, 1979.

———. "'Thou Idol Ceremony': Elizabeth I, *The Henriad*, and the Rites of the English Monarchy." In *Urban Life in the Renaissance*. Ed. Susan Zimmerman and Ronald F. E. Weissman, 240–66. Newark: University of Delaware Press, 1989.

Merrix, Robert P. "The Vale of Lillies and the Bower of Bliss: Soft-core Pornography in Elizabethan Poetry." *Journal of Popular Culture* 19 (1986): 7–16.

Miller, David Lee. "Allegories of Allegory: Metalanguage and the Function of Truth." Session response at conference "Spenser at Kalamazoo," May 1988.

———. *The Poem's Two Bodies: The Poetics of the 1590 Faerie Queene*. Princeton, N.J.: Princeton University Press, 1988.

Miller, Nancy K., ed. *The Poetics of Gender*. New York: Columbia University Press, 1986.

Montrose, Louis Adrian. "The Elizabethan Subject and the Spenserian Text." In *Literary Theory/Renaissance Texts*. Ed. Patricia Parker and David Quint, 303–40. Baltimore: Johns Hopkins University Press, 1986.

———. "'Eliza, Queen of Shepheardes,' and the Pastoral of Power." *English Literary Renaissance* 10 (1980): 153–82.

———. "Gifts and Reasons: The Contexts of Peele's *Araygnement of Paris*." *ELH* 47 (1980): 433–61.

———. "*A Midsummer Night's Dream* and the Shaping Fantasies of Elizabethan Culture: Gender, Power, Form." In *Rewriting the Renaissance: The Discourses of Sexual Difference in Early Modern Europe*. Ed. Margaret W. Ferguson, Maureen Quilligan, and Nancy J. Vickers, 65–87. Chicago: University of Chicago Press, 1986.

Moi, Toril. *Sexual/Textual Politics: Feminist Literary Theory*. New York: Methuen, 1985.

Moore, Sally, and Barbara Meyerhoff, eds. *Secular Ritual*. Amsterdam: Van Gorcum, 1977.

Muir, Edward. "Images of Power: Art and Pageantry in Renaissance Venice." *American Historical Review* 84 (1979): 16–52.

Mullaney, Steven. *The Place of the Stage: License, Play, and Power in Renaissance England*. Chicago: University of Chicago Press, 1988.

Mumby, Frank A. *The Girlhood of Queen Elizabeth: A Narrative In Contemporary Letters*. London: Constable & Col, 1909.

Murrin, Michael. *The Veil of Allegory: Some Notes Toward a Theory of Allegorical Rhetoric in the English Renaissance*. Chicago: University of Chicago Press, 1969.

Neale, John E. *Elizabeth I and Her Parliaments, 1559–1581*. London: Jonathan Cape, 1953.

———. *Elizabeth I and Her Parliaments, 1584–1601*. London: Jonathan Cape, 1957.

———. *Queen Elizabeth I: A Biography*. 1934. Reprint. Garden City, N.Y.: Doubleday, 1957.

Neely, Carol. "Constructing the Subject: Feminist Practice and the New Renaissance Discourse." *English Literary Renaissance* 18 (1988): 5–18.

Norbrook, David. *Poetry and Politics in the English Renaissance*. New York: Routledge & Kegan Paul, 1984.

Norhnberg, James. *The Analogy of The Faerie Queene*. Princeton, N.J.: Princeton University Press, 1976.

Orgel, Stephen. *The Illusion of Power: Political Theater in the English Renaissance*. Berkeley: University of California Press, 1975.

———. *The Jonsonian Masque*. 1965. Reprint. New York: Columbia University Press, 1981.

———. "Making Greatness Familiar." *Genre* 15 (1982): 41–48.

Palliser, D. M. *The Age of Elizabeth*. London: Longman, 1983.

Panofsky, Irwin. *Studies in Iconology: Humanistic Themes in the Art of the Renaissance*. 1939. Reprint. New York: Harper & Row, 1962.

Parker, Geoffrey. *The Dutch Revolt*. Ithaca, N.Y.: Cornell University Press, 1977.

———. *Spain and the Netherlands, 1559–1659: Ten Studies*. Short Hills, N.J.: Enslow, 1979.

Parker, Patricia. *Literary Fat Ladies: Rhetoric, Gender, Property*. New York: Methuen, 1987.

Parker, Patricia, and Geoffrey Harman, eds. *Shakespeare and the Question of Theory*. New York: Methuen, 1985.

Parker, Patricia, and David Quint, eds. *Literary Theory/Renaissance Texts*. Baltimore: Johns Hopkins University Press, 1986.

Patterson, Annabel. *Censorship and Interpretation: The Conditions of Reading and Writing in Early Modern England*. Madison: University of Wisconsin Press, 1984.

Patterson, Lee. *Negotiating the Past: The Historical Understanding of Medieval Literature*. Madison: University of Wisconsin Press, 1987.

Pearl, Valerie. "Change and Stability in Seventeenth-Century London." *London Journal* 5 (1979): 3–34.

Peck, Linda Levy. *Court Patronage and Corruption in Early Stuart England*. Boston: Unwin Hyman, 1990.

Perry, Maria. *The Word of a Prince: A Life of Elizabeth I from Contemporary Documents*. Woodbridge: Boydell Press, 1990.

Pollard, A. F. "Local History." *Times Literary Supplement* 11 (March 1920): 1, 162.

Pomeroy, Elizabeth W. *Reading the Portraits of Queen Elizabeth I*. Hamden, Conn.: Archon Books, 1989.

Prior, Mary, ed. *Women in English Society, 1500–1800*. New York: Methuen, 1985.

Prockter, Adrian, and Robert Taylor. *The A to Z of Elizabethan London*. London Topographical Society Publication No. 122. London: London Topographical Society, 1979.

Prouty, Charles. *George Gascoigne: Elizabethan Courtier, Soldier, and Poet*. 1942. Reprint. New York: Benjamin Blom, 1966.

Pulman, Michael. *The Elizabethan Privy Council in the Fifteen-Seventies*. Berkeley: University of California Press, 1971.

Quilligan, Maureen. *The Language of Allegory: Defining the Genre*. Ithaca, N.Y.: Cornell University Press, 1979.

———. *Milton's Spenser: The Politics of Reading*. Ithaca, N.Y.: Cornell University Press, 1983.

———. "Sidney and His Queen." In *The Historical Renaissance: New Essays on Tudor and Stuart Literature and Culture*. Ed. Heather Dubrow and Richard Strier, 111–96. Chicago: University of Chicago Press, 1988.

Rabinow, Paul. *Symbolic Domination: Cultural Form and Historical Change in Morocco*. Chicago: University of Chicago Press, 1975.

Ramsay, G. D. *The City of London in International Politics at the Accession of Mary Tudor*. Manchester: University of Manchester Press, 1975.

———. "Clothworkers, Merchants Adventurers and Richard Hakluyt." *English Historical Review* 92 (1977): 504–21.

———. "The Foreign Policy of Elizabeth I." In *The Reign of Elizabeth I*. Ed. Christopher Haigh, 147–68. Athens: University of Georgia Press, 1987.

Rappaport, Steve. "Social Structure and Mobility in Sixteenth-Century London: Part I." *London Journal* 9 (1983): 107–35.

————. "Social Structure and Mobility in Sixteenth-Century London: Part II." *London Journal* 10 (1984): 107–34.

Read, Conyers. *Lord Burghley and Queen Elizabeth*. New York: Knopf, 1961.

Rich, Adrienne. *Diving into the Wreck: Poems, 1971–1972*. New York: Norton, 1973.

Riggs, David. *Ben Jonson: A Life*. Cambridge, Mass.: Harvard University Press, 1989.

Robertson, Karen. "The Body Natural of a Queen: Mary, James, *Horestes.*" *Renaissance and Reformation* n.s. 14 (1990): 25–36.

Roche, Thomas P., Jr. "The Challenge to Chastity: Britomart in the House of Busirane." In *Essential Articles for the Study of Edmund Spenser*. Ed. A. C. Hamilton, 189–98. Hamden, Conn.: Archon Books, 1972.

Rodriguez-Salgado, M. J., and the staff of the National Maritime Museum. *Armada: 1588–1988: An International Exhibition to Commemorate the Spanish Armada*. Harmondsworth: Penguin Books, 1988.

Rosaldo, Michelle Zimbalist, and Louise Lamphere. *Women Culture & Society*. Stanford, Calif.: Stanford University Press, 1974.

Rose, Mary Beth. *The Expense of Spirit: Love and Sexuality in English Renaissance Drama*. Ithaca, N.Y.: Cornell University Press, 1988.

————, ed. *Women in the Middle Ages and the Renaissance*. Syracuse, N.Y.: Syracuse University Press, 1986.

Rubin, Gail. "The Traffic in Women: Notes on the 'Political Economy' of Sex." In *Toward an Anthropology of Women*. Ed. Rayna R. Reiter, 157–210. New York: Monthly Review Press, 1975.

Russ, Joanna. *How to Suppress Women's Writing*. Austin: University of Texas Press, 1983.

Said, Edward. *The World the Text and the Critic*. Cambridge, Mass.: Harvard University Press, 1983.

Sargent, Ralph M. *At the Court of Queen Elizabeth: The Life and Lyrics of Sir Edward Dyer*. New York: Oxford University Press, 1935.

Saunders, Ann. *The Art and Architecture of London*. Oxford: Phaidon Press, 1981.

Schleiner, Winfried. "*Divina Virago*: Queen Elizabeth as an Amazon." *Studies in Philology* 75 (1978): 163–80.

Scott, David. "William Patten and the Authorship of 'Robert Laneham's *Letter*' (1575)." *English Literary Renaissance* 7 (1977): 297–306.

Seaver, Paul. *The Puritan Lectureships: The Politics of Religious Dissent, 1560–1662*. Stanford, Calif.: Stanford University Press, 1970.

Sedgwick, Eve Kosofsky. *Between Men: English Literature and Male Homosocial Bonding*. New York: Columbia University Press, 1985.

Sharpe, Kevin, and Steven Zwicker. *Politics of Discourse: The Literature and History of Seventeenth-Century England*. Berkeley: University of California Press, 1987.

Silberman, Lauren. "Unsung Heroines: Androgynous Discourse in Book 3 of *The Faerie Queene*." In *Rewriting the Renaissance: The Discourses of Sexual Difference in Early Modern Europe*. Ed. Margaret W. Ferguson, Maureen Quilligan, and Nancy J. Vickers, 259–71. Chicago: University of Chicago Press, 1986.

Spivak, Gayatri Chakravorty. "Displacement and the Discourse of Woman." In *Displacement: Derrida and After*. Ed. Mark Krupnick, 169–95. Bloomington: Indiana University Press, 1983.

———, ed. *In Other Worlds: Essays in Cultural Politics*. New York: Routledge & Kegan Paul, 1988.

Stallybrass, Peter. "Patriarchal Territories: The Body Enclosed." In *Rewriting the Renaissance: The Discourses of Sexual Difference in Early Modern Europe*. Ed. Margaret W. Ferguson, Maureen Quilligan, and Nancy J. Vickers, 123–42. Chicago: University of Chicago Press, 1986.

Stallybrass, Peter, and Allon White. *The Poetry and Politics of Transgression*. Ithaca, N.Y.: Cornell University Press, 1986.

Starkey, David. "Intimacy and Innovation: The Rise of the Privy Chamber, 1485–1547." In *The English Court: From the Wars of the Roses to the Civil War*. Ed. David Starkey et al., 71–118. New York: Longman, 1987.

———, ed. *Rivals in Power: Lives and Letters of the Great Tudor Dynasties*. New York: Grove Weidenfeld, 1990.

Starkey, David, et al., eds. *The English Court: From the Wars of the Roses to the Civil War*. New York: Longman, 1987.

Stimpson, Catharine R. "Ad/d Feminam: Women, Literature, and Society." In *Literature and Society: Selected Papers from the English Institute, 1978*. Ed. Edward Said, 174–92. Baltimore: Johns Hopkins University Press, 1980.

Stone, Lawrence. *The Crisis of the Aristocracy, 1558–1641*. New York: Oxford University Press, 1967.

———. *The Family, Sex, and Marriage in England, 1500–1800*. New York: Harper & Row, 1977.

———. "Social Mobility in England, 1500–1700." *Past and Present* 33 (1966): 16–55.

Strong, Roy. *Art and Power: Renaissance Festivals, 1450–1650*. Woodbridge: Boydell Press, 1984.

———. *The Cult of Elizabeth: Elizabethan Portraiture and Pageantry*. London: Thames and Hudson, 1977.

———. *Gloriana: The Portraits of Queen Elizabeth I*. New York: Thames and Hudson, 1987.

Strong, Roy, and J. A. van Dorsten. *Leicester's Triumph*. Leiden: Leiden University Press, 1964.

Stuard, Susan Mosher. "Did Women Lose Status in Late Medieval and Early Modern Times?" In *Restoring Women to History*. Vol. 1. Ed. Elizabeth Fox Genovese and Susan Mosher Stuard, 176–97. N.p.: Fund for the Improvement of Post Secondary Education and the Lilly Endowment, 1983.

Suleiman, Susan Rubin, ed. *The Female Body in Western Culture: Contemporary Perspectives*. Cambridge, Mass.: Harvard University Press, 1986.

Teague, Frances. "Elizabeth I: Queen of England." In *Women Writers of the Renaissance and Reformation*. Ed. Katharina M. Wilson, 522–34. Athens: University of Georgia Press, 1987.

Tennenhouse, Leonard. *Politics on Display: The Politics of Shakespeare's Genres*. New York: Methuen, 1986.

Terdiman, Richard. *Discourse/Counter-Discourse: The Theory and Practice of Symbolic Resistance in Nineteenth-Century France*. Ithaca, N.Y.: Cornell University Press, 1985.

Thickstun, Margaret Olofson. *Fictions of the Feminine: Puritan Doctrine and the Representation of Women*. Ithaca, N.Y.: Cornell University Press, 1988.

Todd, Margo. *Christian Humanism and the Puritan Social Order*. Cambridge: Cambridge University Press, 1987.

Todorov, Tzvetan. *The Poetics of Prose*. Trans. Richard Howard. Ithaca, N.Y.: Cornell University Press, 1977.

Travitsky, Betty. "The 'Wyll and Testament' of Isabella Whitney." *English Literary Renaissance* 10 (1980): 76–95.

Trimpi, Wesley. *Muses of One Mind: The Literary Analysis of Experience and Its Continuity*. Princeton, N.J.: Princeton University Press, 1983.

Turner, Victor. *Dramas, Fields, and Metaphors: Symbolic Action in Human Society*. Ithaca, N.Y.: Cornell University Press, 1974.

Tuve, Rosemond. *Allegorical Imagery: Some Mediaeval Books and Their Posterity*. 1966. Reprint. Princeton, N.J.: Princeton University Press, 1977.

———. *Elizabethan and Metaphysical Imagery: Renaissance Poetic and Twentieth-Century Critics*. Chicago: University of Chicago Press, 1947.

Van Dyke, Carolynn. *The Fiction of Truth: Structures of Meaning in Narrative and Dramatic Allegory*. Ithaca, N.Y.: Cornell University Press, 1985.

Veeser, H. Aram. *The New Historicism*. New York: Routledge & Kegan Paul, 1989.

Vickers, Nancy J. "Diana Described: Scattered Woman and Scattered Rhyme." In *Writing and Sexual Difference*. Ed. Elizabeth Abel, 95–109. Chicago: University of Chicago Press, 1982.

Walker, Cheryl. "Feminist Literary Criticism and the Author." *Critical Inquiry* 16 (1990): 551–71.

Wayne, Valerie. Introduction to Edmund Tilney, *"The Flower of Friendshippe": A Renaissance Dialogue Contesting Marriage*. Ed. Valerie Wayne. Ithaca, N.Y.: Cornell University Press, 1992.

Weimann, Robert. *Structure and Society in Literary History: Studies in the History and Theory of Historical Criticism*. Baltimore: Johns Hopkins University Press, 1984.

———. "Text, Author-Function, and Appropriation in Modern Narrative: Toward a Sociology of Representation." In *Literature and Social Practice*. Ed. Philippe Desan, Priscilla Parkhurst Ferguson, and Wendy Griswold, 29–45. Chicago: University of Chicago Press, 1989.

Wells, Robin. *Spenser's Faerie Queene and the Cult of Elizabeth*. Totowa, N.J.: Barnes & Noble, 1983.

Wells, Susan. *The Dialectics of Representation*. Baltimore: Johns Hopkins University Press, 1985.

Wernham, R. B. *The Making of Elizabethan Foreign Policy, 1558–1603*. Berkeley: University of California Press, 1980.

Wharton, Thomas. *Observations on the Fairy Queen of Spenser*. 2 vols. London: C. Stower, 1807.

Whigham, Frank. *Ambition and Privilege: The Social Tropes of Elizabethan Courtesy Theory*. Berkeley: University of California Press, 1984.

White, Hayden. *Metahistory*. Baltimore: Johns Hopkins University Press, 1973.

———. *Tropics of Discourse: Essays in Cultural Criticism*. Baltimore: Johns Hopkins University Press, 1978.

Williams, Penry. *The Tudor Regime*. Oxford: Clarendon Press, 1979.

Williams, Raymond. *The Sociology of Culture*. New York: Schocken Books, 1981.

Williams, Sheila. "Two Seventeenth Century Semi-Dramatic Allegories of Truth the Daughter of Time." *Guildhall Miscellany* 5 (1963): 207–20.

Williamson, Judith. *Decoding Advertisements: Ideology and Meaning in Advertising*. London: Marion Boyars, 1978.

Willson, David Harris. *King James VI and I*. New York: Oxford University Press, 1967.

Wittig, Monique. "On the Social Contract." *Feminist Issues* 9 (1989): 3–12.

Woodbridge, Linda. *Woman and the English Renaissance: Literature and the Nature of Womankind, 1540–1620*. Urbana: University of Illinois Press, 1986.

Woolf, Virginia. *Mrs. Dalloway*. 1925. Reprint. New York: Harcourt Brace Jovanovich, 1953.

———. *A Room of One's Own*. 1929. Reprint. New York: Harcourt Brace Jovanovich, 1957.

Wright, Louis. *Middle-Class Culture in Elizabethan England*. Chapel Hill: University of North Carolina Press, 1935.

———. "Reading of Renaissance Englishwomen." *Studies in Philology* 28 (1931): 671–88.

Wright, Pam. "A Change in Direction: The Ramifications of a Female Household, 1558–1603." In *The English Court: From the Wars of the Roses to the Civil War*. Ed. David Starkey et al., 147–72. New York: Longman, 1987.

Yates, Frances. *Astrea: The Imperial Theme in the Sixteenth Century*. London: Routledge & Kegan Paul, 1975.

———. "Queen Elizabeth as Astraea." *Journal of the Warburg and Cortauld Institute* 10 (1947): 82.

Zimmerman, Susan, and Ronald F. E. Weissman, eds. *Urban Life in the Renaissance*. Newark: University of Delaware Press, 1989.

Zizek, Slavoj. *The Sublime Object of Ideology*. New York: Verso, 1989.

Index

217